9.95
604

D0802021

THE LAST GENERATION

The Last Generation

WORK AND LIFE IN THE TEXTILE MILLS

OF LOWELL, MASSACHUSETTS,

1910–1960

Mary H. Blewett

The University of Massachusetts Press

AMHERST

Copyright © 1990 by
The University of Massachusetts Press
All rights reserved
Printed in the United States of America
LC 89-77124
ISBN 0-87023-712-8 (cloth); 713-6 (pbk)
Designed by Jack Harrison
Set in Linotype Walbaum by Keystone Typesetting, Inc.
Printed and bound by Thomson-Shore, Inc.

Library of Congress Cataloging-in-Publication Data
The Last generation : work and life in the textile mills of Lowell,
Massachusetts, 1910–1960 / [edited by] Mary H. Blewett.
       p.   cm.
   Includes bibliographical references.
   ISBN 0–87023–712–8 (alk paper) — ISBN 0–87023–713–6
(pbk. : alk paper).
     1. Textile workers—Massachusetts—Lowell—History—20th century—Sources.
2. Textile workers—Massachusetts—Lowell—Interviews.
I. Blewett, Mary H.
HD8039.T42U6525   1990
331.7′677′0097444—dc20   89–77124
                                  CIP

British Library Cataloguing in Publication data are available

Frontispiece: Doffing boy. Courtesy of MATH (Museum of American Textile History)

TO MY COWORKERS:

Martha Mayo,
Donna Mailloux,
Paul Page,
and
Diane Novelli

Contents

THE CHILDREN

List of Illustrations

Acknowledgments

I am grateful to the Lowell National Historical Park, especially to Larry Gall and Mike Wurm, and to the Lowell Historic Preservation Commission, especially to Paul Marion, Rosemary Noon, and Martha Norkunas, for three generous grants that supported the research for and the publication of this book. I am thankful for the variety of ways in which Peter Blewett, Andrew Gill, Louis Eno, Robert Weible, Brian Mitchell, Douglas DeNatale, Martha Norkunas, Edward Pershey, and Shomer Zwelling encouraged this undertaking. I especially wish to thank Linda Smith Rhoads for her warm encouragement and helpful interest during the initial phases of manuscript development.

The Last Generation could never have been written without the diligence, sensitivity, and dedication of my coworkers on the oral history projects, especially my coproject director Martha Mayo, the Lowell Park's oral historian, Donna Mailloux, and the dozen undergraduate student interviewers at the University of Lowell, especially Paul Page and Diane Novelli, who demonstrated intelligent commitment to the research process. I am also grateful to Janine Whitcomb, Audrey LaRose, and JoAnn Paré for the often thankless but absolutely vital work that they did transcribing the tapes.

At many points in the publishing process, I was buoyed by editorial enthusiasm from the University of Massachusetts Press, especially from that prince among editors, Bruce Wilcox, and from my excellent and demanding editorial reviewers, Milton Cantor and Ken Fones-Wolf. The technical aspects of this work benefited from the skills of my consulting editor, Laurence Gross of the Museum of American Textile History (MATH), and from the willingness of my friend John Goodwin to let me exploit his encyclopedic knowledge of the technical aspects of textile production and to lend me a copy of *The Cotton Handbook*. I was unusually fortunate to be able to work with a skilled oral historian of the Vietnam War, Clark Dougan, at the University of Massachusetts Press, who knew all about the pitfalls of oral history, lavished time and energy on the manuscript, and helped me improve the coherence of the narratives and develop their interpretation.

I was also encouraged by the ongoing interest of former mill workers in the development of the book and by their willingness to lend me family photographs: Grace Burk, Valentine Chartrand, Lucie Cordeau, Hubert LaFleur, Mary Karafelis, Sidney Muskovitz, Ronald Bacon, Nicholas Georgoulis, and James Simpson. I also wish to thank MATH, the Center for Lowell History, and the Lowell National Historical Park for letting me use their photograph collections, and the Lowell Museum for giving me permission to use the interviews with Yvonne Hoar and James Ellis. Kenneth Merrill generously permitted the use of Gilbert Merrill's drawing of a ring spinning frame, and Edward Golec allowed the use of his drawing of the weaving process.

Finally, I thank the scores of former mill workers who crowded the Visitors' Center at the Lowell Park on Labor Day 1985, demonstrating their skills and knowledge, reliving old times, and being honored for their contributions to the history of the city. That day's fascinating activities led directly to the writing of this book.

In 1965, I arrived in Lowell from the Midwest where I had been born, raised, and educated. Initially I viewed the city in ways that seemed contradictory. Lowell then bore the scars of decades of industrial decline. Its downtown was shabby; some of its ethnic neighborhoods had vanished to make way for public housing projects and urban renewal. What textile mills remained had been abandoned entirely or were partially rented to indifferent tenants interested in profiting from local cheap labor. Unemployment ran at well over 10 percent with little prospect of easing.

Despite the apparent decay, at first I saw only the romance in the remains of nineteenth-century industrialization and the richness of multicultural life, both a relief from the all-white, middle-class suburb near Chicago where I spent my youth. It was not until I caught glimpses of the anonymous men and women who had worked in this once-vital center of New England textile production that I could reconcile those two conflicting images of the city.

In the history classes that I taught at Lowell State College, I came in contact with the sons, daughters, grandsons, and granddaughters of mill workers. I began to become aware of the human costs of textile industrialization, and this understanding put the achievements of nineteenth-century Lowell in a new light. I particularly remember one young man whose immigrant grandparents had been buried at public expense during the depression years of the 1930s. His relatives had prospered in postwar America, but when they tried to rebury his grandparents, they were told by city officials that the exact grave sites were unknown. The poignancy of their loss had a powerful effect on me. This book is an attempt to rescue from anonymity those mill workers whose lives shaped and were in turn shaped by the twentieth-century textile industry in decline. Their stories tell us of their struggles and dignify their lives.

In the early 1970s I became involved with many others in community history projects that culminated in a rejuvenation of the local historical society, the publication of a bicentennial history of the city, and the development of a local history museum. Sporadic attempts by my students and by the staff at the Lowell Museum to interview mill workers became part of these efforts. Some of these interviews appeared in

Surviving Hard Times: The Working People of Lowell (Lowell: Lowell Museum, 1982), which I edited. Historian Marc Miller was also gathering oral history on the World War II experience in Lowell to write *The Irony of Victory: World War II and Lowell, Massachusetts* (Urbana: University of Illinois Press, 1988).

When Congress authorized the establishment of the Lowell National Historical Park in 1978, new sources of energy and funding became available to recapture the human story of the mills. In 1979–1981, Judith K. Dunning organized the first serious effort by the National Park Service to gather oral histories of Lowell mill workers. Between 1984 and 1986, a second major attempt to record the memories of mill workers and ethnic groups was made for the park by its oral historian, Donna Mailloux, in combination with the University of Lowell's Special Collections librarian Martha Mayo, me, and a number of undergraduate liberal arts students. The material in *The Last Generation* draws on interviews from all of these projects.*

The oral history project from 1984 to 1986 was intended to document the experiences of mill workers for use in the park's major exhibit on textile industrialization to be opened at the Boott Cotton Mills in 1990. The students who conducted the interviews were trained in the humanistic approach described in Paul Thompson's *Voice of the Past: Oral History* (New York: Oxford University Press, 1978). They were encouraged to ask questions about mill work, beginning with the training process and including experiences with coworkers and mill managers, and at the same time, to probe the individual's memories of family, ethnicity, and childhood. Most of all, they were told to keep their mouths shut, listen, and ask follow-up questions only when the informant had finished the story. Eager interviewers struggled to keep to those guidelines.

The results of the interviews are strikingly articulate, as if each person had silently mulled over for years the good times and the bad within the family and at work. When asked to speak, they were ready. Their memories were neither anecdotal nor unfocused. Sometimes grudges and resentments toward family members appear as potent as those against the bosses at the mills.

---

*In 1988–89, historians participating in the "Shifting Gears" project, funded by the Massachusetts Foundation for Humanities and Public Policy and by the Heritage State Park System, interviewed former mill workers in the cities of Lawrence, Fall River, Holyoke, North Adams, and Gardner, who had had experiences similar to mill workers in Lowell (*Boston Globe*, Nov. 18, 1989).

I still wonder at the generosity with which each person shared his or her feelings and experiences with us. Everyone interviewed was a volunteer. Donna Mailloux circulated recruiting brochures and contacted senior citizens' groups, churches, and service agencies to build a network of former mill workers who could identify others willing to tell their stories. To celebrate their efforts, the park sponsored a Mill Workers' Reunion Day on Labor Day in 1985.

Understandably, those who agreed to talk were the hardiest survivors of mill work who had held skilled jobs such as loom fixing or drawing-in. Most of these people had positive memories; those whose memories were too painful refused to be interviewed. These narratives thus represent neither a systematic sample nor a reliable cross section of working-class life in Lowell. But they do provide a compelling if impressionistic view of the economic, political, social, cultural, and psychological worlds of these textile workers. What the informants told us provides many insights into working-class life in a twentieth-century American city that was undergoing industrial decline and depression.

When I discovered that the exhibit designers for the Boott mills planned to use very little from these narratives, I became determined to

A former silk weaver with Mary Blewett and Martha Mayo on Mill Workers' Reunion Day, 1985. *Courtesy of Lowell National Historical Park.*

write this book. With it, I intend to deepen the appreciation of industrial life for the many visitors to the tours and exhibits at the Lowell Park.

Seeking to include as many different jobs and skills as possible as well as a cross section of ethnic groups in the city, I selected thirty-four interviews from over one hundred. Then I removed the questions posed by the interviewer, rearranged sections of the narrative when necessary to provide continuity, and added words in brackets for clarification. The women's narratives revealed a pattern of free association different from the more linear path of the men's interviews, but both were edited to provide the reader with a coherent chronology. I also deleted material that seemed tangential to the main story, but tried to convey in detail both the personality and the cultural circumstances of the person's life. My goal was to capture the character and experiences of individual mill workers, although many of them worked in the same mills and some knew each other. The complete transcripts of all the narratives are available to researchers at the Center for Lowell History, University of Lowell, Mogan Center.

I tried to balance men's experiences with women's experiences because the textile industry continued to employ a relatively high percentage of women in the early twentieth century. The introductions to the sections on the women and the men explore the different meanings and circumstances of womanhood and manhood, ethnicity, and age group for this last generation of mill workers. Some of the original narratives involved persons whose parents worked in the mills but who themselves escaped any significant involvement in mill work. I added four of these interviews to document the unique perspective of the children of the last generation.

Of the thirty interviews with mill workers, fourteen are with women of Irish, Swedish, French Canadian, Italian, Greek, and Scottish descent. Many of these women spent their entire adult lives working in textile mills as spinners, weavers, velvet cutters, twisters, quillers, drawing-in girls, menders, or weave room inspectors. Their stories illustrate their training, their experiences in the mills with bosses and coworkers, their reactions to their jobs, the possibilities of access to certain kinds of skilled work, and the restrictions on opportunities for women in the textile mills. Although many women workers quit the mills when they married, others continued to work even after they married and had children. Some were self-supporting women with dependents. They faced the challenges of child care and housework after working long, exhausting hours for low wages, but often did so with ingenuity, vitality, humor, and affection. Late twentieth-century women who commonly work full time throughout their adult lives, including unpaid housework and child care, will find unexpected parallels with the experiences of these working-class women.

Sixteen of the interviews are with male workers of diverse background: Lancashire English, Irish, native New England, Scottish, French Canadian, Jewish, Greek, Polish, and Portuguese. These men had jobs as sweepers, bobbin-boys, mule spinners, slashers, carders, dye house workers, weavers, loom fixers, foremen, efficiency experts, or paymasters. Male mill workers benefited from a job ladder that provided some diversity and opportunity. Because mill wages were low even for skilled male workers, however, they often worked a second job. Sometimes they helped out with housework and child care. Their relationships with women workers at the mills reveal complex patterns of family and ethnic ties, tensions over participation in strikes and union activity, and cooperative efforts with female coworkers to manage machinery and the process of work.

Historians of textile workers in the early twentieth century have used oral history to produce a number of fine studies of mill workers. Elizabeth Robert's *Woman's Place: An Oral History of Working-Class Women, 1890–1940* (Oxford: Basil Blackwell, 1984), which focuses on the social and family lives of English women in Lancashire, presents a group of textile workers who, unlike many Lowell women workers, generally disliked their work except for the opportunities it offered for female companionship. In contrast to these Lancashire women, Lowell mill workers often demonstrated a commitment to and, for the relatively skilled, a fascination with their machines and work.

Victoria Byerly's well-written *Hard Times Cotton Mill Girls: Personal Histories of Womanhood and Poverty in the South* (Ithaca: Industrial and Labor Relations Press, 1986) is largely concerned with the family context of women's work in southern mill villages. Byerly used edited interviews to demonstrate the exploitation of women mill workers. Labor protest is analyzed only briefly, and the greatest strength of *Hard Times Cotton Mill Girls* is its focus on gender and race.

In *Like a Family: The Making of a Southern Cotton Mill World* (Chapel Hill: University of North Carolina Press, 1988), Jacquelyn Hall et al. analyze the early twentieth-century experiences of white mill-village workers from rural homes in the Piedmont area who were the first in their families to encounter industrial life. The writers interweave

short quotations from their extensive interviews with mill workers into a
text that, despite the many admirable strengths (including attention to
gender experience), deprives the reader of the chance to hear distinct,
individual voices and stories.

In the lavishly illustrated *Amoskeag: Life and Work in an American
Factory-City* (New York: Pantheon, 1978), Tamara Hareven and Ran-
dolph Langenbach enrich the narratives of male and female workers in
Manchester, New Hampshire, with information drawn from the records
of the giant Amoskeag Corporation that dominated textile work in the
city. Hareven's analysis of the connections between work and ethnic
family life is a major contribution to the understanding of working-class
life in America. However, the material that introduces each interview
offers little help to the general reader in assessing the meaning of the
mill worker's experiences. Gender analysis remains undeveloped. The
book's focus on the 1922 strike dominates the approach, and the organization of separate sections into "The World of Work" and "Family"
does not support the major argument of the book, which is about the
interconnections between work and family life.

Rather than separating the worlds of work and family, *The Last
Generation* uses the narrative flow of its interviews to emphasize the
continuities between life at work and in the family. Although the recruitment of workers through family and neighborhood networks was
the same in Lowell as in Manchester, shifting the focus from family to
individual workers and dividing the material on the two sexes into
different sections highlight the gender-specific nature of both work and
family experience. The personal narratives also examine the childhoods
of both sexes and explore how young women were protected by their
families during puberty, how working women experienced motherhood, and how men and women viewed episodes of sexual harassment
in the workplace.

Hareven argues in *Amoskeag* that, before the 1930s, jobs and work
routines were flexible, that workers accepted centralization and hierarchy within the mill because it was similar to their family and religious
experiences, and that women workers obtained special status as wage
earners. In contrast, the Lowell narratives describe a rigid sexual division of labor and distinct job ladders for men and women that limited
opportunities for women workers and kept their wages low. Some Lowell workers accepted the hierarchy inside most mills and others came to
appreciate the benefits of paternalism, but many other workers resented
the bosses, resisted their directives, and organized in protest. Their

varying reactions to mill conditions reflect the views of labor activists and shop stewards, on the one hand, and of opponents and critics of unions, on the other.

Textile operations in the Lowell area provide another contrast with the practices at the Amoskeag in the one-industry city of Manchester. As did workers in many other New England cities, mill workers in Lowell found themselves in a complex local labor market created by light industries that utilized semi-skilled, non-union labor. Multiple corporations offered jobs in food preparation, electronic assembly, and the making of garments, hosiery, shoes, or plastics. Many mill workers finished their working days in these operations.

In John Bodnar's *Workers' World: Kinship, Community, and Protest in an Industrial Society, 1900–1940* (Baltimore: Johns Hopkins University Press, 1982), Pennsylvania workers, including some who worked in textile mills, are presented as primarily cherishing security and conservative values. Lowell mill workers provide a more diverse reaction to industrial decline. Some mill workers clung to family and ethnic culture, but others did not. Political interests ran across a spectrum, from political apathy to intense interest in homeland politics to activism in the local Democratic party to labor organization and radical politics in the 1930s. Discontent in the mills took many forms, including high turnover rates, open and covert resistance, strikes and episodes of damage to mill property, expressed and unexpressed contempt for the ignorance of managers and their decisions, and the ultimate indictment of mill work by mill workers: the resolve never to permit their children to do it. One of the frequent complaints of mill managers after World War II was that young people refused to work in the mills. The local work force for the mills had disappeared; their parents had been the last generation.

Although the work force at Amoskeag, unlike that of multiethnic Lowell, was dominated largely by workers of French Canadian background, one similarity with Lowell was the prevalence of American-born workers of immigrant backgrounds who saw themselves as the inheritors of their parents' skills and places in mill work. Lowell mill workers found themselves enmeshed in a mature industrial system that was struggling to stay profitable in the face of stiff competition from the South. Their experiences take the historian well beyond the issues of the survival of preindustrial culture within an urban, industrial context to an examination of work and life in a declining sector of industrial capitalism.

Like managers in American industry in the late twentieth century, the supervisors of textile mills in Lowell tested ways of increasing productivity through the use of new technology, new markets, new products, and the introduction of scientific management techniques, such as time- and motion-studies. In contrast to the *Amoskeag* accounts, the narratives of the Lowell mill workers depict a system of textile production that depended on covert networks of cooperative effort among workers. The motive of this cooperation was both practical and subversive: to make the piecework system (paying by measured output), which had been designed by the mills to reduce labor costs, yield the highest possible weekly wage.

By participating in the recruitment and training of new workers, by coaxing the aging machines to run, and by coordinating the process of work, mill workers contributed to managing the mills in ways that were crucial to production but taken for granted or ignored by the mill managers. In contrast to the workers at Amoskeag, Lowell mill workers created a decentralized and sometimes oppositional work culture unappreciated by managers. However, the issues of markets, competition, and profits that ultimately determined the fate of the Lowell mills remained far beyond the reach of mill workers. While tensions over job opportunities and labor protest often divided men and women workers, other experiences united them. The bonds forged among mill workers during the training process and while making cloth reinforced the cultural and social bonds experienced alike by the sons and daughters of immigrants.

The narratives are preceded by two introductory sections. The first presents the historic setting of economic development and subsequent decline of the textile industry in Lowell. The second is a brief explanation of the production process wherein the last generation of mill workers expended so many of their skills and so much of their energy.

THE LAST GENERATION

Textile Industrialization in Lowell

L o w e l l has always meant the mass production of cotton textiles. The city's place in American history began in the 1820s even before railroad tracks connected its mills with Boston's docks and the seaborne trade with the cotton South. Financed with profits from Boston merchant traders and built on a transportation canal once used to float timber down the Merrimack River from the White Mountains of New Hampshire to the shipyards of Newburyport, Massachusetts, Lowell was an early phenomenon of American industrialization.

Nineteenth-Century Background

The innovations at Lowell extended the scope and potential of earlier, smaller companies. Integrated machine production of cotton cloth in a single factory began at Waltham, Massachusetts, in 1815, but the company's capacity was restricted by the limited water power from the shallow and sluggish Charles River. Excited by the possibilities of large-scale production and big profits, the Waltham investors searched for a place with a vast water-power potential and undeveloped land. They found it in 1821 at the turbulent falls of the Merrimack River and in the nearby pastures of the village of East Chelmsford.

By 1830, large factories turned raw cotton from the plantations of the American South into cheap, serviceable cotton cloth. Inside those factories, young women from the rural villages and towns of New England tended machinery powered first by water wheels and later by turbines. These Yankees had been attracted to factory work by the unprecedented opportunity for women to earn wages. Their parents' fears about their daughters' involvement in factory work were calmed by the protective care promised in a system of boardinghouses maintained by the factory owners. Farm families, southern slaves, and workers in growing northern cities began to wear the cloth made at Lowell.

Cotton was not the only textile made in early nineteenth-century Lowell. In spite of Lowell's reputation as a place where cotton was king, small woolen mills, like the Middlesex Company organized in 1830, also drew water from Lowell's two rivers to produce both narrow and broad woolen cloth. Scottish and English woolen and carpet workers from Paisley and Gloucestershire as well as calico printers from Lancashire joined the growing population of Yankee operatives and Irish construction workers. Diversified textile operations intensified in Lowell after the Civil War.

The enormous profits of the ten large Lowell corporations from mass production of cheap staple cotton goods inspired swift imitation and serious competition in the 1840s. New textile factories built in Massachusetts, New Hampshire, and Maine prompted the mill managers of Lowell to cut their production costs to maintain their profits and stock dividends. Mill agents began to increase the speed of the machinery, while giving workers responsibility for third looms and extra spinning frames. Women workers saw these speed-ups and stretch-outs as unfair and exhausting. When the mills cut the wages of their Yankee women operatives in the 1830s and again in the 1840s, conflict erupted between labor and capital. Some women workers went out on strike and formed labor organizations to resist wage cuts, while others left the mills in disgust to return home or seek other work.

These conflicts and the stiff resistance of Yankee women to mistreatment led the mill managers to consider other kinds of workers. In the 1840s, families of Irish settlers who had dug the canals and built the mills were joined by new immigrants fleeing the potato famine in Ireland. The Yankee workers stayed in the highest paying and most skilled jobs, but Irish faces slowly appeared in the mills, first as sweepers and laborers and later as spinners and weavers. The Irish also proved unruly. In 1859, a rebellion of Irish spinners against a wage cut showed that women from Irish families would resist mistreatment in much the same way Yankees did.

The Civil War ended Lowell's golden age of expansion, high profits, and notoriety as a successful model of American-style textile industrialization. When the war curtailed the southern supply of cotton, the Lowell mills cut production sharply and sold raw cotton for quick profits, while the woolen mills boomed, producing the navy-blue cloth worn by Union soldiers. After the Union victory, the mill owners of Lowell became eager to compete once more with the growing cotton centers of Fall River and New Bedford, Massachusetts. Mill managers began to recruit new workers from the eastern provinces of Canada. French-speaking people abandoned the worn-out land and depressed farm prices of Quebec to immigrate in large numbers to the textile centers of New England. Many of them came to Lowell. They were followed in turn by other emigrants from southern and eastern Europe and the Middle East: Greeks, Poles, Portuguese, Italians, Russians, Jews,

Syrians, and Lebanese. The great surges of late nineteenth- and early twentieth-century population movements to the United States coincided with an expanding American economy eager to put them to work.

These new immigrants worked at jobs in a diversified textile economy in Lowell. By 1900, in addition to the big cotton mills and small woolen mills, the city had factories that knit stockings and underwear of cotton and wool and that wove floor carpets and mohair plush for the upholstery of furniture and train seats. Small cotton mills produced narrow, specialty products: thread, elastic, shoelaces, tapes, cords, suspenders, and ribbons. Machine shops turned out textile machinery and machine parts. Mill supply operations provided dyestuffs, leather belting, stair treads, paper and wooden boxes, and the countless other needs of textile factories. A huge tannery, the American Hide and Leather, added its pollution to the river water, as did a big bleachery and various cloth printing and dye works. In the decades following the Civil War, Lowell grew into a mature industrial city with a population dominated by people of immigrant backgrounds.

Lowell as an Industrial City in 1900

When the twentieth century began, New England remained preeminent in cotton textile manufacture, with twice as many spindles and three times as many looms as any other region. Lowell had over ninety thousand residents. More than thirty thousand men, women, and children in their early teens worked in manufacturing jobs of all kinds, the majority in textile production. Fifty-eight percent of the textile workers labored in cotton mills, 20 percent in knitting operations, 12 percent in woolen and worsted production, and another 10 percent in the construction of textile machinery and parts.

In 1900 75 percent of the city's population was first- or second-generation immigrants, and 42 percent was foreign-born. A decade later, only 20 percent of the more than 100,000 inhabitants were native-born Americans of native parents. The remaining 80 percent were split roughly between English-speaking people from Great Britain, Ireland, and Canada and non–English-speaking first- and second-generation immigrants. Half of the non-English-speaking group (20,000) or about 20 percent of the total population was French Canadian, followed by smaller but important populations of Greeks (8,000), Jews (2,500), Portuguese (2,500), Swedes (2,000), and Poles (2,000).

Many of the parents of the last generation of textile workers in Lowell

Bird's-eye view of Lowell in 1939. The Boott mills are located to the left of the Bridge Street Bridge and the Massachusetts mills to the right. *Courtesy of the Center for Lowell History.*

had worked in the mills, laboring in aging, dilapidated brick buildings on worn-down machinery, six days a week, usually ten hours a day except for a half day on Saturdays. The work was hot, dangerous, and difficult, as it had always been. Wage cuts were common when the market for cloth was overstocked or the economy was depressed.

The cotton mill managers in Lowell worked together and with other New England mill managers to avoid competition, oppose state regulation of working conditions, and undermine labor unions. Only skilled workers such as mule spinners and loom fixers were able to create labor organizations with enough strength and continuity to win a little respect from the mill agents. Important strikes in 1903 and again in 1912 that organized both skilled and unskilled mill workers ultimately failed to create viable unions. Except for the building trades, Lowell remained an anti-union city in the early twentieth century. The last generation learned to associate better times only with the two world wars, when the military required huge quantities of cloth for uniforms, parachutes, flags, blankets, and tents. Unions did not begin to come into the textile mills until after the outbreak of World War II in Europe. By then many of the textile mills in Lowell had gone out of business or moved South.

Many members of the last generation entered the Lowell mills in the 1920s and 1930s when the industry faced regional depression and intensifying competition, initially from the growing cotton industry in the South and later from Asian imports. The twelve thousand jobs in cotton manufacture in 1919 shrank to three thousand in 1936, a decline of 75 percent. In the ten years between 1926 and 1936, twenty thousand looms fell silent as five of the original textile companies shut down or moved South. From a work force of four thousand in 1920, only 250 men remained to build textile machinery.

By 1936 the woolen and worsted industry had replaced cotton as Lowell's most valuable manufacturing sector. Forty percent of the city's 100,000 residents, many of them cotton mill workers, received some

Mill worker housing in the Acre, 1939. *Courtesy of the Lowell Housing Authority and the Center for Lowell History.*

form of public relief. Cotton mill buildings were either razed to their granite foundations, abandoned to disuse, or used for storage, retail sales such as auto dealerships, and small industries such as cracker factories. King cotton had abdicated. Of the ten major cotton mills organized to weave cloth in the early nineteenth century, only two (Boott and Merrimack) remained by 1936, and they had already substituted specialty lines of corduroys, velveteens, and towels for staple goods like flannels, sheetings, and shirtings.

Why had this happened? The causes of the decline were multiple. The tastes of consumers had shifted from cotton goods such as ging-hams to silks and rayons. Whatever demand remained for cotton cloth could be satisfied by cheaper southern textiles made possible by the lower wages of mill workers. State regulation of industrial labor and higher taxes on machinery and profits in Massachusetts magnified this southern advantage. As their share of the market declined in the 1920s, many mill owners in Lowell refused even to think about modernizing their buildings or their equipment. The Great Depression of the 1930s finished off many of them.

If they could find them, cotton mill workers moved into better-paying textile jobs in small factories that produced silk, wool, and rayons. The local supply of cheap semiskilled, non-union labor drew other light industry to Lowell as the cotton mills declined. By 1950 the only good news in textiles was rayon manufacturing, while seventeen shoe fac-tories, fourteen garment-making shops, and three manufacturers of electrical equipment occupied mill space and employed hundreds of workers.

When the two remaining cotton textile mills shut down in the mid-1950s, the last generation of mill workers in Lowell spent the final years of their working lives in a complex local labor market of high turnover and multiple light industries. In spite of these jobs, widespread unem-ployment was a persistent reality throughout the city by the 1960s. Unemployment figures fell only when Defense Department contracts in the 1970s stimulated the local electronics industry and when com-puters, many of them designed and built in Massachusetts, became a commonplace in American society.

Members of the last generation had survived the worst that economic decline and hard times could deliver. Their experiences in the mills had taught them one hard, essential lesson that they all shared, whatever their religion, their ethnic background, their sex, or their abilities. They never wanted to see their children at work in any mill.

The Production Process

A TYPICAL WORKING DAY in the early twentieth-century Lowell mills began very early.

> Every morning at quarter of six, every door in the Acre would open, and we'd all troop out, down to the Merrimack, the Prescott, the Boott, or the Tremont and Suffolk. We'd all be going down Merrimack Street in those days in the early morning. It was crowded with the mill workers going to work.

Mill bells rang out at 5:45 A.M. to signal the approach of the next shift. Quickly the streets became jammed with hundreds of workers. Some talked and laughed to each other, others sang to themselves, but all hurried to beat the closing of the mill gates at 6 A.M. sharp and thus avoid the fines for stragglers and the humiliation of being made to wait while the rest went to work. Whether the streets were slippery with warm summer rain or icy and cold, the atmosphere inside the mill was always the same: hot, stuffy, linty, humid, and noisy. Each day of the work week was identical, except for Saturday mornings when young mill workers restlessly anticipated their pay envelopes and the freedom and pleasures of Saturday night.

Once inside the mill yard, workers headed up the old spiraling iron staircases to their sections. In the weave room as the looms pounded away, a red light flashed the signal that the third shift was over and the first shift had begun. Weavers rushed to their machines and reset the pick-counters that measured productivity for each shift, the basis for weekly wages. After that, the pick-counters would credit the workers on the first shift for each movement of the shuttle in the looms. Then the weavers took off their coats and hats and put on their mill clothes and work shoes. Loom fixers picked up their tool boxes and surveyed the looms for those most likely to break down. In the spinning rooms, the carding rooms, and throughout the mill, the first-shift men and women replaced those late-shift workers who were headed home to sleep and report back at 11 P.M. In the dye houses and cloth-finishing areas, boilers spewed steam into the atmosphere, making it difficult to see.

Although the ethnic background of Lowell mill workers changed over the decades, the experience of mill work remained essentially what it had been since the founding of the city. Most mill workers had little formal training or what the managers recognized as skills. They taught each other the work. If a worker got hurt around the machinery, the boss did not want to hear about it, and if someone told him, the injured got blamed. Mill workers were fined for defects in their work, which were often caused by conditions beyond their control. They rarely saw new machinery or improvement in the condition of the deteriorating mill buildings. The market determined how much and what kinds of cloth to make, and, when that market became depressed, workers got laid off. Mill work seemed routine and timeless: the bells tolled, the shifts changed, and sons and daughters followed their parents into the mills.

Yet it was impossible to make cloth without actively engaging the energy and judgment of mill workers in the complicated process of production. Turning a five-hundred-pound bale of raw cotton into cloth by using many different operations and intricate, powered machines is one of the miraculous achievements of industrialization. Even late twentieth-century observers can be dazzled by watching perfectly woven fabric emerge from the crashing noise and dirty grease of an automatic loom operating in a weave room filled with heat, steam, sweat, and lint. In order to grasp the meaning of textile work for the last generation, it is essential to understand the fundamentals of textile production as it was performed before 1950.

Fiber into Yarn

The first step in preparing cotton fiber for spinning into yarn is to loosen or open up the compressed bale of raw cotton and clean out the dirt and plant debris. Cotton from various bales is then mixed together and blended to achieve greater uniformity. These procedures are called opening and picking. Both were men's jobs. The hazardous work of cutting open the steel bands on the tightly compressed bales and mixing up the highly flammable cotton was performed in separate buildings, at some distance from the rest of the machine operations. The picking process produces a lap or roll of cotton about an inch thick and usually forty to forty-five inches wide that weighs about forty pounds. These laps are carried or trucked to the carding room.

In the carding room the cotton lap composed of mixed cotton fibers that still contain some debris is fed into a carding machine. The carding operation both disentangles and cleans the fibers so that they can be spun into yarn. The mechanism inside the large, whirling cylinders of the massive card grabs at the cotton lap with rows of tiny sawlike teeth and wire brushes. They strip and work the cotton, plucking it apart and straightening the fibers into more parallel lines. The cotton emerges from the carding machine as a fine web that is immediately reshaped into a sliver or ropelike strand of soft cotton about the size of a broomstick. The sliver is then coiled into a can (see figs. A and B). Most of these jobs on either cotton or wool were done by men, although additional operations to carding such as combing were the work of women (see the narratives of Sidney Muskovitz and Emma Skehan). In combing, those slivers intended for fine yarns of high quality are combed by several rows of needles to remove any short fibers and to straighten them further.

The process following carding is called drawing. The coiled slivers are recombined several times with other slivers for additional strength and uniformity. A drawing frame straightens and blends the slivers by running them through a series of rollers that are operating at progressively faster speeds, drawing them out so that what emerges from the process is no larger than those slivers fed in. The action of being pulled through these rollers does not stretch the cotton but rearranges the fibers and makes them more parallel within the sliver. One drawing operation is never enough, and repeated drawings help straighten and blend the cotton fibers for uniformity. The sliver is then ready to be reduced to a size suitable for spinning.

Many of the jobs in textile production involve twisting and winding the fibers in preparation for actual high-speed spinning. Each combination of operations gives the yarn specific characteristics. In the first step, called roving, the sliver is transferred from its can, twisted slightly and reduced in size, and wound onto a bobbin. Made of hard wood with holes drilled through the center, bobbins represent one of the most easily recognized artifacts of textile production. Many hands were required to insert the bobbins into the winding, twisting, and spinning machines and to doff or remove them when they were full of yarn (see fig. C). Most men and women began to learn textile work by doffing bobbins. Workers had to clean any remaining cotton roving off the bobbins by hand before they could be reused.

Spinning converts roving into yarn. Most spinners were women (see the narratives of Valentine Chartrand, Martha Doherty, and Jean Rouses). It was their job to watch the spinning frames carefully and repair or piece up any broken roving or yarn with a twist of their fingers. Roving is converted to yarn by reducing its size and giving it strength

FIGURE A: Cotton web emerges from a carding machine and is reshaped into a sliver. *Courtesy of MATH.*

through twist. If the material is filling yarn (or weft), to be used crosswise in the loom during the weaving process, it might be spun on a mule spinning frame by men. Filling yarn requires less twist than warp yarn.

Mule spinning involves huge machines that move back and forth on tracks in the mill floor (see p. 169). The mule spinner oversees the drawing out and twisting of the yarn and then reverses the action to allow the spun yarn to be taken up on filling bobbins. Next he doffs and replaces the full bobbins. The skill of the spinner permits him to produce the correct specifications of the yarn required, while he pieces up broken ends as the machine is operating. (See the narrative of Charles Costello.)

As spinning technology advanced in the twentieth century, most cotton filling yarn was spun on ring spinning machines (see fig. D), which were operated by women workers who needed less skill and could be paid lower wages than the mule spinners whom they replaced (see p. 134). Many of the spinning jobs required workers to pace around or "patrol" the work area, stopping only to piece up or clean off excess cotton. Mabel Mangan recalled: "I never had a job that I sat down." Filling yarn is wound onto filling bobbins to be inserted into the shuttles either by hand or by an automatic machine, called a battery, attached to the loom. While they refilled the batteries for the looms as battery hands, aspiring weavers began to learn their jobs by watching those who were experienced.

Warp yarn composes the lengthwise construction of fabric. Warp yarn is spun on a ring spinning frame that adds enough twist to give it additional strength and elasticity to stand up to the pounding action of the loom. After it is spun, it is wound from the spinning bobbins onto spools or double-headed wooden bobbins to form large packages of yarn for the warping process. The spools are placed into creels behind the warping mechanism.

Warping involves the assembly of warp yarn into a sheet of hundreds and hundreds of parallel yarns that are wound around a large wooden double-headed warp beam. In an intricate, painstaking process involving creels or racks loaded with spools of warp yarn, a woman worker carefully arranges each piece of yarn on the warp beam (see the narrative of Lucie Cordeau). Each yarn must be aligned parallel to the next piece while the beam slowly revolves to take up the yarn from the spools in the creel (see fig. E).

FIGURE B: Cotton carding operation. *Courtesy of MATH.*

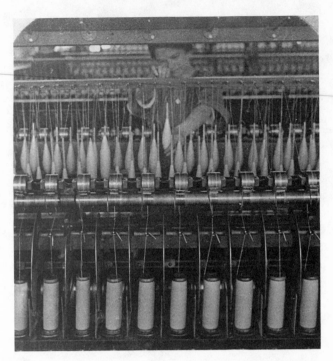

FIGURE C: Twisting, one of the processes of turning fiber into yarn. *Courtesy of MATH.*

After warping, the slashing process unwinds the warp yarns from the beam, passes them through a hot bath of starch or size, and then dries and rewinds them onto another beam ready for the loom (see p. 270). The sizing adds durability to the warp. The warp beam is inserted into the back of the loom just before weaving begins. Slashers or slasher tenders were usually men (see the narrative of Del Chouinard), but during wartime when labor was scarce, women also did the job of slashing. Warp riggers or change-over men inserted the beams into the back of the looms (see the narrative of Henry Pestana).

Before the loom can weave cloth, every warp end has to be drawn through the complicated weaving mechanism of the loom. This intricate and demanding operation, called drawing in, was once skilled women's work. Drawing-in girls (see the narratives of Grace Burk and Leona Pray) threaded the warp ends through the eyes of the heddles that were attached to harnesses that moved up and down when the loom began weaving (see p. 108). Finally, each warp yarn is pulled through the appropriate space or dent in the reed before the warp is placed in the loom. Some looms produce patterned weaves by using as many as forty harnesses and thousands of warp ends. Machines that were introduced to replace the drawing-in girls swiftly tied knots between the yarn on a

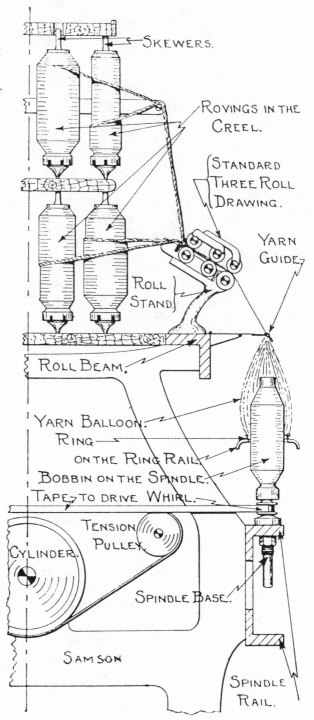

FIGURE D: Cross section of a ring spinning frame. Gilbert R. Merrill drawing. *Courtesy of Kenneth Merrill.*

SKEWERS.

ROVINGS IN THE CREEL.

STANDARD THREE ROLL DRAWING.

YARN GUIDE.

ROLL STAND.

ROLL BEAM.

YARN BALLOON.

RING

ON THE RING RAIL.

BOBBIN ON THE SPINDLE.

TAPE TO DRIVE WHIRL.

TENSION PULLEY.

CYLINDER.

SPINDLE BASE.

SAMSON

SPINDLE RAIL.

Figure E: Creels feeding warp yarn onto a warp beam. *Courtesy of MATH.*

new warp beam and the almost exhausted warp yarn still in the loom. After the machine process was completed, the warp rigger, standing in front of the loom, pulled the new warp yarns through the heddles and reed of the loom with the utmost care, trying not to break too many.

Yarn into Cloth

The warp yarn, wrapped around the beam in the back of the loom and threaded through the weaving mechanism, forms the lengthwise system of yarns in the fabric. The filling yarn wound onto bobbins placed in the shuttle of the loom creates the crosswise system of the cloth. But in order for the fabric to hold together, the warp and the filling yarn must interlace. This interlacing is achieved as the harnesses lift up alternating warp ends to form a shed or opening. The shuttle carrying the filling yarn passes through the shed created by alternating sets of lifted warp. Shuttles are made of hard wood with steel-pointed ends. They deliver the filling yarn to the weaving process through a hole or eye in the side of the shuttle. Each pass of the shuttle across the shed is called a pick. This opening and closing of the sheds formed by alternating yarns allows the interlacing action of weaving to take place (see fig. F).

After each pick or sideways movement of the shuttle, the reed that guides the warp yarn bangs hard against the filling yarn to tighten the weave. As the loom weaves cloth, the woven fabric is taken up and wound onto a cloth roll in the front of the loom, the warp beam slowly lets off more warp yarn, and the filling bobbins are replaced in the shuttles by hand or by battery. The noise is tremendous.

Heavy use of looms, hour after hour and day after day, inevitably results in both minor and major breakdowns. Loom fixers, who were always men, attended to the looms, making adjustments, replacing broken parts, and conducting general overhauls. Because the loom was the most complicated mechanism in the cotton mill, the loom fixers were regarded as the most skilled mechanics. Other male mechanics took care of the machinery for the rest of the operations.

The weave room was probably the most dynamic and interesting place in the cotton mill. Many workers including men and women weavers, loom fixers, cloth boys (who carried away the woven cloth), change-over men, battery hands, and smash-piecers (men and women

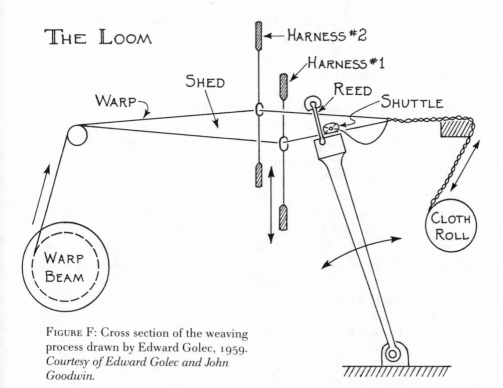

FIGURE F: Cross section of the weaving process drawn by Edward Golec, 1959. *Courtesy of Edward Golec and John Goodwin.*

who repaired breaks in the warp yarns caused by malfunctions in the looms) cooperated in complex and systematic ways to weave a product of first quality that earned the highest weekly wage. Their relationships with other workers, with their supervisors, and to their machines were shaped by the special vocabulary, behavior, and tensions of mill work.

Getting a place in the weave room usually did not depend on decisions made by mill managers or programs run by supervisors, but instead on personal connections. Experienced weavers recruited and trained young men and women and then certified their readiness to take on a full week's work. In most cases, neither the teacher nor the learner was paid for this training process. The fund of collective knowledge about mill work was passed on as a gift or favor from one generation to the next. One such skill was the tying of small, smooth weaver's knots that would pass easily through the eye of the heddles and the dent of the reed and would not slip. This pattern of being taught and teaching others created a bond among textile workers and represented one of the many ways that the workers themselves helped manage the process of making cloth.

The shared commitment of mill workers to production defied the divisive values of competition and wage incentives imposed by the piece-rate system. This commitment reflected those social bonds forged during the training process through which each person became a member of a common family of workers, each individually and all collectively in need of a decent weekly wage. There was no cash incentive when a weaver took time to train a younger person, when a smash-piecer started up a stalled loom, or when work was shared to allow time for someone to buy coffee. Mill managers did not pay a dime for these activities, which were critical to sustaining the pace of work.

Textile production depended on cooperation among workers, and in many mills, this coordination took place face-to-face. For example, weavers who needed help signaled the fixer with special hand motions or by placing bobbins on the loom in particular ways. The weavers' need to make the most money off the piece rate and the willingness of "good fixers" to make speedy repairs kept the looms going. In the 1930s, some mills, seeking even greater efficiency, replaced the worker-driven system by taking over the delivery of these messages. When weavers raised various colored flags on the looms, supervisors directed the fixers to make repairs. When managers gave the orders to workers, the system appeared more orderly, although speed and informal cooperation were sacrificed.

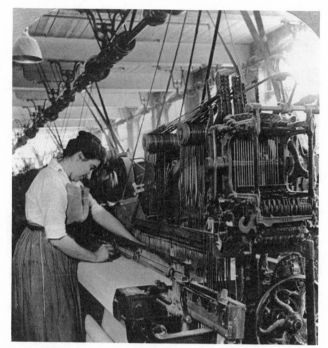

Weaver at a fancy loom with a dobby head. *Courtesy of MATH.*

After arriving for the first shift in the morning and resetting the pick-counters, the weavers changed into their work clothes, after shaking out the cockroaches. Many had walked or run to work, hoping to get into the mill before the gates were closed. One woman worker remembered that "the bells would ring at quarter of six, and my mother used to say, the gates would close on her heels. I'd have to run all the way down Worthen Street to get into the mill before the gate closed, for then you had to wait till the boss came out and got you." Another worker recalled that the bosses would ring the bell, and you would be right there, but "he'd shut the gate right on you." But others remembered that the gateman or the watchman might "feel sorry for you; he'd let you in sometimes." The tensions in the mill between supervisors and workers began with each shift.

Supervisors, overseers, or simply the "bosses" kept the time clock, collected data on production, enforced order, and demanded greater effort (see the narratives of James Simpson and Fred Burtt). One of these bosses was Joe Stewart who "went up the hard way" from an unskilled job to being an overseer at the Merrimack mills. He remembered:

I had to be mean to the help. Mean to your help to get the production out. You had to discharge people, and you hated like hell to do it because they hated to be discharged. I hated to tell anybody they were laid off. And I hated to give anyone hell for doing bad work. Being in a supervisory capacity, you had to do things that you wanted to cut your throat for the next day.

The woven cloth from the looms has to be finished and dyed, sometimes mended, and always inspected. Much of the finishing process depends on the type of cloth and its market. Cotton goods produced in Lowell were routinely bleached and dyed or bleached and printed in many colors. Men who worked in the bleacheries and dye houses of the cotton mills faced hazardous conditions (see p. 285), performing some of the worst kinds of work near scalding steam, dangerous chemicals, and indelible dyes. (See the narratives of Sidney Muskowitz, Nicholas Georgoulis, and James Ellis.) Heavy rolls of cloth are soaked in caustic, bleach, or dye and fed by hand into the steaming baths. Constant attention keeps the color even on the cloth, which when wet with dye weighs close to five hundred pounds. After dyeing, the water is spun out and the cloth dried.

Woolen fabrics dyed in the yarn and then woven are inspected by menders who carefully repair any flaws in the weave (see p. 129), thereby rescuing the cloth from being a "second" or inferior grade (see the narrative of Evelyn Winters). Women worked in the cloth room with its atmosphere of relative peace and quiet, inspecting cotton velvet and corduroy for imperfections or folding cotton towels (see the narratives of Yvonne Hoar and Mabel Mangan). The last step in the mill is packing up and shipping the cloth to its market.

Boott Cotton Mills

Organized in 1835 to mass-produce cheap cotton cloth, the Boott was typical of the large, integrated mills of Lowell. Its woes in the twentieth century were symptomatic of the slow decline in New England textiles, and workers at the Boott shared similar experiences with those at the Merrimack mill, the Massachusetts mills, and other large cotton mills in Lowell.

In the nineteenth century, managers at the Boott mills stuck to the production of long runs of a limited number of styles of cheap cloth that returned steady profits. Intensifying competition after the Civil War brought some changes to the kinds of cloth made at the Boott, but not to the primary goal of returning profits to shareholders and owners. By

1900 the Boott had one new mill building: the last significant investment in its operations. Managers hoped that different products like cotton velvet and corduroy would tap new markets, maintain profits, and justify that investment. By the 1890s, the Boott mills had bought Draper automatic looms whose batteries of bobbins fed the shuttles and required little assistance from workers, who could then be made responsible for additional machines. Boott managers used both this stretching-out of worker effort and the speeding-up of machines to increase levels of productivity.

Massachusetts law in 1874 limited work for textile operatives to ten hours a day, six days a week. In 1893, legislation further reduced the work week to fifty-eight hours, and in subsequent reforms, to fifty-four by 1912. Weekly earnings varied with the prices on the cloth market and the level of prosperity in the national economy, but the average yearly wage in 1902 for Lowell cotton mill workers was less than $300. In 1900, most of the work force at the Boott were second-generation Irish and first-generation French Canadians. Women performed many mill jobs, while male emigrants from Britain got the most skilled work and a chance at supervisory positions. Unions did not exist in the mills. By 1912, 85 percent of the Boott workers were foreign-born.

A corporate reorganization in 1905 set the Boott on its downward course in the twentieth century. Frederick A. Flather and his sons, Frederick and John Rogers, who ran the company until it closed in 1954, saw hope in restructuring production and cutting labor costs. Measured output by time clocks or devices such as pick-counters on looms and adjustable piece rates determined wages. Attempts to use scientific management policies to redesign work and increase productivity, however, remained partial. Engineering and management consultants were ignored, and planned outlays for reorganization or new buildings always fell victim to salaries and dividends. Haphazard spatial arrangements within the old mills and the problems created by running aging machines alongside new ones made efforts to tap new markets difficult. While managers talked about rebuilding the antiquated and delapidated brick structures and dreamed of new machinery, profit-taking always came before investment in new mills or equipment.

Production was buoyed temporarily by wartime orders for cotton canvas (duck) for the army, for white and black twill required for naval uniforms, and by occasional but strictly limited investments in new looms with dobby heads for patterned weaving in towels. The Boott

The Boott mill yard c. 1930 during the first shift. *Courtesy of MATH.*

management, however, refused to build for a future. An almost inevitable but lingering slide into bankruptcy followed key decisions made in the late 1920s to run the operations at the Boott into the ground. With the Flather sons in charge of this policy, workers lost hope in trying to make anything at the Boott work right (see the narrative of Harry Dickenson).

The Depression of the 1930s forced the Flathers to return to the production of cheap goods, which competed in markets already dominated by southern mills that had the advantages of cheaper labor and better equipment and plant. Demand created by military needs during World War II kept the mills operating, but also ushered in the first effective union organization. Beginning with the loom fixers, the Congress of Industrial Organizations (CIO) organized the Boott in 1942. The mills continued to produce a simplified line of goods: curtains, towels, corduroy, and twill for the navy, but this production was carried out by overworked and disgruntled employees in unheated buildings with leaking roofs, buckled floors, broken windows, and antiquated machinery, some of which dated from the late nineteenth century. These conditions created high labor costs that historian Laurence Gross has argued had nothing whatever to do with state labor laws or unions.

Contract talks between labor and management encouraged the use of time- and motion-studies and job standardization that worsened working conditions. Dissatisfied workers left the Boott for better work in other textile mills (see the narratives of Albert Morrissette and Albert Cote). As the result of a general textile depression in the early 1950s, the Flathers declared in 1953 that unless the union negotiated give-backs in wages, the mill would close. The union refused to believe this, but in May 1954, the Boott mills suspended operations.

Abbot Worsted Mills

In contrast to the large cotton mills, woolen and worsted production was often small and decentralized. Employees numbered in the hundreds rather than the thousands. Although woolen mills like the Bay State Mills, Uxbridge Worsted, and United States Bunting in Lowell and the Navy Yard in nearby Dracut made finished products, others like Southwell Combing in North Chelmsford, near the Lowell city line, concentrated on carding and combing operations. Abbott Worsted specialized in yarn production and did not weave cloth.

Abbot Worsted began in 1855 at the rural village of Graniteville in the town of Westford, ten miles west of Lowell. Owned by partners of Yankee and Scottish background, the small mill first made carpets and upholstery goods, but when it expanded its operations to Lowell in 1910, Abbot Worsted was specializing in spinning worsted yarn for new markets in automobile upholstery. During the 1920s Abbot, unlike most cotton mills, developed paternalistic projects for worker welfare including low-rental corporation housing in Westford, company-sponsored team sports, and free health care. The managers also introduced careful product measurement in testing laboratories and time- and motion-studies on the mill floor. Some employees had trained at the Lowell Textile School where scientific management and measurement techniques were part of the curriculum since its founding in 1895 (see the narratives of James Simpson and Fred Burtt).

In the 1930s woolen and worsted operations replaced the failing cotton mills as the city's most valuable industry and provided higher wages and better conditions. War orders for khaki yarns during World War II kept the woolen and worsted mills of Lowell prosperous, but the postwar years brought declining markets for pure worsted yarns and increasing uncertainty. The mills began to spin wool yarn mixed with synthetics like Orlon and nylon. Company housing, land, and mills were sold off, while the worsted mill that Abbot set up in South Carolina never made any money. In a telling decision in the early 1950s, the sons of the Abbot partners refused to become involved in the worsted busness. In 1956 Abbot Worsted disappeared, and former managers sold off its machinery.

The production of worsted and woolen cloth differs in some significant ways from the production of cotton textiles. Sheeps' wool is much more costly than cotton. The average eight-pound fleece is permeated with a greasy substance (refined into lanolin) that must be removed along with various kinds of vegetable debris, animal manure, and stains. The first step is to trim and sort the fleece into grades and then to wash or scour the wool in a washing process that for years polluted countless streams throughout New England. After the wool is dried, it is sent to the carding operation to be turned into slivers coiled in cans. Abbot Worsted did its own sorting, scouring, and carding, but Southwell Combing, known as a top mill, sold its product off as wool roving or tops. Different processes turned wool tops into worsted yarns.

Woolen yarn is soft and fuzzy with less twist than worsted yarn. Wool sorters choose fleeces with longer fibers and more natural crimp from breeds like the Merino sheep for worsted yarns. This wool provides better twist in spinning and a harder and more resilient finished appearance. Differences in the process of carding also distinguish woolen from worsted. Accumulations of soft wool lint made the carding process difficult by clogging the bearings and forcing Sidney Muskovitz, who worked at Southwell, to wipe his glasses every fifteen minutes. Uniformity in fiber intended for worsted cloth is achieved by combining carding, fine combing, and a process like cotton drawing called gilling. The English or Bradford spinning system done on gilling and spinning frames produced smooth, thin, durable worsted yarns with a lot of twist.

Fiber intended for woolen cloth emerges from carding as softer and more tangled. It goes directly to the spinning process without combing or drawing. The French system, usually carried out on mule spinning machines, produced soft, thick woolen yarn with little twist. Mule spinning continued in woolen and worsted operations long after the cotton mules had been junked, but by the mid-1930s mule spinners had lost their jobs in woolen factories (see the narrative of Charles Costello).

The weaving of woolen and worsted cloth is similar to cotton, but it is done on machines that are heavier in construction than cotton looms. More intricate patterns of finer detail are used in worsted where they are more visible than in woolen. The mending and inspection process for worsted often required the reconstruction of those complicated patterns by women menders whose work truly represented a trade in the industry (see the narrative of Evelyn Winters).

Newmarket Manufacturing Company

The silk industry in Lowell moved in after 1920 to replace older textile operations such as carpet weaving. Like woolen and worsted mills, silk mills were small and employed fewer workers than cotton mills, but they usually paid better. In 1934, Abbot Worsted employed 450, the Newmarket 1,000, while the Boott and the Merrimack employed a total of 3,700 workers. The movement of the Newmarket Manufacturing Company to Lowell represented new diversification of textile production in the twentieth-century city.

The Newmarket mill originated in the town of Newmarket in southern New Hampshire where it had been organized in 1823 as a small cotton mill. By the early twentieth century it was known for the silk cloth it wove and the silk yarn that it sold. In 1924, the Newmarket opened a subsidiary mill in Lowell called the Lowell Silk Mill where it introduced the production of artificial silk or rayon. Caught in unresolved and persistent labor troubles at its location in New Hampshire, Walter Gallant moved all the Newmarket operations to Lowell in 1931. John Falante and Joseph Golas were among the silk workers who relocated with the mill (see their narratives).

The Newmarket produced cloth for casket linings made partly of silk and partly of rayon, but it also made fancy silk cloth and intricate weaves depending on market demand. The mill's management was known among its own supervisors as a "tight outfit" that paid lower wages than necessary, even during the depression years. Each month, late shifts were alternated among the work force to avoid paying any worker the special higher wages for night work. Warp rigger Henry Pestana (see his narrative) observed the efficiency of the operations at the Newmarket in the 1930s that depended on speedy communications, an intense pace of work, and short cuts that workers devised to enable them to earn some money.

Efficiency at the Newmarket demanded stern opposition to unions, but strikes supported by weavers (see the narrative of Narcissa Hodges) continued to plague the managers throughout the 1930s until the CIO organized the mill in the late 1940s. In 1954 the Newmarket was purchased by Textron, Inc., a Providence, Rhode Island, corporation based on New England textile companies run by Royal Little. Textron quickly closed the Newmarket and wrote off the losses for tax advantages. Newmarket workers drifted into the production of synthetics or left the textile industry.

Silk fiber is produced entirely by the silkworm as it spins a long, very fine filament for its cocoon. Raw silk unwound from the silkworms' cocoons by skilled workers and rewound onto reels was exported to the American silk industry by Asian companies like Mitsubishi of Japan. Raw silk is spun or thrown into yarn without any need for carding, combing, or drawing processes.

At the Newmarket, workers took the silk yarn already dyed from its packages and rewound it onto quills or filling bobbins that were then inserted into shuttles (see the narrative of Dori Nelson). This meant that the Newmarket was essentially a weaving operation. Silk was troublesome yarn for weavers; it was delicate, slippery, and full of static electricity. Silk weavers earned the best wages working on Jacquard looms that used programmed instructions on punch cards to manipulate the warp yarns one at a time and produce intricate patterns. Women silk workers gloried in the colors and beauty of the cloth.

Wannalancit Mills

In 1933 the Wannalancit Mills began to make rayon textiles from manufactured filaments of cellulose. Much less expensive than silk, rayon became popular in the late 1920s and 1930s, replacing some light cotton goods. Occupying empty mill space at the old Appleton cotton mills, this small operation set up by Alan Larter and later run by his son Edward wove Celanese and rayon satin, taffetas, and crepes. One of the mill's backers was Louis Olney, a professor of textile chemistry at the Lowell Textile Institute.

The military's need for synthetics during World War II, especially for nylon parachutes, stimulated the industry in Lowell. Synthetic Yarns occupied additional mill space in the old Lawrence mills, while the Atlantic Parachute Company assembled and packed parachutes in other empty mill space. After the war, the Wannalancit moved into the old Tremont and Suffolk mill that in the 1920s had been bought by the Nashua Manufacturing Company of New Hampshire to produce sheeting, but it had closed in the 1930s. In the 1950s, as most cotton, woolen and worsted, and silk operations closed down, Larter acquired their cast-off machinery and workers and began to weave nylon and Dacron cloth.

The Wannalancit operated as a weaving subcontractor, buying synthetic yarns from chemical companies like American Viscose or DuPont and converting them into fabric. As bosses, Larter and his son proved paternalistic and even generous, an approach that contrasted with the Newmarket managers and one that stimulated loyalty and kept the union out. Workers who wanted to stay in textiles could find jobs at the Wannalancit, but their numbers continued to dwindle in the 1960s and 1970s until, after an unsuccessful endeavor at hiring Latin American textile workers, the Wannalancit finally closed its doors in 1980.

Natural cotton and wool fibers have short lengths. The beauty of manufactured synthetic filament yarns lies in their smoothness, uniformity, and long length. Textiles such as rayons, Orlon, Dacron, polyester, and acrylic are various compounds of cellulose and chemical mixtures. Manufactured yarns are extruded through metal caps or nozzles into liquid chemical baths or other mediums. The chemist imitates the silkworm. The filaments are then twisted like raw silk to make yarn. The weaving process for manufactured and synthetic yarns is much like that for silk.

Whether they worked in mills that made cotton, woolen, worsted, silk, or rayon cloth, the mill workers of Lowell lived and worked in a city beset with decay in all branches of its basic industry. The uncertainty and confusion made it difficult to find any steady work at a decent wage. In the 1930s and 1940s, workers moved from job to job in the remaining mills, adapting to the requirement of each process. As old companies collapsed and new enterprises tried unsuccessfully to fill up the huge, empty mill space with activity, high turnover among the labor force became commonplace. But the choices for jobs in the mills were few. Mill work as a way of life was slowly vanishing.

Sources

Blewett, Mary H., ed. *Surviving Hard Times: The Working People of Lowell.* Lowell: Lowell Museum, 1982.

Davison's Textile Blue Book. Ridgewood, N.J.: Davison Publishing Co., 1908–1960.

Dublin, Thomas. *Women at Work: The Transformation of Work and Community in Lowell, Massachusetts, 1826–1860*. New York: Columbia University Press, 1979.

Eno, Arthur L., et al., eds. *Cotton Was King: A History of Lowell, Massachusetts.* Lowell Historical Society. Somersworth, N.H.: New Hampshire Pub., 1976.

Gross, Laurence F. *Public Morals and Private Interests: The Boott Cotton Mills and the Pattern of American Industry*. Baltimore: Johns Hopkins University Press, forthcoming.

Lowell City Directories.

Merrill, G. R., et al. *American Cotton Handbook*. New York: American Cotton Handbook Company, 1941.

Miller, Marc Scott. *The Irony of Victory: World War II and Lowell, Massachusetts*. Urbana: University of Illinois Press, 1988.

Mitchell, Brian C. *The Paddy Camps: The Irish of Lowell, 1821–61*. Urbana: University of Illinois Press, 1988.

Norkunas, Martha K. "The Ethnic Enclave as Cultural Space: Women's Oral Histories of Life and Work in Lowell, Massachusetts." In *Cotton Was King*, edited by Robert Weible. Vol. 2. Nashville, Tenn.: The State and Local Historical Association, forthcoming.

Parker, Margaret Terrell. *Lowell: A Study in Industrial Development*. New York: Macmillan, 1940.

Potter, David M., and Bernard P. Coleman. *Textiles: Fiber to Fabric*. 4th ed. New York: McGraw-Hill Book Co., 1967.

Shanahan, Kevin. "Study of the Abbot Worsted Mills of Westford, 1855–1956." Unpublished paper, 1970, at the Center for Lowell History.

Transcriptions of group interviews conducted by Mary Blewett and Paul Page, and by Mike Wurm and Andy Chamberlain on Mill Workers' Reunion Day, 1985, at the Center for Lowell History.

The Women

Introduction

G ROWING UP FEMALE in a working-class family that lived in early twentieth-century Lowell meant learning hard lessons early. The general parameters of life for working-class children regardless of ethnic background were distinct. For most girls, school ended at fourteen; chances to earn a high school diploma vanished. After giving up their formal education, these young women appeared to accept their lot with resignation and a clear understanding of their lack of alternatives: "You got used to it"; "We had to take what came"; "We had no choice"; "I knew my place"; "We had to work for a living"; "We had to make a week's pay in order to survive." Still, the challenges of work and family life offered women mill workers the opportunity to develop abilities and strengths in which they took justified pride as they remembered their lives.

A working-class family rented a small house or tenement large enough for many brothers and sisters, sometimes for grandparents. Everyone walked or rode the trolleys. Families owned little; there were no savings. The work week stretched from Monday morning at six to Saturday afternoon when the first shift got paid. Families were absolutely dependent upon the combined wages of their working members to meet household expenses for basic necessities: "three squares a day," heat, clothing, and rent. At fourteen, girls were expected to contribute. Young women as well as young men were ready to help out.

The domestic setting for many mill worker families in the early twentieth century was the grim world of cold-water tenements filled with cheap, galvanized objects like beds, tubs, and lunch pails. Coal fires were essential to heat water in boilers for the endless washes, even during the summer swelter. In the winter, the kitchen was often the only heated room. Getting ahead meant having a hallway toilet instead of an outhouse. Kerosene lamps lit the table where the family gathered for meals, for homework, and for instruction in the language and customs of the homeland. Bath night in a crowded tenement presented special problems for maintaining modesty and containing sexual curiosity. Mothers usually resolved these difficulties by separating the boys and girls and locking one group into their rooms until the washing had been performed.

Working-class girlhood. Interior of Acre housing, 1939. *Courtesy of Lowell Housing Authority and the Center for Lowell History.*

In these tenements, little girls watched their mothers and grand-mothers work tirelessly on behalf of the family. Mothers enforced high standards of domestic cleanliness that meant scrubbing the warped, wide-board floors and scouring the battered stairs and hallways. They stretched the small wages paid for mill work by baking bread and cooking large thrifty meals, filling dinner pails for noontime at the mill, and by making most of the family's clothes. On Monday mornings, the neighborhoods dripped with huge washes of coarse work clothes and family linen done on washboards and hung out to dry. Women knitted for the winter, and in the summer, if they could, they grew vegetables and tended fruit trees, using agricultural skills that they brought with them from Poland or Quebec.

Mothers swapped services such as nursing, midwifery, child care, and sewing with their neighbors, sometimes for pay, more often in barter. They brought medical skills from their homelands where doctors had been scarce and cures depended on observant amateurs. Occasionally a neighbor would bake the bread left to rise by a busy mother who worked the second shift. One mother fed Lowell businessmen their midday dinner until she had her fifth child and the effort became too much.

Other women took in industrial homework supplied by local shoe shops for a few cents in payment. The image left in a daughter's mind was one of lifelong, significant activity by her female relatives in support of family life.

Whether a mother worked for wages depended on the number of children in the family and on the occupation of the father. The larger the family, the less likely a mother was to be able to earn income, but some managed to. Then the household chores and child minding fell to school-age daughters, especially the oldest daughter who gave up her childhood for adult duties. If the father was a mill worker, it was likely that both parents worked, and, for as long as the mills offered steady employment, parents prepared their children to enter the work force as early as possible. A mother with young children who was deserted or abused by her husband faced dreadful alternatives. The death of a spouse usually presented a stark choice between hasty remarriage or extreme difficulty.

Some women demonstrated inexhaustible physical vitality, helpful medical know-how, and a readiness to fight to protect their families and their friends. They earned the respect of their neighbors and co-workers and left indelible impressions on their daughters. Some mothers worked full time in the mills. More mothers were forced into work during the hard years of the Depression of the 1930s. Daughters took pride in their mothers' courage, their willingness to learn, and their skills on the job and in dealing with the bosses. Still, strong mothers could be difficult. Some Greek and French Canadian mothers arranged marriages for unwilling daughters. Objections went unheard. Pious mothers forced their resisting children to unwanted religious observances. Harried mothers turned on complainers with "If you think you can do better elsewhere, go!" Some energetic mothers wrestled unruly children to the floor; some had rolling pins used for making pita bread handy to keep the kids in line.

As important as a mother was, the relationship of a young girl to her father was often crucial to her sense of self-worth as a woman and to her enjoyment of a decent marriage as an adult. Fathers who ignored their daughters' needs or blocked their opportunities and then callously exploited them for the family welfare were remembered by them with barely concealed pain and resentment. A girl who felt abandoned or rejected by a father who cared little for her future faced life at great risk. But fathers who showed interest in and taught their daughters how to do things—to make music, to cook, to fish, to enjoy nature—forged strong and loving ties that were immensely important. Memories of paternal concern and kindness helped provide courage and confidence in later life.

Many first-generation, French Canadian immigrants, men and women, refused to become American citizens. Quebec Province was close enough to Lowell so that it was hard to abandon the idea of going back frequently to maintain family ties or even of returning for good. These immigrants built Little Canadas all over New England where young, unmarried sisters, brothers, cousins, and whole families came and went, moving from one textile city to another, depending on their connections. Because of the distance and the expense of travel, the break with the homeland was sharper for Polish, Greek, and Portuguese immigrant women. In the ethnic communities they built, new arrivals were cushioned against the shocking unfamiliarity of their American industrial environment. Each day after their shift, mill workers returned to these neighborhoods.

Religion and religious practices defined each ethnic community. Ethnic neighborhoods crowded around the separate Catholic churches for Poles, Portuguese, French Canadians, and Irish with priests of their own nationality and distinct festivals and holidays. Some French Canadian families said the rosary together after every meal; all the children, no matter what their age, were expected to join in. Misbehaving children were punished by being sent by their mothers to church. Some Greek Orthodox women cooked and baked on Sundays for their large families, while their husbands, as the head of the family, took the children to church. These women performed their own religious duties during the week, unobserved. For older kids, Saturday night fun ended abruptly at midnight if they wanted to take communion at Sunday Mass.

The "old Irish mothers" maintained family devotions no less rigorously than those from Quebec. Irish Catholic workers rose especially early on Holy Days of Obligation to get to five o'clock Mass before they went to work at six. Young Catholic women learned they would have no control over the number of children that they might have. As with many other aspects of their lives, they had no choice.

Language, customs, religion, festivals, food, and music preserved the central core of national feeling. Mothers and grandmothers cooked in the homeland ways, making Portuguese soups, Polish cabbage dishes, and French Canadian pork and fish suppers. First-generation immigrant women who stayed at home and took care of their large families usually did not feel the need or have the time to learn English. A working woman who entrusted her youngest to a day nursery where English was spoken actually risked having a child who could not understand her own mother's French or Greek. Schools run by religious organizations or by ethnic communities preserved and transmitted the native tongue to American-born children of immigrants. Knowing the English language could be helpful in the mills, in school, and in contacts outside the ethnic neighborhood, but conversing in the native language often eased the way to a better job in the mill and tied some coworkers together, though excluding others. Still, a knowledge of English or the ability to make yourself understood by people of other nationalities at moments of crisis could help when managers and workers of diverse backgrounds needed to understand each other.

In the Little Canada enclaves of French culture, language, and piety, the American-born second generation grew up in households where their mothers stayed home, taking care of large families, using huge pots and pans, and doing enormous washes. The children went to work as soon as they were able. Daughters of immigrant mothers left school at fourteen and went into the mills, and this employment made their lives different from their mothers. Second-generation French Canadian women married later, bore fewer children, and did not suffer the tragedies from high infant mortality that their mothers had. Others who had lost their mothers to ill-health and overwork cared for their families until the father died. When at last they married within their ethnic communities, they often left the work force but their families remained small.

The parochial school and the ethnic family taught obedience to religious, educational, and parental authority. Family life was loving but strict and controlling. Discipline for childhood errors could be direct and physical, but as one mill worker remembered, "there was so many of us, just like a pack of rats," there was safety in numbers. The strong ties of family life could promote a daughter's sense of self-worth and usually offered some protection for young girls as they entered puberty. Mothers and fathers watched their growing daughters closely; attitudes ranged between benevolent oversight and stern vigilance. Older women of the community handled whatever reproductive information seemed appropriate to share with young women, but vague warnings often served as uncertain guidelines. For most girls, sexual morality seemed to require ignorant virginity.

At fourteen and with school days behind them, working-class daughters were recruited by networks of family and friends into mill work.

French Canadian weavers, Boott Cotton Mills, 1905. *Courtesy of the Lowell Museum and the Center for Lowell History.*

Many interrupted their schooling on the exact day of their fourteenth birthday. There was little choice. They already knew what the inside of a mill looked like; they had carried dinner pails to their parents or had been shown their work. Working mothers not only brought their daughters into the mills but often taught them how to spin or weave. As mothers taught daughters, aunts taught nieces, and sisters taught sisters, their skills, experience, and knowledge of short-cuts were passed from one generation to another. But to a fourteen-year-old girl, learning to run the complex and deafening looms could be an overwhelming and frightening responsibility. Many ended up working as doffers while they learned to spin.

Young working women frequently learned just one job in the textile mill, and that job often became their life's work, unlike the opportunities to learn many jobs that were available to men. This training period was short because their families needed their wages immediately. Some mill workers' families lived so close to the edge that for Christmas to fall on a Thursday was "terrible." The loss of pay for three consecutive days (Thursday through Saturday) meant an even tighter budget and no presents.

Aspiring girls who hoped to escape mill work soon learned through the community grapevine that no Catholics worked as secretaries in the front offices of many textile mills and that Yankee and Irish women dominated the profession of nursing. Anti-Catholic and antiforeign feelings ran deep in the politics of Lowell, beginning with the arrival of the Irish in the early nineteenth century and reviving with each new wave of immigration. Contacts with Protestant women through such organizations as the Young Women's Christian Association could either blur or intensify ethnic feeling. The YWCA offered lessons to young women from immigrant families in how to cook, how to play, how to sew, and how to behave in American ways. Yet some girls chose to take from the experience only what they enjoyed most: making fudge and taking shower baths. The annual Miss Lowell Contest occasionally produced a blonde, blue-eyed winner from the ranks of mill workers whose girlfriends thrilled to see one of their own beat out more privileged candidates.

During their first two years, daughters worked the "short hours" of a forty-hour week with one afternoon of school. Then at the age of sixteen, they began to work a full week of forty-eight hours or more, five full days a week and a half day on Saturdays. Although a small minority attended high school or trade school hoping to land an office job, those young women usually ended up working in the mills. These working daughters turned their pay envelopes over unopened to their families every Saturday. Their mothers gave them an allowance of less than a dollar, usually whatever was in coin, for their own use. Working daughters were also expected to do domestic work for their families at the end of the day: scrubbing floors, washing dishes, ironing their brothers' shirts, and minding the younger children. They learned early about the double job of adult women: paid work in the mill and unpaid housework for the family. There was little distinction between work and home life for women workers; their families' survival depended on their incessant efforts.

Older women wore cotton dresses and aprons in the mill; after World War II younger women wore dungarees. Street clothes hung on hooks during the working day. Everybody wore old shoes or loafers with rubber soles to keep her footing on the slippery, oily floors. In the 1940s, spinners at the Merrimack put on blue aprons with big patch pockets for cotton waste. They carried thin, sharpened brass hooks to clean the cotton from the spinning frame mechanism. Weavers used round-headed scissors, hooks, combs, and picks.

Hair and braids were tightly bound to avoid catching them in the belting and having part of your scalp ripped off. Fingers got caught in unboxed gears and wheels. The atmosphere was gloomy; the Boott was known for its penny-pinching use of twenty-five-watt bulbs. A flashlight was essential if a worker really needed to see. The air was stuffy, overheated, and full of lint that got into hair, eyelashes, and lungs. There was no hot water for washing. Lunch breaks ran from fifteen to thirty minutes in most cotton mills. There were no lunch rooms. Women workers ate cold sandwiches and drank cold tea by their machines unless they had access to a steam pipe. The cockroaches and rats in the mill were legendary. Toilet breaks occurred while the machinery was running, and of the toilets, one woman worker reported, "the less said, the better!" The noise of the weave room deafened, and no children were permitted near the looms because of the danger of a shuttle with its pointed metal tip flying loose.

Physical hazards were matched by human abuses. The network of older family members recruiting younger workers offered some protection for women mill workers, but supervisors misused their authority and male workers misbehaved. Any presentable young woman who walked into a mill looking for work became an easy target. Taking their cues from the petty tyrannies practiced by the bosses, some male work-

Workers at a Lowell woolen mill in the 1930s. *Courtesy of the Lowell National Historical Park.*

ers felt free to annoy and molest women in the mill. Most bosses remained indifferent to such sexual harassment. Young women who needed to keep their attention on the work and the dangerous machinery were taken advantage of. Even then bosses rarely intervened. Many women regarded their bosses as "hard" and felt that they could make no complaint for fear of being fired. Women workers often appreciated the personal politeness and formal courtesy of their English immigrant overseers which they preferred to the rough manners of the other men who were bosses.

Female heads of families like widows eagerly sought the best-paying work they could find. There were different job ladders for women and men in the mills, however, and wages were lower for women's work. Women never gave orders to or supervised men, and they were discouraged from working with or learning to fix their machines. The highest job a woman weaver could aspire to was that of a weave room inspector. On the other hand, mending wool represented a genuine trade for women. Both mending and the clean, quiet work of cloth inspection in the cotton mills were generally reserved for well-connected women of Irish and French Canadian backgrounds.

Most women mill workers were spinners and winders of all sorts. Weaving was the only job performed on equal terms by men and women. Jobs requiring patience, dexterity, and the physical coordination of threads, like smash-piecing, drawing-in, and warping, were usually done by women. Women workers objected strongly to doing physically heavy jobs that they regarded as men's work: lifting heavy wooden boxes of bobbins and pushing trucks loaded down with cans of cotton slivers.

The best wages went to the wool menders and to the velvet cutters. Velvet cutters, who made ten dollars a week in 1920 when other workers were getting only six, were something of an elite; they called themselves the "400" of Lowell. When a local retailer offered fur coats for a dollar down and a dollar a week, most of the velvet cutters at the Merrimack bought them. Their bosses regarded the parade of fur coats through the mill yard in the morning as excessive, however, and cut their piece rate in retaliation.

At one time or another, especially during wartime when many of the men were in the service, women performed almost every kind of job in textile production except for the most dangerous or the most skilled. Opening cotton bales, picking and carding, and loom fixing remained out-of-bounds. During World War II, when the federal government suspended state laws against night work for women, they worked all shifts. Textile production boomed during both world wars, and wages rose. During World War II, new work on war contracts offered higher wages and better conditions. Women sewed parachutes, tents, and jungle hammocks; they stitched electrically wired suits to warm the pilots and crews of bombers; and they made bullets. Women worked double shifts, saved money, and entertained soldiers from nearby Fort Devens. The wages that women earned producing war goods during World War II became the nest egg that allowed many to purchase a first house or tenement when the boys came home.

Lowell was a city of many light industries attracted by the reputation textile workers had of being unorganized and low paid. Women workers became part of a local labor pool with a high turnover rate, moving in and out of jobs as difficulties arose or opportunities seemed better. Most were looking for some kind of "nice little job": steady, good money, and not too demanding. Many women worked throughout their adult years, shifting around through the cotton, silk, and woolen mills, garment-making operations, electronic assembly work, cookie or candy packing, and shoe shop jobs. As one woman put it, "I was in every mill in the city until it folded."

Courtships took place openly on Saturdays: at the afternoon movies and at night in the ballrooms and dance halls crowded with eager young men and women. Dancing was one of the pleasures that tied the families of mill workers together; mothers and fathers had enjoyed themselves the same way. But vigilant parents kept control over their daughters with rigid, early curfews and cautious scrutiny of the young men. Spontaneous attractions had to gain approval or risk real trouble. Still the shining moment of winning the dance contest on Saturday night with a fancy-stepping partner marked the romantic high point of many women's memories. On Sundays after church, it was possible to meet girlfriends and stroll around the neighborhood, inevitably bumping into boys.

Most married with little fanfare in their early twenties. Marriage and motherhood could be a real challenge for female mill workers. If their husbands had a steady job outside the mills as a telephone lineman, a railroad worker, an auto mechanic, or skilled tradesman, they could drop out of industrial work, usually with their first pregnancy. But if their husbands were mill workers, even loom fixers, the most skilled job for men, the wives usually worked too. These women stayed at their jobs throughout their pregnancies, and some returned to work a few weeks after childbirth depending on the difficulty of the delivery. The most common practice was home birth with a doctor or midwife in attendance. However it was accomplished, the women of the last generation of mill workers did not bear the large numbers of children that their own mothers had.

Infants and school children were usually cared for by female relatives—a grandmother, older sister, or aunt—or by neighbors for pay. A few families could use private charitable institutions such as the Lowell Day Nursery, which was established in 1890 to serve a small number of working mothers. Some parents avoided the costs of day care by working different shifts. While the father worked the early shift, 6 A.M. to 2:30 P.M., the mother would get the children off to school and prepare lunch and supper. The wife worked the second shift, 2:30 to 11 P.M., and her husband fed the children, bathed them, and put them to bed. The children's needs were taken care of without expense—at whatever cost to the marriage. By the time the oldest child was fourteen, it was time for work in the mills.

Distracted by burdensome work in the mill and in their households and bearing the special responsibilities of females of all ages for taking care of children, these women workers were rarely involved in the planning and execution of acts of protest or organization among textile workers. Yet when opportunities arose for joining in and supporting collective action during strikes in the early twentieth century, women workers demonstrated a deep and widespread sense of outrage over injustices. Some of the acts that resulted remained individual: quitting, telling a boss what he could do with that job, and finding another. Repeated instances of female insolence and defiance contradict the stereotype of passive French Canadian, Greek-American, or Italian-American women. Although home was the place where women learned the limitations of being working class and the obligations of being female, they also learned in their families and at their parochial schools a fundamental sense of what was right and what was wrong and that everyone should pull together for the common good. These lessons provided a yardstick to measure the difference between mill values and family life. The high regard that many mill workers at the Wannalancit had for Alan and Edward Larter, genuine paternalists who took good care of their employees, seemed to confirm family values of mutual responsibility and joint effort.

Individual outbursts gave momentary satisfaction, but high turnover rates were endemic to mill life. A few skilled women workers such as silk weavers could refuse to be intimidated by their bosses and could even join in destructive acts against mill property. When many women textile workers shifted to garment stitching under the protection of the International Ladies Garment Workers' Union (ILGWU), they participated actively as shop stewards and served on price committees. For the two women who became most active as shop stewards, Valentine Chartrand and Yvonne Hoar, their relationships with fathers who tried to keep them under control or disapproved of union activity may have been significant. Their ability to defy management seemed to follow from the recognition that their own fathers could be wrong.

During the early years of the Depression, however, many Lowell mill workers, both men and women, were discouraged about strikes and union organization. One woman recalled, "We got nowhere!" and reported the general attitudes of Lowell workers as acceptance: "Half a loaf is better than none; you lost a day, you lost your pay." She remembered, "If they cut us, what could we do? We were all poor people. We had no money, living hand-to-mouth. If that was cut off, we went hungry." Many were afraid that if they missed work or refused to work overtime, they would lose their "place on the mill." Market ups and downs and the closing of mill operations in the 1920s and the early 1930s underscored the economic vulnerability of mill workers. Although the few remaining textile operations in Lowell were organized by unions in the late 1930s and 1940s as profits increased from wartime government contracts, the most powerful legacy of women mill workers to their children was a deep determination to keep them out of the mills.

Offsetting their resignation to the limitations on their lives and the pressures of their duties, women mill workers often expressed deep interest in and commitment to their work and took pride in their endurance and vitality. Although they disliked the long days, the bad conditions in the mills, the low pay, and the harsh treatment by their bosses, they enjoyed the company of their coworkers and took an interest in the machinery they ran and the work they produced. Under pressure to make money on piecework, women workers responded to the challenges of starting up a spinning frame faultlessly and of learning the intricacies of the weaving process. They appreciated the beauty of the vivid silk thread that they wound on bobbins and the glories of the colorful cotton velvets and woven silks. They worked together helping each other to maximize their weekly earnings by intensifying the pace of work and providing essential coordination for production. They worked hard and well.

I Learned Right Away

Valentine Chartrand
SPINNER

*Valentine Chartrand learned many hard lessons as a mill worker. Family
needs always came first for working-class daughters. Drawn along with
many others of her age into the work force during the prosperous years of
World War I, she reluctantly abandoned her hopes for a high school
education, her chance to avoid lifelong industrial work.*

*Hard work gained her little. Her father kept her under close control with
deferred promises and strict surveillance. So did her employers. Her bosses
appeared to contribute nothing to production, while she and other women
labored at difficult jobs that male workers refused to touch. She repeatedly
expressed her dissatisfaction by walking out of one job and into another.
Such actions were typical of the high turnover rate among mill workers
that was common in an industry where union organization was feeble
and management's demands for increased productivity created widespread worker discontent.*

*Like many women workers who were children of immigrant parents,
Valentine Chartrand married within her ethnic community and continued to work full time, despite a series of difficult pregnancies. As a
stitcher in the garment shops that had been drawn to Lowell in the 1930s
by the local supply of cheap labor, she became a member of the ILGWU.
This union encouraged its women members to run the local themselves.
Her years of subordination to family needs and her bosses gave way to
active involvement in fights over prices and other management decisions.
As a shop steward, Chartrand came to resent, for different reasons, both
her Jewish bosses and her Greek coworkers, but divisions among workers
from diverse cultures who spoke different languages weakened the union
local. As a final lesson, she learned the meaning of a "runaway" shop
when an owner took off, locking the door and taking the payroll.*

I WAS BORN in Lowell, but my parents were born in Canada. They
met in Lewiston, Maine, and they were married there, then moved
down and settled in Lowell. My father, Frank Beaulieu, was a contractor and a builder, and he done that practically all of his life. He became

a citizen after he was here about twenty or thirty years. He was seventy-four when he died. My mother was always at home with a big family, twelve children. She never had a chance to work outside; she had all she could do.

I was the fourth child and the oldest girl. There was two that were in the First World War, and they died over there in Germany. We lived way outside the city in a house near the Tewksbury town line, and I went to Immaculate Conception School which was the nearest [parochial school] coming from Tewksbury. Before that I had gone to an orphanage as a resident student for four years because we were too far away from the school. We were Catholics, and my father wanted me to make my first communion. So he put me in St. Peter's Orphanage on Stevens Street. He was the one that built that building. I was there four years, room and board for four years. I made my first communion when I was six. I skipped a grade because they thought I was advanced. When I came back home, I was about eleven. I went to the Immaculate Conception grammar school until my birthday, December 18, 1917. I was fourteen, and about a week and half later I had a job in the woolen mills in North Chelmsford.

We had a talk, my father and I. He asked me if I would mind quitting school. He was crying, and he needed help, you know. And I was the oldest, the oldest at home then. And he asked me if I wouldn't mind very much if I quit school. And I said, I did like school, and I hated to leave it. I wanted to go to high school. But when he asked me that I said okay, and I remember telling the Sister (we had nuns up there) that I was leaving school, and she felt bad about it, she did. She said, I hate to see you go because you're doing good in your grades and everything. And (in tears) I said, Well, my father needs the extra money, and I have to leave.

I went by myself to the employment office at the city hall to find out if I could get a job. I'd take anything. I never went to a French school even though I'm French, so I could talk good English. They told me one job was open, but I was not of age. And they asked me, Isn't it kind of hard to leave school? And I said, Yes, it is but I've got to help my father. I said, I'd take anything, so they had this place in North Chelmsford. I worked six hours a day because I was only fourteen. I took a trolley car for a five-cents fare. I told my father what kind of work it was and that I was gonna have to learn. And he said, Well, do you like it? And I said, I don't know, but I'll try it until I get something better. Within a year I got something better in Lowell at the old Massachusetts mill.

Valentine Chartrand in 1917 at the age of fourteen. *Courtesy of Valentine Chartrand.*

At my first job, I was on the frame, spinning and doffing. You have to take the end of the yarn and bring it down to the steel rollers on the side of the frame. You pass the thread between them. And then on the side of the frame below, there's bobbins. You've got to put that yarn on the bobbin, and it spins when you start the frame. That was spinning. And then when you doff, you have to stop your frame, and you have to put an empty bobbin to replace the one that's full. They call it doffing. Those who were experienced people older than me showed me how.

I worked mostly with women. The bosses and the machinist who fixed the machines were men, and they had the boys bring the empty bobbins in for us loaded on big trucks. And we'd take them from this big box, put them in a little truck, and bring them to our frame. When a bobbin was full, we knew just when to stop the frame. We had to stop it ourselves. Make sure the yarn was twisted around the bobbin when we started the frame; if the threads break, you got to piece it up right away. I learned right away; I learned quick in everything.

I was a little scared about the belts. In those days they didn't have security; they weren't as organized like they are today with everything boxed in. In those days those big wide belts, some of them about a half a foot wide, went way up on a pulley to make the frame run. And there was a handle on the end of the frame that you pulled to stop and start it. And it was dangerous. Once I saw a girl with long hair get her hair caught in the pulley. They had belts eight feet wide there. We heard the screech. I never heard a screech like that before; I hope I never hear another one like that. I ran and stopped her frame. She happened to be turning fast, and her hair caught on it, and she went up with it. I'll never forget that sight. It pulled out a lot of hair, and she died not long after. In the winter the windows are all closed, and you get that lint flying around. And you breathe a lot of that. I always had a feeling that it wasn't good for your lungs.

My first week's pay that I ever made was $9.65. I think it was. That was considered pretty good pay for the hours I worked and for the times. I worked six hours a day, six days a week. There were no coffee breaks; we had our lunch at noontime. We stopped our machines and had our lunch all together. Then at a quarter to one, we had to start up again. There were quite a few that were my age or a little older.

There were a lot of people in the mill from Canada. There was a few Greek, a lot of Polish, Portuguese, and Irish, but most of the while they were French. In those days, they'd come to Lowell, Lawrence, and Manchester [New Hampshire] for the textile mills. They'd come down this way, and some of them would settle here, and others would go back after a while. I remember my father talking about taking me to Canada and meeting my aunts and uncles. Now they're all gone. My Uncle Joe, my father's brother, was the last one. Once after my father died, I went to Canada on a visit, and of all things Uncle Joe had been buried that morning. I never met him or talked to him. My father had wanted to take me a long time.

When I was gonna turn fifteen, I wanted a better job. And I wanted to get nearer to the center of the city because it was so far out in the country where I lived. But I had no high school diploma. I went to an employment office, and they told me I could go to the Massachusetts mill. It was a cotton mill. I said, Well, I've had experience spinning wool, so they put me in the spinning room. I worked more than six hours, and I had a little bit more money. My father was working, but he was the only one working. I gave him my pay envelope, and he'd give me a dollar for expenses and fifty cents for my car fare. That's what I had a week out of it, and he kept the rest. It wasn't much, but it helped. 'Cause we always ate good. We always had plenty of food, and he always worried about that.

The work at the Massachusetts was different. It was finer work. On wool it's heavier and thicker. The first time I worked on cotton it was so fine, it was hard. It was hard trying to get it pieced together. Sometimes my thread would break from a defect, like seconds in the cloth, and we'd have to piece that up. And I'd get mad because [the cotton] was so thin, and it was hard to get at it. Sometimes it would stay pieced, and sometimes it wouldn't. We had to have a hook and a knife to cut off the cotton yarn when it got all twisted around the steel rollers. We had to be careful. That's the first thing we learned. We were told the dangers, and we had to make sure that nothing would happen. I worked in all the mills in Lowell: Appleton, Hamilton, Prescott mills. And I worked in the Newmarket mills at weaving. But I stayed at the Massachusetts for a while because I was thinking that I'd like to go to night high school.

I asked my father about it, but he was worried because the trolleys cars only ran until a certain hour. And he was always afraid that I might get stuck downtown. And there was no way he could come after me, and I was young then. And then I got sick for eight months with typhoid fever and lost all my hair. I was afraid to go out with no hair on. So I used to wear a turban, and I stayed in the mill. I said, Oh well, I'm never going to school; that's where they laugh at you and everything. I was thanking God every day I hadn't died because I was in the hospital a long time. And when I came out of the hospital, I had lost my place at the Massachusetts. I went to the Prescott mill across the street. I did the same kind of work. I guess it was meant to be that I'd be a mill worker all of my life anyway.

Spinning and doffing was hard work. You're on your feet all day, and you can't sit down. Maybe a second, a minute maybe, and there were no chairs nor stools around. We weren't supposed to sit. You sit down for lunch, and that was it. We had what they called a second hand, and there was a supervisor; he was in his office all day, doing nothing. The second hand would be walking around and watching us to see that we did everything just right, and that was it. The only time I remember ever stopping work was when I had to go to the ladies' room. Some of these jobs that I did in my life, I don't think they should have been women's jobs. They should have been men's jobs. But you'd hardly ever see a man doing these jobs that I did. They wouldn't go for that. They worked as machinists or in the stockroom. They'd bring out the stuff for us, but they wouldn't work on those frames. It was mostly all women then.

When you were running a spinning frame, some yarn you have to doff [only] once a day because it's very fine thread. The coarser yarn you had to doff three times, sometimes four times a day. If your machines were running all the time, the more work you put out. They had that all marked down, what you put out. If you didn't put it out, something was wrong. They called it piecework. The more you did, the better for the company. And a little more money for you. I started with one frame on wool. When I came over to the cotton, they gave me two frames, then three, then four.

Sometimes the machines would break down. The machinist would have to fix it, and by the time he'd fixed it, we'd lose money. We had the same machines every day. Everybody was busy. We'd talk when we'd meet at the end of the frame. We'd walk up and down the end of the aisles. And sometimes we'd help each other. [For example,] poor soul, sometimes she'd have so much cotton on her steel rollers she couldn't catch up to tie up her threads. So I'd go and help her. Sometimes I had the same thing too.

I started to go out with boys at seventeen. We had to bring them home then and only once a week. I used to go out with my girlfriends once a week to the dance at Lakeview where they had a big ballroom. I loved to dance. I had to be home by ten-thirty. The dance started at eight-thirty; nine-thirty I had to decide to come back on the trolley to Lowell and then home. And I can see my dad even today. He had a big stick in his hand, and he was sitting near the coal stove. And he would be looking at the clock. And one night I came home late, and my mother had the front door open. She was worried for me. My father asked, Where is she, what is she doing? She told him, She's upstairs sleeping. Mothers, they're the best. He scolded me for that the next day. Parents in those days were very strict. It was always please and thank you.

Then I met my husband. He worked as a weaver at the Bay State Mills. And that closed down just the year we were getting married. He was a wonderful dancer! He used to go out two or three times a week. Well, I happened to be dancing with a fellow, and he cut in. He wanted to dance with me. And we danced a few dances, and then I went back to the girls. And they said to me, Who's that fellow you were dancing with? I don't know. I never met him before. So the last dance we had together, he asked if he could take me home. I said, Oh no, I came with the girls, and I'm going back with the girls. He said, Okay. So that was it for six months. I didn't see him. Six months later I was at the Royal Theater on Merrimack Street. And the ushers in those days placed you in your seats. There weren't many seats left that afternoon, so the usher seated me between two guys. And who was it but him, the one I danced with. And Ah, he says; Oh, he says; and I says, Ya. This time he had a car, and he took me home. I told him that my parents were strict. And I said, You'll have to come to the house, and if my father says, Yes, okay; No, then no. And then we started to go out.

I was at the Hamilton then to make more money. When I could make more, I'd change. I did change a lot. We thought the weeks were long because we had to work six days to start with, and we only had Sundays and Saturday night if you wanted to go out. But then Sunday you had to go to church, and in those days you couldn't eat after twelve midnight if you're going to church the next morning to take communion. You couldn't eat or drink water. That was a short weekend. Then Monday morning off again. I remember seeing people take a day off, and they were fired. They wouldn't keep them.

I worked overtime a lot of times. If the boss asked you, you didn't dare refuse. There were no unions then. We had arguments with the boss. We'd tell him we should get more pay, but we never won. Sometimes we'd be promised, but we would never get it. If we had a union, it would have been different. Some would say maybe worse, maybe better. I would go to other places. That's why I changed so often. I even went out on strike once. I never went back to that place. Once I did twisting. It's the same idea as spinning but the thread twists onto the bobbin.

We were supposed to be married in February 1923, but my father died in February. My husband was twenty-one years old, and my father died on the twenty-first of February. His family lived in Little Canada in Lowell. They were from Canada, the whole family. The first place we lived was in Little Canada. I didn't stop working because I got married. I always worked all through my life until I was sixty-eight. It was over four years before my first pregnancy. I only have two children; I lost three children at birth. I had a hard time wtih every one of them. I worked until I was ready to go; there was no embarrassment about it. We were proud; we're gonna have a baby. We didn't even have to go to the hospital. We had them right at home. I remember with my first daughter I was in the Boott mill, and they called an ambulance. I thought I was going to have her in the ambulance. I stayed out of work for three or four months because I had such a hard time that the doctor wouldn't let me go back.

My husband knew what it was to work in the mill, but we never worked in the same mill. He was a weaver, a loom fixer, and later on he became a foreman and then a supervisor. I wove silk for a while at the Newmarket mills. We were making silk pongee. It's nice and soft. We made linings for caskets. We had to keep cleaning the loom all the time so no dust or anything would get on it. I liked that job, but when they had a big strike and went out, I never went back. I could have gone back, some of them did, but it shut down anyway. That's when I went into stitching.

The first place I stitched was in a stitching shop called Paris Lingerie They were making slips and night gowns for women. There they had a union [the ILGWU]. And we had so much out of our pay every week to pay for that union. A lot of people are never satisfied. There's always some that want more. So they'd bring up things they wanted done, and sometimes they'd get it, sometimes they wouldn't. It was hard to win anyway. That's why I first got into the unions. Later on, I was chairman of the union and on the price committee. And I'm a fighter. Sometimes I'd win; sometimes I wouldn't.

They stopped the shop once. We were making bathing suits up on Jackson Street where the old Appleton mill used to be. The owners had taken over and were making bathing suits and sweaters. In the winter we'd make bathing suits, and the summer we'd make sweaters. And that guy, the owner, he was a Jewish fella; I remember his name because we had more problems with that guy. He was a rich guy, and he thought he could get us to work for nothing. And we got the union in there anyway, and we were fighting. He was a stubborn mule. You couldn't make him understand anything. He was rich, and he didn't care as long as he had the work out. We were on piecework. So we started getting mad at him and said to him one day, We'll all walk out. He didn't believe it, but we did. And when we did, he went bankrupt or something, I don't know. And one of his sons took over, and he opened a shop up on Bridge Street, and I went to work for his son. I liked the son better than the father. I was there about six or seven months, and one day he closed the shop. We come into work, and the shop was closed. Nobody there. It was three or four months before we got our last pay. He had done like his father. He had taken his money from the company and went off, disappeared.

When I left the mills, I stayed on stitching. We were on piecework but it paid better. If you worked fast, you could make good money on it. I made over $150 a week. It was sitting down but, Boy, it is tiresome! You sit there for four hours without getting up. We had a service girl that would bring you your work. She'd throw it in a box next to you, and you take it from there and stitch and do whatever you had to do. Then you throw the work that's done in the front, and they'd pick it up. So we just sit there until lunch time. And it was like that all day. And when you get up from that chair, you were tired! The mills, they were going down, this one here and this one, all to the South. First thing you know they were all empty here, one after the other. There were a lot of people out of work, those that had never done anything else. They had to go out of town. My husband went to work in the Manchester mills. He went other places too.

During World War II, I made jungle hammocks on Jackson Street in the old Hamilton mill where I used to spin. They have a net all around the hammock, and they hang these in the jungles during the war. It was all water and swamps, and they had to sleep in these hammocks so the mosquitoes won't get at them. They just zipped themselves in there. I worked in the Marginal mills making the suits for the air force with the electric wires in them. I stitched tents for the army and made bullets. We worked on parachutes right in the old Lawrence mill. They had a whole floor there the length of the mill they were using for that. In the Second World War, that's where I made a lot of money. During the war, we women tried to do the best we could. We couldn't go there, but we did our share right here. I thought I was one of them anyway.

On the sewing machines, I was better than the machinist. The machines had big motors, and I would never go into the motors. I was always afraid of electricity. But in the machines themselves, I'd lift up the head, and I could tell right away what was wrong. I have all kinds of tools, little screwdrivers and special things to work on the sewing machines. I'd fix my machine every day, clean it, and make sure it went good! When there was something wrong in the motor, I'd get the machinist. I tried out every kind of sewing machine in the shops: the button-hole machine, that's hard, that's tiresome. Tacking machines and all different kinds. When I could see I could make more money on one thing or if they needed help on one type of work, I'd take it. I never refused; I always said, Okay.

After the world war was over, I remember working in a shop where there was about 70 percent Greek people and maybe 10 percent French and a few Portuguese and Irish. We wondered why there was so many Greek people there. Not because we resented them, but they were always squawking about the pay. I was always running to the office and speaking up for them. And some of them couldn't say a word of English. In those days we had signs in the shops: speak English only. So we did.

Valentine Chartrand in 1984 when she was interviewed. *Photograph by Daniel Donovan*, Lowell Sun.

That's the place I nearly lost my job a couple of times. Because they wanted my job. They came from their own country, and these Greek people had been here in Massachusetts only a few years. And the first thing we knew they were all in Lowell. And they had jobs. And when they'd get into a shop any place in Lowell, they wanted the best. We got mad and nearly went on strike a couple of times on account of them.

I've been a busy person all my life. I worked all through the depression years; that's why I figure nothing can scare me anymore. We had a hard time during the Depression. It was a Republican that was in office. And I registered Democrat. I stayed Democrat, and I'll never change. This year [1984] I don't care about the other one, the cowboy. I'd like to see him face to face. I'd tell him right to his face. I'd say to him, Go back to Hollywood.

I worked fifty-four years. And the doctor was after me to quit. You've had it; let somebody else work. Well, we needed it. My husband's pay wasn't that big, so I needed the extra money. When I was sixty-two, I was working part time, and I wasn't well. I had to keep going. Because my husband was sick for four years and a half, in and out of the hospital, and I could see the money going out and getting nothing in. When he died twenty-five years ago, I nearly gave up for two years. I didn't feel like doing nothing, and then I said to myself, Well, you can't give up, you gotta keep going. And I just kept going. I went back to work.

[In] 1980 when Carter was running, I went to vote like everybody else does in the primary and then the elections. I went to three different places but my name wasn't on that board. They couldn't find my name. So I said, I'm going to the commissioner's office 'cause I helped out on the elections lots of times. I says, I want to vote, and they don't have my name. It had to be somewhere. I haven't moved; I'm in the same place. So she took out the big record book, and she opens it up to "C" where my name was. "Valentine Chartrand, deceased." I banged the desk hard. I have a temper, you know. I hurt my hand by banging away. I was so mad, I just said right out, Like hell I'm dead! I'm very much alive! And the poor woman said, I think you are. I had to fill out forms to be able to vote; I was going all over the place that day to vote. I found out later I had this sister-in-law, Emma Chartrand. She died in 1980, and my middle name is Emilia. So they explained to me that the computer had made the mistake.

But you know what happened? They stopped my Social Security for about a year. Then I got it all back eight months later. They thought I was cashing a check that didn't belong to me. I had to see a guy from Boston, and I signed fifteen papers without reading them, and then it dawned on me, What the heck did I do that for? My son was mad at me. You signed your life away, Ma. What did you do that for? Well, I said I was nervous, I was supposed to be dead. The computer makes me dead, and they're asking me all these questions. I haven't done anything to nobody, and I didn't do no wrong. I was scared. Everything is gonna be run by computers. Well, I don't want to be around to see that. The heck with that; I want a human being.

Pinching, Nicking, and Tucking
to Make Both Ends Meet

Grace Burk

DRAWING-IN GIRL

Grace Burk's memories of her early childhood capture the stark domestic reality of early twentieth-century working-class life. She remembered a household crowded with her grandfather and grandmother whose deaths were part of her growing up. But in some ways, Grace Burk's girlhood and work in the woolen mills surpassed the experiences of most mill workers. Her father's attentions to her as the oldest daughter seemed to give her resiliency and strength. Her protective family made sure that she learned a skilled job and continued her education. As a drawing-in girl, she was one of the last in the industry when new technology undermined this skill.

Grace Burk became a modern woman of the 1920s. After her marriage she was convinced she should have her babies in a hospital, unlike her mother. When her first child came, she gave up mill work but continued to copy her mother's thrifty ways, especially with the onset of the Great Depression. And like her bankrupt grandfather, she could never refuse a hungry man at her back door. She knew what it was not to have much.

MY MOTHER'S PARENTS came from Waterford County, Ireland. My father's parents were born in Sweden, and my husband's parents were Germans who settled in Peoria, Illinois. My mother, Elizabeth Gallagher, came from a family of ten, and she worked as a spinner in the Boott mill. My grandmother kept house for all the kids. My grandfather took a mortgage and bought a little cottage with a storefront on Lakeview Avenue, and he used to run a grocery and a meat market there. They lived in the back in the cottage. My grandfather was a soft-hearted guy and got bled to death. Anyone that had any trouble, they'd come to him for their meat and groceries on credit. Or if they needed medicine, he'd give them a dollar. They thought he owned a store, so he had money. Well, he bankrupt himself in that way and had to go out of business. They had to sell the cottage, and they came to live with my mother and father in 1904 when I was only about ten years old.

My father's parents came from Scandinavia, and we still have that Swedish Bible recording their experiences coming on sleds across the mountains from Sweden to Norway. When my father, Einar Ecklund, was two years old (in 1867), they came to Canada and gradually migrated down to the United States. They settled in New Hampshire for a while, and then they heard about the woolen mills of Dracut [just north of the city of Lowell], so they came to Dracut and worked in the Navy Yard for the [J. P.] Stevens woolen company. They called it the Navy Yard because when the war was on, they manufactured navy blankets and material to make the sailors' uniforms. My father went as a young boy to work there as a bobbin-boy and sweeping the floors. Gradually he got interested in looms and learned how to weave. And he was a weaver for quite a few years. He was mechanically inclined and learned how to fix looms. Eventually he became a loom fixer. I don't know [if] he liked it, but what else was there? They had to live. They had to have money. You had to like it whether you wanted it or not.

My mother and father got married after they met at the Saturday night dances held in the little halls in Lowell. My father was quite a dancer, and my mother too! That's how they met, at the dances. They won many a prize for being the best waltzers. They moved out to Dracut, when I was six months old. They had a little three-room apartment in a four-tenement block. In those days, there was no conveniences. There was no running water, no hot water, no indoor toilet, no bath. Just a pump in the sink to get your drinking water and an outhouse in the back. They heated with coal in a black stove. If you wanted to take a bath, my mother would get out the big washtub and put it in front of the stove and fill it up with lukewarm water. I used to say the cleanest got in first. We'd wash ourselves, and she would wash our backs. Then they moved to Lowell because my father got work in the Bay State Woolen Mills as a loom fixer.

I went to work in the mill when I was fourteen (in 1908) after I graduated as valedictorian from the Butler [Junior High] School. I went to work that summer. I suppose I could have gone to high school. Some of my class did, but things were getting hard.* We needed the money, and I knew it. They weren't getting much pay then. The highest pay my father ever made was fourteen dollars a week. When I went to work as a

---

*A general economic downturn in 1907–08 depressed the textile industry throughout New England.

hander-in where my father worked, I used to make from $2.25 to $2.75 a week. My mother would have the $2, and I'd have the rest for spending money. When I started making more money as a drawer-in, making twenty, thirty,—if they were busy—thirty-five dollars a week, I'd give her my pay envelope, and she'd take ten dollars out and put it under the oil cloth where the dishes were in the closet. That was my spending money; that's for the future. She'd take ten dollars out for each of us, and the rest was house money.

As a hander-in, I used to sit in a chair under the [drawing-in] frame and hand these threads to the one who was putting them through. I held a bunch of yarn there and would pull a thread out one at a time, and she'd put the hook in through the eyelet [of the heddle] and pull it through. That was a hander-in. I was one of the last of them. I did that for two or three years, and then I learned to be a drawer-in and sat on the outside of the frame. We used to make the old-fashioned coatings, fancy woolen blankets, and worsted men's suitings. And the plaid back blankets they called steamer robes.

I liked drawing-in; it was interesting. I tacked the pattern for the weave that the textile designer had prepared onto the wooden frame with a thumb tack. A dresser arranged the spools of thread for me. There were between six to sixteen harnesses to draw-in depending on the pattern, but wool was usually sixty inches wide. We were paid by the number of threads on the beam; the piece rate was per thousand. For wool serge there was five thousand on the beam. For the plaid backs, three thousand on each side and for coatings two thousand to twenty-five hundred. I kept a notebook for the office and entered the number of the beam and the number of the threads. It wasn't fair being paid by the thousand threads because if you had sixteen harnesses there was a lot more work than with six or eight. It's harder to reach and to see. A starter checked the drawing-in work by running the loom for twelve inches or so. If there was anything wrong like a doubled thread [in one eyelet], I had to leave my work and fix it. I was able to make thirty-five or forty dollars a week sometimes at that job. I worked there until I was twenty-eight [in 1922] when I got married and left.

We rented a tenement on Bleachery Street when I was ten years old. We had come up in the world then and had a built-in toilet. It was a little cubby hole with a one-seat toilet and a tin bathtub. Still only cold water, and you had to keep the coal fire going all the time to heat your water. My father insisted that we get a gas stove. My mother was scared stiff;

afraid we'd blow up. But that helped in the summer when you didn't have to put the coal fire on. In the summer you could use the gas for cooking and heating water.

When my grandfather had to give up his store and come live with us, we had to give up the living room to be a bedroom for my grandparents. He ended up working at a dirty job in one of the cotton mills, the Appleton mill, down there on Central Street. He used to walk in the coldest weather to work in there for five dollars a week. He'd bring that five dollars home, and my grandmother would give my mother three dollars a week. They said, I won't live for nothing. So she gave her three dollars a week for their food. She and my grandfather would keep a dollar [each] for themselves.

They lived with us until he died; I remember he died on Christmas Day of pneumonia. The undertaker came to the house and shut the door off the kitchen. They did their embalming and everything in there and laid him out right there. When everything was ready, he opened the door and had us come in and see him. For a day and a half, people came by to see him. Some of them would sit out in the kitchen and talk. There was always a bowl of tobacco on the table. The men would sit with her [the widow], and she'd make a pot of coffee. He was brought to the church in a hearse for the Mass. They had hacks, the horse-drawn two-seater closed carriages. They figured on how many were going, and they'd order so many hacks from the stables in the city. You had to wear black for a year, and then black and white for six months to let it be known you were in mourning. Six months later my grandmother took a shock, and she couldn't talk or eat or swallow or anything. She just laid there for ten days [and then] she died. No one went to the hospital. People just stayed at home and took their medicine and waited to see what happened.

When I was fifteen, my father bought a little cottage out in Wigginville, a section of Lowell named after the man who owned all the property around there over a hundred years ago probably. My father went down to the co-op bank with a hundred dollars or so and got a loan.* He bought the house for fifteen hundred dollars. The place in Wigginville [had] an enamel tub and toilet right off the kitchen. In the cellar we had a coal bin because in the winter we used to have a coal

*The Lowell Co-operative Bank specialized in lending sums of money at low interest rates to families with small assets. The borrower had to buy at least one share of bank stock for one dollar.

furnace. The coal man carried his bags of coal and just put it down the slide through a window into the bin in the cellar.

My mother always baked her own bread whenever we'd run out. She'd bake five or six loaves and a couple of pans of biscuits every time she would bake. She'd go up to the store and get a shinbone for a nickel. She used to have a great big iron pot, and she'd make a big pot of vegetable soup or pea soup. And we'd have a couple of big meals of the soup, whatever it was. Then she'd keep the meat and chop it up the next day with onions and stuff and make another meal of hash for a nickel. We always had oatmeal porridge for breakfast, but my father had soft-boiled eggs. I would get up early in the morning to see if he had left any in the shells. My favorite was oyster scallop and johnnycake. We used to have johnnycake with pea soup. There was a little rhyme that went with that. "Pea soup and johnnycake, makes a Frenchman's belly ache." It's because it's so good, you'd eat so much of.it, you'd have a stomach ache. A regular down-to-earth cook, plain cooking. She was able to buy more meat later on when we all got working. I was the oldest of the six children in the family. My mother made all my clothes. I learned from her. I couldn't go out and buy everything. Times were hard.

Then there was the rag man. My mother got all her things from the rag man. She always had a great big sack for a rag bag, and each scrap of rag would go in that bag. And every so often, he'd come around on his wagon, and he'd have old things, brooms, washtubs, and washboards. All kinds of pans. And he had a price on all of them. He'd come calling, Rags, rags! Of course we'd run out with the rag bag. And he'd weigh them and give so much a pound. And then you'd pick out what you wanted. He had a little book, and he'd say, Well, if the thing's a dollar, and you have seventy-five cents worth of rags, you could have it, but next time he'd come, you wouldn't get anything till you paid that up. He used to sell the rags to the paper mills.

Then we had the iceman. We had the old-fashioned ice chest, lift the cover and put the ice in it. When you needed ice, you had a card, "Ice," and you'd put it up in the front room window. And when he come by and see that card, you needed ice, and he'd bring the ice in. There would be a pan underneath the ice chest, and you had to empty it every night or it would overflow on the floor. We had the old-fashioned heavy, heavy irons. You had to have a coal fire or a gas fire with a plate over the gas for these heavy irons until they got good and hot. And a holder, lift it off and iron your clothes while the iron was hot. And then put it back and go and get the other hot iron, one heating while you're using the other.

My mother always washed with the old scrub board. It got to be a terrible chore for her. Wash for all of us. She'd change the beds on Sunday morning while we were all at early Mass. Then she would go to Mass. My father brought up the big copper boiler from the cellar on Monday morning and filled it with water for her. She used to be exhausted at night and knocked out. So we said, Now Ma, you get the wash ready on Monday night. When we got home from work [at six o'clock], we'd each scrub a tub of clothes. The three sisters and my mother. She'd have everything sorted out and have the water all heated on the gas stove. Then we'd wring them out through the wringer into a tub of water, then a last rinse with blueing for everything, and then wring them again into the basket, and then she'd take them out and hang them on the line, winter or summer. By ten o'clock at night, she had all the wash done. So it wasn't like her doing it the whole day long.

I used to get up and walk to the mill about a mile with my father in the morning and back at night. We used to start at six-thirty in the morning and work till five-thirty at night, five days a week. I also went to evening high school. They had classes in typing and bookkeeping. So for three years, four nights a week, I'd work in the mill all day. Come home at six o'clock. Grab my supper, change my clothes, and walk all the way downtown to the high school until nine o'clock and walk back home again. I learned the basics of bookkeeping, debit, credit, journal, and trial balance. I never put it to practical use because I went to work in the mill. Then when my husband started working for himself, he had to have some way to keep his records. He'd bring me home his slips, and I'd keep track of the money.

On Saturday you got out at noon, big deal! You had Saturday afternoon off. When I was a teenager, there was a group of about six girls, and every Saturday night, they'd have dances. I'd go down to the end of my street and get the electric car and meet my chums under Page's Clock [at the corner of Bridge and Merrimack Streets]. And we'd go up each Saturday night and meet on a certain part of the dance floor. And there used to be a bunch of fellows too, and we'd all meet. Then at a quarter past eleven, you'd hurry up to get the last electric car back home to Wigginville. If you didn't get that last car, you'd have to walk a long way.

When my father was a young man, he learned to play the guitar, and he played in a mandolin, guitar, and banjo band in Lowell. My mother had these green trading stamps she saved, and when they went down to redeem them, he saw a mandolin up on the wall. He said to her, Let's get a mandolin and let Grace take lessons. I was only ten. So they got the mandolin, and there was this teacher who had a studio downtown in Lowell, and I took lessons there for fifty cents till I went into the mills. My father would tune up the mandolin and accompany me on the guitar.

I taught my sister to play and then another sister, and we became known in Lowell as the Ecklund sisters and played for free entertainment at church sociables and clubs. Later we kinda harmonized the popular songs of World War I, like "There's a Rose That Grows in No-Man's Land, And It's Beautiful To See." When the soldiers came back to Fort Devens to be processed and let go from the war, there was a community service in Lowell to entertain the soldiers. We'd go down in big seven-passenger rented touring cars called jitneys to Fort Devens, me and my two sisters for volunteer work. That's where I met my husband. He was working at the garage, and he was one of the drivers. Everybody sat in the same seat all the time, so that's how I got to know him.

My husband came from a family of coal miners. As he grew up, even the young boys went into the mines early. He went to work at fourteen years old in Peoria, Illinois. Then he got hurt falling off one of those trucks that go through the mines carrying coal. Got his knee run over, so he couldn't go back in the mines anymore. He and his brother and a couple more fellows, they decided to go to Flint, Michigan, and work in the automobile factories making parts for the Hudson cars. He also took a correspondence course on automobile repairing. While he was there, he met a fellow from Lowell who had a little roadster, and the fellow asked him if he'd like to ride home with him. And my husband said he always wanted to see one ocean or the other, so he gave up his job. As they rode East, he learned how to drive a car. When he came to Lowell, he got a job in the auto repair shop of the Hudson and Essex agency.

I worked at the same mill for fourteen years until I was twenty-eight. When there was slack time instead of laying me off on drawing-in, my English boss would give me a job in the clothroom where the cloth was examined when it came off the looms. It was examined for knots and imperfections. He did this to hold on to me because there weren't many drawers-in. Many couldn't do it. Then when the work came in, he'd take me off and put me on drawing-in again. The work was dirty. You'd get your hands dirty. I used to have an old apron I'd put on over everything. And in the morning, you had to grease your hands with oil to make those [heddles] work. At lunch we'd go in the washroom and wash up. Go to a big long sink with eight faucets and eight wash pans. The looms would stop at twelve for one hour.

My mother used to send our hot dinners down to the mill in two dinner pails. She had a little girl that went to school in Wigginville for a "dinner carriage," they called them. My mother got her to come and carry dinners down to the mill. The bottom part of the pail was hot coffee, then potatoes and vegetables, meat cakes or whatever meat she had, and the top would be a piece of pie or cake. One of my sisters worked in the mill with me, and the other one worked in the [United States] Bunting. And she used to come over from the Bunting to where we were. And my father. There was dinner for four. We had plates and knives and forks and cups there. After we got through, I'd go down in the washroom and wash the dishes and stack them up again until the next day. And then be ready when the bell would ring, be ready to start up at one again till five-thirty.

The floor was oily, but they had floor sweepers every day that swept up the dirt and refuse. We used to see cockroaches; people never took any notice of them. It was terribly noisy. When the looms started up, you couldn't hear yourself talk. If you wanted to talk to someone, you had to get right up close and holler. I had to get used to it like everybody did. If you did your work right, you didn't have any trouble with the bosses. I think I vaguely remember the mills being on strike. I was pretty young then. We were in Dracut, and my father couldn't get work. He and a couple of other men, they had bicycles, and they used to ride all the way to Lawrence [about ten miles] to find work and then back on those bicycles. Just to get a couple of dollars until the strike was over.

I got married in 1922. No special thing. A friend of my husband's at work was his best man, and another fellow he got a four-passenger car and drove us to the rectory. They didn't have big church weddings then. You had to be the mayor's daughter or some big high-society person to have a church wedding. I made my dress, a white satin dress, and a pink chiffon bridemaid's dress and hat for my sister. My mother had a caterer come in and serve a buffet lunch at the house. We went out to Peoria for a honeymoon. A friend loaned him his car, and we drove out to visit his folks. There were no highways as there are today. We had got a manual from the automobile people, and you'd read it: so many miles on this road or on this street. And take this road, and you go so many miles until you come to the next town. You had to read the book all the way. We stayed about two weeks, getting to know his family.

When we got back, the man in the next house from us, he was a boss in the Bunting mill, he come to the door one day, and he says, Are you gonna work, anymore? And I said, No, I gave up work when I got married. He says, Do you suppose you could come back for a week or two and help me out? I need some drawers-in. And my mother says, Go ahead. We lived with my mother. You might just as well than hang around the house. So I went to work for him, and I worked a year there until I got pregnant, and I gave it up then. Then in 1924 we bought a piece of land, and we had a house built. I had saved a little money, and he had a little, so we put it together for a down payment to get a mortgage at the co-operative bank to build our house. My brother was an electrician, and he put in all the wiring.

I had seven children. The first was in 1924, and I went to the hospital. People were starting to go. When I was going to have my first, my mother was kind of getting ready to have it at home. There was a doctor who used to go to my husband's garage to have his car fixed, and he told him. I was six months pregnant before I saw a doctor. He told him I was gonna have a baby. He said, How far was she? Bring her in; I'll see her. I said, My mother was getting ready for me to have the baby at home. And he said, Don't. It's better if she's in the hospital for the first one anyway. So we gave up the idea of having the baby at home, and he was my doctor for all of them after that. That's the only vacation I had. Two weeks; stay in bed in the hospital for ten days. You couldn't put your foot on the floor for ten days; then the doctor would let you walk around. With all my kids, I was always out of diapers; every day two lines of diapers. Seven kids in eleven years.

The kids were raised during the depression years. You had to do a lot of pinching and saving, but I didn't work in the mills. My husband wasn't making much money then, and there was the house to pay off. It was always a case of pinching, nicking, and tucking to make both ends meet. There used to be hungry men around. Come to the door asking for a sandwich. My mother would say, never let them in the house. But I'd make up a couple of sandwiches and give it to him, and he'd go. Yes, many a time.

It Wasn't Difficult to Learn
But You Didn't Get Paid

Martha Doherty

SPINNER

Martha Doherty and Blanche Graham (see next narrative) were daughters of mill workers, friends since childhood and of similar background—Scotch-Irish, Scotch–French Canadian—but Martha Doherty had a good life and Blanche Graham did not. Adolescent daughters needed family protection. A good relationship with her father seemed crucial to a girl's chance for a decent marriage.

Youngsters like Martha Doherty sometimes lied about their age to get full-time mill jobs when their families needed the extra few dollars. Her father's illness and his membership in a Scottish fraternal organization saved her from the anger of her boss. During the deadly influenza epidemic of 1918, Doherty's father located a doctor to save her life. A year later, she was the sole wage earner in the family.

Even at fifteen, she refused to take a man's job during a strike when the boss tried to turn her into a strike breaker. Like some women mill workers, after her marriage she worked only until she became pregnant and then left to raise her children. The fact that her husband had steady work outside the mills made this possible.

I WAS BORN in Lowell in 1904. My mother worked in the Boott mill as a weaver, and her father was an overseer. She worked for her father; he was one of the bosses. She used to put us in a day nursery so she could work. My father worked in the machine shop. I was kept in the day nursery till she came after me, and my father took us home. When a baby had to be nursed, she came home to nurse it. Her father was the boss; he let her go home and nurse it, then back to work. There were nine children in the family. I was the fourth. My father comes from Scotland, and his people were all Scotch. He came to America when he was a little boy. My mother's people come from Nova Scotia. They were all fishermen up there, and they were Irish. My mother was born in Biddeford, Maine.

I graduated from the Immaculate Conception school after ninth grade, but I was at work [in 1918] at fourteen. I just graduated and gotta job the day I was fourteen, right on my birthday. I just walked in the Merrimack mill with another girl, she was sixteen, and she was going for a job and I went with her. And the boss said, How old are you? And she said, Sixteen. And he said, How 'bout you? I lied; I said, I'm sixteen too. He says, Good, I need ya. So he put us right to work—and two days later he said, Now you have to go get your working papers at the city hall to show how old you are.

So, I went to city hall. I got a fourteen, and I come back. He was furious. He said, Why did you do that? Why did you lie? I said, If I told you I was fourteen you wouldn't hire me, and I need the job. He said, Yes, but you could have got me in trouble because I employed you on long hours [forty-eight hours a week]. I was supposed to be on short hours [forty hours a week], and I said, Well, I'm sorry, but I do need the work. So he looked at me, and he says, Your father Scotch? I said, Yes, are you? He said, Yes, and he said, Does he belong to the Scotch club? I said, He goes there. He said, Well, I'm going to keep ya, but he says you'll have to put in short hours for the next few days for the hours you put in that you shouldn't of put in.

My parents didn't know I was doing that, and the boss got a hold of my father in the Scotch club and told him. He said to me, You should always be honest. And I said, I know, Dad, but you're not well. He had a bad heart. He knew that I was only trying to help. He was a very calm man. He was strict, but he didn't abuse us in any way. He taught us to be honest and go to the Immaculate Conception Church; if you didn't, you didn't go out.

The boss put me in the card room. I was the only little girl in that room. I was by myself all the time, and that was too lonesome for me. I was a live wire. I had to lift the tin container with the coiled sliver in it. It was a big tin can filled up from the card, and I had to lift that up and bring it over, but I started getting lumps under my arms because it was too much for me. I was too young and wasn't fit for it. I got a ruptured appendix from lifting. I was out two months and almost died from peritonitis; the appendix had burst. The company did pay for the operation and the doctor. So then he put me in another job just putting bobbins in a box. I was making $9.45 a week. I only stayed about a year, when I went to the Massachusetts [mill], and I learned to spin and doff. They tried to teach me how to spin, and I kept trying to do it [piece the yarn] and trying, and the ends kept falling down. So one of the boys who was in the room, he was watching me, and he came over to me, and he said, Are you left handed? I said, I don't think so. He said, Well, try it with your left hand; you look awkward to me. So I did, and it worked. He said, That's all that's wrong with you. You're doing it with the wrong hand.

It wasn't difficult to learn but you didn't get paid. You had to work for almost two weeks without pay. And if you jacked up during that time, that is, if you stayed for a week and you didn't like the work, you didn't get any money or a job. If you stayed two weeks to prove you could do it and you liked it, then you were on the payroll. You'd get paid right away if you were experienced, but if you were learning something, you had to learn for nothing. Usually you didn't have time to learn anything else. I was fifteen. I made good money. I started making nineteen, twenty dollars a week. Then the state man comes in and asks me how many at home and who was working. I said, I'm the only one working now 'cause my father had a heart attack, and my mother was home with the children, so he said, Oh, well, we can't touch you because your money has to go for the support of a house.

We had a nice boss, and I enjoyed myself very much. I got too good, I guess. The boss put me upstairs where it was mostly men, and they needed somebody up there. It was heavier work on big bobbins. You spinned your own work, and then you doffed your own frames off. I had three sides to keep doffed every fifteen minutes so it kept me running. I had a partner on the other side of the frames. I had one side, and she had the other. When she doffed one side, I'd be doing the other, and then we'd start the machine up fast so we could make more money. You had a clock on the end of the machine, and the more ya kept the machine going, the more money you made. She was a married woman that I was on with. She was nice; and she liked me and I liked her. I could run around and help her more because, like I said, I was a live wire. I could run around.

I remember a strike at the Massachusetts mill around 1919.* They started going out on strike. I didn't know what it was all about. Then the boss came over to me and said, They've gone out on strike. I didn't know what they were talking about. And he said to me, Want to go over there and do so and so's job? It was some fellow I knew that was in there [on that job]. I said, No way, and he says, Well, you have to do that; there's

*Post—World War I strikes hit many American industries and spread throughout the textile industry in the Merrimack Valley region.

nothing else. So I went out; I went out [on strike] too. So they settled it; they settled it right away. It was only a few days. Maybe it was the beginning of some strikes, I don't know. I don't remember the grievances. It was more among the men; that's why I didn't go out [immediately], but when he wanted me to do that fellow's job—maybe it was more money for the men, I don't know. But when I went out, the fellows said, Ha, you come out too! I said, Well, he was giving me your job, but I wouldn't take it. He said, I would have broke your neck! Whatever it was I wasn't mixed up in it. I wouldn't know what it was, but there was a strike.

I went on forty-eight hours, seven in the morning to five at night, when I was sixteen. We had an hour for dinner, and we worked a few hours on Saturdays. There was no place to heat anything; we had cold sandwiches. And we drank water unless you wanted to bring your tea and have cold tea. I stayed there until they closed up. I had a good boss, and they were real good, the people that worked; we had a lot of fun. I was married when I was twenty [in 1924], and I was still working there until it closed. Five or six years [in all]. I didn't have any children till I was married for four years, so I still stayed working, but they closed up, and then I went to a woolen mill out in North Chelmsford [just west of Lowell]. Doff and spin, but it was on wool instead of cotton. It was easier because the machine runs longer, and we had about five girls on one side doffing, then we'd run to another machine and five girls again. We could sit down in the meantime, and when that machine would stop, the [head] spinner would holler, Doff here! and we'd all jump, and we'd run down, and we'd start doffing the machines.

If you were sick, you went to the first aid to see if [the nurse] could help you. They'd make sure that you were sick before you left the mill. Otherwise you couldn't. You didn't get paid for when you were out. It could be Christmas, and if Christmas came on a Thursday, well, you were out Thursday, Friday, and Saturday. You lost three days' pay. Which was terrible, 'cause then you had only a couple of days' pay for the following week instead of having money for Christmas.

One day I was drinking an awful lot of water, and my face was flushed, and the boss came over to me and he said, Don't you feel good? And I said, No, I don't. I suppose he noticed I wasn't jumping around as I usually did. That's when I took the flu during the First World War. They were dropping right and left then.* It was hard to get a doctor, but

*A deadly influenza epidemic swept through the world in 1918–19. It killed thousands in the United States.

my father got one, and he said, You'll have to keep her soaked in whiskey. I said, I never took a drink. This time you gotta. There was aspirin, and that was it. And quinine. Quinine and whiskey. And he said, Isolate her from the rest of the family. So they did. I was in a room by myself. They'd come in and wash me, but none of the rest of the family got it, only me. When I come out of it, many of my friends were dead.

When I had children, I didn't go back. My husband didn't let me work once the children come. He said, They need a mother. His mother and father were dead, and he had missed his home life. He says, I didn't marry ya to have you work. He was a boxer, a carpenter who made coffins. Plain wood coffins, so he had pretty steady work. I had a very good husband, one of the best. I had a good life, thank God!

I first met Blanche Graham at the day nursery when we were kids and going to school together and playing hopscotch. She lived right around the corner. Sometimes we went to the Young Women's Christian Association. They had a gymnasium so we did that. They taught us how to cook and make fudge, and they let us have shower baths which we didn't have at home. We had a galvanized tub. They had a playground, and we were taught how to play, how to sew, and get along with each other. Then one day we'd go up to Eliot Street to a Protestant church. We had a shower there too, which was good because it was better than getting into a galvanized tub. We used to walk out to Lakeview where there's dancing and roller skating. Sometimes we'd hire a bicycle for five cents a day and ride out there. We swam together. We all tried to help one another. No matter where you lived, whether she was Polish or Greek, we helped one another.

Blanche and I were together when they picked Miss Lowell. After work, we took a girlfriend Mary, and we were gonna go to the Associates' Hall in downtown Lowell to see who Miss Lowell was. We had just a little skirt and little white blouse on. It was free. So they started to dance. They were supposed to pick Miss Lowell, and we were waiting around, and then they said this dance was for Miss Lowell. And some of the girls there were beautiful; they had nice gowns. But they didn't pick her right away. So they started up more dancing, more music, and these men that belonged to the Kiwanis Club or something, these elderly men—we thought, they were about thirty or thirty-five, but to us they were old—so they come over and ask Mary and me for a dance. The first thing we know they're getting near the stage, and Mary gets off the floor with this elderly man. The one I am with, he said, Thanks for the dance, and he lets me sit down. They were eliminating, you know. Mary's up there, and her face is so red. She has this little skirt and blouse, and the other one's beautifully dressed in a gown. It was between these two girls. The other had a long gown, and I thought she'd get it. But who did they pick? My friend Mary. I said, That's something. I went up to see Miss Lowell, and I didn't know I was walking with her. And she was crying, but she was pretty. She had nice red cheeks, a Polish girl. Blonde, blonde hair and blue eyes. She was really pretty. And she had no makeup. Just natural.

My Father Just Didn't Bother Too Much with Me

Blanche Graham

SPINNER

Blanche Graham's hard-working mother protected her as much as she could, preferring to have her by her side in the lint-filled spinning room on summer afternoons than leave her at home or on the streets. After her mother died when she was twelve, the young girl was left emotionally adrift. She found herself pregnant at fourteen, abandoned by her pious, unforgiving father, and forced to leave school.

Her marriage and family life became so difficult that she eventually left her abusive husband. She worked at a round of routine jobs in various light industries in which she took little pride or interest. The one bright spot seemed to be her friendship with Martha Doherty.

I WAS BORN in Lowell in 1906, and my mother and father lived in the corporation boardinghouse on John Street while they worked in the Boott mill. He was a weaver in the Boott, a first-class weaver. My mother was a very good spinner. We moved around to other mill towns and stayed in boardinghouses. I remember they had to work from six in the morning to six at night. My mother would take me over to the day nursery and leave me there while they worked, and then she'd pick me up at night and take me home. There was only three of us. My father says there was seven children, but four died when they were very young. There were only three of us living, my brother, my sister and me. I'm the baby.

Both of my parents came from Canada; my father was a Canadian Indian. My grandmother was a thorough-bred Scotswoman with red hair. My father said that's where I got my red hair from. She married a Canadian Indian and lived in the Province of Quebec. From the time my father was thirteen, he lived with his uncle, who was a priest. So he was going to be a priest. He went to the seminary, but before he could take his last vows, he fell in love with a pair of shoes.

There was a wall around the seminary, and all he could see [under-

70

neath it] was these shoes walking by at six o'clock in the morning. They bothered him every morning and every night. So when it came time to take his vows, the priest had a good talking to him. He said, It would be better for you to go out and meet them—those shoes—and marry the woman because with that in mind, you wouldn't make a good priest. But my father was very strict when it came to religion.

I met Martha [Doherty] in the nursery school. As I got a little older, I couldn't speak French, and my parents spoke French. My mother talked to me, and I wouldn't know what she was saying, so I'd say to my sister, What is she talking about? So they sent me to St. Joseph's Convent when I was about five years old to learn French. Sent there to live; it was all girls. I moved to the Acre [in 1916] when I was ten. I went to St. Patrick's School that was all Irish-Americans, I was the only little French girl in the Acre, so they used to say I was the best-looking French girl in the Acre. I was the only one.

When I was twelve years old, I used to help my mother. She worked in the Appleton mills. She was a spinner. I used to spend my summer vacation in the mill with my mother from twelve noon to closing time. She used to teach me how to do it, but she said, I don't want you to come work in the mills when you get bigger. I want you to do something else. I used to clean her frames for her and put the bobbins in, and she'd tie up the ends because I didn't know how to tie them up. I would have been at home alone, so rather than to be on the street or alone at home, my mother would take me in there, and I'd spend the afternoon with her. Just pass the time.

I left school [in 1920] at fourteen 'cause I got married. I [had] lost my mother that year I was twelve. There was just my father and I, and of course he was a young man, and he just didn't bother too much with me, so I got myself in trouble and had to get married. I couldn't go to school no more; I left school when I was in the sixth grade. Instead I had to go to the Green School,* and they taught me how to cook and things like that. After I had my baby, they said, Don't bother coming back, so I stayed home.

When I was first married and had the baby, I was too young to work. I was only fourteen; you had to be sixteen. I was living with his folks. After I got married, my father lived with his sister in New York. My husband didn't work in the mills; he didn't work period. I jumped out of

---

*Located in the Acre, close to the mills, the Green Grammar School offered special services to its neighborhood including the city's largest number of state-mandated night classes in English language instruction for adults.

the frying pan into the fire. When I first went into work, I was sixteen. It was like a hosiery, the Hub Hosiery. I had to cut the neck of the shirts or something. I had to cut with scissors, and they were big scissors. I had blisters on my fingers. But the work didn't go good, so I stayed home. I started having another one and another one. I had five children. I went back to work when the children were grown. I left my husband after thirteen years 'cause I was badly bruised. So for thirteen years I stood it on account of the children, but then I left.

I went in the Boott mill during the Second World War. I was learning twisting on the second shift, three in the afternoon until eleven at night. We was making something for the navy or the army. I don't know what it was. My mother told me when she was working in the mills, she had long hair, and her hair got caught in the belt. Took her scalp right off her, so they used to wear nets on their hair. Then you had to be careful when you cleaned your machines. I used to clean mine and climbed up to clean the top part—there was something caught up there—and got my finger caught in it. It was the little finger, and I almost lost it. I got scared then. It was a twister machine, so I was cleaning the gears and my little finger was stuck up. I had a habit of keeping that finger out, and it got caught in the gear. So I pulled it out quick. It was squashed. I seen stars. I came down and showed it to the boss, and he said, Oh, my God! what happened? I told him, and he said, Well, you had no business getting up there!

Then from there when that slacked down, I went to another mill. I worked there as a twister on nylon for parachutes and for [use in the manufacturing of] shoes. At the end of the war, I went on stitching, making dresses or jackets, pants or lingerie. Eighteen years on stitching, but then my eyes began to go bad. Then I went to Symphonics Electric, radios and things, and then back to Lowell Lingerie. That's where I had to quit because my heart gave out, and I had to give up working. That was the end of my working days.

You Had to Be on Your Toes, All the Time

Lucie Cordeau

WARPER

Very large numbers of people who were born in the French provinces of Canada immigrated to Lowell and found work in the textile mills. Often relatives were waiting for them with advice, jobs, and housing. In most New England mill towns, there were Little Canadas where the French language and the customs and pieties of French family life flourished.

The daughters of French Canadian families had special responsibilities, and when her mother and oldest sister died, Lucie Cordeau became the family's "second mother." This responsibility had a disastrous effect on the social life and marriage prospects of a young woman of twenty-three. Because they began work in the mills at fourteen and often delayed marriage, daughters like Cordeau usually did not bear the large numbers of children that their mothers had.

Lucie Cordeau worked for years at various mill jobs; the most skilled was preparing the warp threads for silk looms. Warping required great mental concentration and precise and careful attention to a procedure that took several days to complete. The challenge of the work and the good money she earned gave her deep satisfaction.

I WAS BORN in Joliet, Canada, in 1895. All of the family was born in Canada only but two, the last two. My parents come to this country, to Lowell in 1900 to better themselves. My father was a farmer and sold his farm in Canada because we were a large family. My uncle, my mother's brother, got him a job. They were already down here for quite a few years. And they got my father a job—and all the boys and girls— in the mill. There were eight children when we came to Lowell, and then two more born in this country. We all have eighteen months difference, and then another one was born. When I came to this country, I was the baby, I was the youngest. There was some more, but they died young. My mother had seventeen children.

We lived in Little Canada where all the French people immigrated.

Get there; [get settled someplace]. Later they get a better place to live. I lived in Little Canada until I got married [in 1931]. My father was doing good and bought a tenement block. There was eight tenements in that big house. We had one, and we rented seven others. My father and my mother never learned to speak English. My father, along the years, he could pick up a few words, but us kids, we learned English at school. We went to the French school, but they were teaching the two languages, English also.

We were a close-knit family. My father was a good provider. We always had something to eat. He was a hard worker, and the oldest [children] were working. When they'd punish us, it was something very bad. My father was the law. If we did anything wrong or if we wanted to go someplace and my mother didn't know what to do, she used to say, Go see your father. And my father says, What did your mother say? We said, Ma says no or go ask your father. And he used to say, Lucie (my mother, her name was Lucie too), what do you think? It's up to you. Okay, you can go. Or, my mother says, No. It's no. What was right was right; what was wrong was wrong.

My father was a handsome man, [and] my mother was a very pretty woman. She had nice reddish hair. Beautiful wavy hair. She had a good carriage. And my mother was a very, very religious woman. We lived near the St. Jeanne [Baptiste] Church. In my house, no fights were tolerated between the kids. Me and my sister would fight, and you're a bad girl. You go to church and say your rosary. And we went so many times, we hated that. That was the biggest punishment we could have. My mother says, Which one started the fight? Go to church.

After a while, my mother was not too well, so one of my older sisters stayed with her all the time to help her with the housework. Me and my sister had special household chores. We had a large tenement, a large kitchen. We had no linoleum, but floors with big wide boards, and every week we had to scrub that floor on our hands and knees. Me and my sister. We had the toilet in the hallway, and we had to scrub that and scrub the hallway. And the stairways. The boys had to lug the wood and the coal and do the shopping. Me and my sister had to wash the dishes, and the pots and pans were big. It was too much work for us.

We always used to eat on time. Three good meals a day. Every day, we always had soup. One day there was one kind, and the other day, there was another. And the leftovers, we never threw them away. We would all sit around the table. My father was at the end, and he's the one that was cutting the bread. And if we didn't behave at the table, there he was. He never cut us, but we got a little sting on the finger. And after we eat, we always had the rosary. Kneeled down and the oldest ones say the rosary. The whole family. The boys when they grew up, they couldn't get up and go out. They had to say the rosary. We didn't fuss; we were the real patriarchal French family.

My mother died in 1911 at forty-nine. She had a bad cold, and she never got over that. I was about sixteen. My sister took over because she always stayed with my mother. And then she died. I was the only girl left, so I had to take over. At that time, the two older girls were in a convent [in Canada.] My sister died during the big influenza [epidemic of 1918].* We lost three members: two brothers and my sister.

I took charge of the family. At that time, when the mother died, the older girl used to take over. As they said, The girl, she has a little bit of heart. My father never remarried, and I married only after my father died. I was tied to my family. I was not [actually] tied; my father told me, Lucie, he said, you better get married. I won't live forever. He told me that when I was twenty-nine, and when I got married I was thirty-six. I buried them all, all ten, my husband, mother, father. But I remember; I well remember. The older girl takes over. She's the second mother. She has to supervise and make all the decisions in anything. And if you had a boyfriend, when you have to go back home and cook supper for your father or cook meals for your brothers, the boys never stay long. The friendship never lasts. They say, You take your family before me.

I left school [in 1909] when I was about fourteen. I really didn't graduate. I left that year; I was in the eighth grade. We were lucky if we could go to high school, because we could get a job at fourteen in the mills. Most everybody went to work. I went to work in the Lawrence Manufacturing Company. That was my first job as a young girl. My father worked in the Lawrence mill for a long, long time; he was a knitter. He was making the material that I was working on. My sister was working there before me. They learned me to stitch knitted men's underwear. Tops and drawers and then union suits. It was all men's underwear. That was the style. If we were making three dollars a week, we were lucky. We gave our pay to my sister. One brother worked for the Boston and Maine, and another was a weaver. My sister was running the house, and we kept the change. Fifty cents or ninety-four cents—

*See p. 67.

that was big—we kept the change. Then the work slowed down, there was a layoff, and I went to the silk mill after that. I worked ten years at the Lowell Silk Mill.

I got my first job at the Lawrence Hosiery through friends. They say, Come. At that time it was easy to get a job. You go in, ask for a job. The boss says, Okay, we'll take her. Take her to this machine and that machine and learn her how to do it. That was it. I could sew at home. It helped but it's altogether different. The work comes on a truck in a bundle. It was by the dozen. We had the ticket [from the bundle]. After each operation, that ticket was marked. My machine had a number, forty-five, and we would put that forty-five on the back of that ticket. At the end of the day, we put them tickets on a piece of sticky paper, and there was a box where we put that. The next day they take that sheet into the office. I finish my bundle, I put it aside, they take it to the next operation, and then another truck. After a while I could do any kind of operation, but at the beginning I was stitching the side. After that I graduated to setting the sleeves; there was a special girl for that. Put the cuffs on; put the collar on. It was open in the front with buttons. We had button-hole machines, button machines, all kinds of machines. Like an assembly line, each girl has her own operation.

I worked on a regular commercial sewing machine run by a pedal. And we push with our foot to make the machine run. The other foot, we never lifted up. Assembly line, you got to go fast. Every now and then, there was a timer to fix a price. They time you for about two to five minutes. How fast you can go. And then they decide on the new price. The more production they have, the more money they have. But you go too fast, they cut you. If you make too much money, they say, We're going to cut that. Rather than give you a penny, they give you three quarters of a penny. Or a half a penny. Or a quarter of a penny. We used to put out two hundred a day. At a cut of one penny, that's two dollars less a day.

I had a nice boss; I work a long time for him. He was born in New Brunswick, Canada. He was mostly English, but he was speaking good French. I worked mostly with French Canadians. We spoke French all the time; my English was worse then than it is now.

We had the first aid in the mill. We'd stick our finger with the [sewing-machine] needle. We'd go so fast that sometimes your finger gets in the way—just happens. We're careful but it happens, even at home. Usually they call the boss. He knew first-aid knowledge. If the needle breaks in your finger, they send you to the hospital. They didn't touch it, but if it just goes through the flesh, they had first aid. It was a very clean place, but of course the noise of the machines. We were about a hundred girls in that very large room. High ceilings, all painted white. I must have been at the Lawrence for eight years. Then there was a layoff, so I had to find a job. There was an employment office at the silk mill. Someone told me, Go there, you get a job. I went a couple of times before I got a job.

I first start to do quilling. You used to take a skein of silk and put that on spools in a big, big frame. On your frame was about twenty spools. We take the beginning of the skein and put the end on the spool. Start the spool to fill it. If it breaks, we have to find the end. It splits sometimes; it was hard. Find the right end and tie it with a weaver's knot. The thread might break, but the knot won't come out and would go through the eye of a needle. It's hard. You think that you have it [the knack of the weaver's knot] and the first thing you know it falls apart. And then start the spool and go to another frame. The spools are for the weaving operation. We call that quilling. You have to be trained, because when the thread breaks, you have to make the weaver's knot by hand. It's quite tricky to learn it so it won't slip. I did the quilling for four or five years.

Then after a while there was an opening in making warp. A girl left, and they offered it to whoever wanted to learn. So I learned that. I had to get two weeks' training on that, two weeks without pay, but I knew they were making good money. Fifteen dollars at that time was good. But warping was very tricky. Very, very tricky. The warping frame was a great big thing. It was made of steel, and it was twelve yards in circumference like a big barrel. On one side of the frame was [the creel that held] hundred and fifty spools and the other side was a hundred and fifty. And all of them three hundred ends come to a narrow space [called a screen], all close together [see fig. E]. If the thread broke—we had to look out all the time—if the thread on a spool broke, we had to part them and tell which row that spool was on where the thread was broke. We had to go all around the frame, pick up that thread, take it all around, and bring it to that narrow space. Usually the material was about forty-five inches wide, [but] we used to work by six-inch strips, so many ends per strip. Then we start all over again until the strip was the width of the material. When we had that [wound], the reel held a thousand yards [and then the reel was wound onto the beam].

We tied each end with a knot to a black-topped pin, then we take these pins and tie it on the beam [that supplied warp threads to the loom]. Each one, even, even, even. So that everything was close. We had to look all the time. Sometimes [when the reel or beam was rotating] the thread breaks, and we had to piece it up. We'd stop the [rotation of the] beam and make a weaver's knot, just to make it even. We start the machine again until the beam was full [of parallel warp threads].

When the beam was full, we put back the pins to keep it even, and then the boys used to take that beam to the weave room. When the beam was full, there would be eight hundred to a thousand yards [of silk warp thread] on it. The beam was for the men to handle; we just put that silk on. It was hard work; it was mental, because you had to remember so many things. You had to watch for when the ends break. You had to know where and why and if the spool was empty. You had to watch the clock [on the machine that measured out sixty-four yards] and you marked it with a thread. If your hands sweat, we had a little bag of white chalk, because it would stain the silk which don't make good material. They'd have seconds. It was very mental. You had to be on your toes, all the time. Watch your clock; watch your silk. You got hell if you wasted time or if they see that you wasted too much silk. So you had to be on your toes, all the time.

The work was not hard, but you had to have it just right or when it went for weaving, it wouldn't make good material. If we missed a warp thread, there would be a line in the cloth. You had to look, and you had to have very good eyesight. You could tell right away. That's why we had to watch all the time. You couldn't wear no rings, no jewelry. You might break the thread. Or make a smash. We had girls [smash-piecers] for that; they had to know their job so the material won't be spoiled. Maybe they lose about two, three yards, but it's better than lose a thousand yards. Each week we made one warp. One thousand yards. Some weeks we made two. The minute we were all done, we start new again [making] another one. It takes three or four days. We were paid by the warp. If your second warp was half full, they paid you for half full [that week] to make up your pay. I was making good money, fifteen dollars a week at the end. At the beginning eight to ten dollars. When I was on quilling, I think we were making nine or ten dollars. At the quilling, we were paid by the case.

They were a nice group of girls. No loud girls. They wouldn't tolerate a fresh girl or a cheap girl. We had some Greek girls, mostly French and Irish. Some Polish. Us girls, we'd talk French, but if she were Irish, they'd talk English. At the silk mill, it was harder work. You were on your feet all day long. The Lawrence Hosiery, you were seated all the time. And the boss never pushes you. At the silk mill, it was harder because you had to concentrate. You had to look all the time; you couldn't lift your eyes off. Because if a thread breaks, you had trouble.

I was married in 1931 to a retired marine. He was older than me. He did thirty years' service and was forty-four. He had to come back to Lowell to meet a Lowell girl. After I got married I quit work. My husband made me quit. In my days, when [a woman] got married, usually she quit. I met my husband in the neighborhood. He came down visiting his sister. He saw me, and that was it. Fell in love with me. I found out; he hung around. I gave my notice, and that was it. The girls at the mill give me a good send-off.

I didn't have any children, and after my husband died [in 1951] I went back to work at fifty-six. It was tough because I had been married for twenty years. I went back stitching in a dress shop on Bridge Street. They had the International Garment Union at the Jay Dress Shop; it was compulsory. The boss, a good boss, was Al Pagano. Once we had a strike about the prices. The material comes all ready cut from Boston in big bundles. We all worked by the dozen. A girl would make the sleeve and tie the bundle all together again. When I first went in it was cotton, but after a while it was all rayon. Nice, clean place.

I worked there for ten years. It was work or starve. I didn't have no Social Security; I never worked [after 1931]. All I had was my husband's pension which was not too much. I had to go to work, so I went back to work. A lot of times we go to work, we don't feel like it. We had a headache or you got a cold or something. But if you miss a day of work, you never get around to nothing. It was tough because I hadn't worked on stitching since I left the Lawrence Manufacturing Company. I enjoy working, and after the first year, I manage, and I make good money. I happened to hit a nice paying operation in stitching: putting the collars and the sleeves on. I worked until I was sixty-seven, and then I retired [in 1962].

After I retired I happened to hit a nice part-time job in a small stitching shop in the Collinsville section of Dracut. I told the boss, I don't want to work piecework. I was independent; I was fresh. I don't want to work full time. In the summer, I don't work. He says, You're just the girl I want! It was such a small shop, and you had to know all the operations. I was taking surplus work. Like a girl, she had her own operation, but the others had to wait for her [to finish her work]. So to allow the other girls to work, I was taking whatever she couldn't do. I was on day pay [not piecework], six hours a day.

So I work until I was seventy, small lots. When there wasn't much work, the boss let me collect unemployment, but he wants to keep me. He'd give me one day's work and let me bring my low wage slip to the unemployment office, and I'd collect. When there was full-time work, I worked three days a week until I was seventy. It was near my house, and I had a ride there. The last month I worked, he says, Lucie, you want to work full time? I have a lot of work, and he says, I know you're leaving, but he says, it will help me. He was good to me. I couldn't say no. I worked five days a week, full. I was so darn tired. So right then I retired; it was time for me to quit.

I Knew My Job and
I Knew My Place

Narcissa Fantini Hodges
WEAVER

Two realities shaped the work life of Narcissa Fantini Hodges: her skill as a weaver, "her job," and the limitations that discrimination imposed on Italian-Americans and women mill workers, "her place."

For weavers like Narcissa Hodges, each hundred strokes, or picks, of the shuttle across the loom determined the contents of the weekly pay envelopes handed out on Saturday afternoon. Bosses deducted penalties for "seconds," or flaws, in the cloth, defects often not the fault of the weavers. Resentment over the penalty system eventually brought Hodges and her coworkers into angry, open conflict with management in the early 1930s.

As a weave room inspector, Narcissa Hodges used her mechanical abilities to identify problems in looms that were about to malfunction and produce seconds. She did so shrewdly without violating the taboo against a woman giving orders directly to the male loom fixers. Her job was to keep the looms producing as flawlessly as possible. Her recognition of the shared needs of all the workers in the weave room helped each to earn a decent weekly wage.

Narcissa Hodges valued competence, in herself and in others. Two things made her angry. Bosses who gave orders but didn't understand the work and unbreakable barriers for women in the mills and for Italian-Americans in New England towns. Her unshakable belief in her own considerable abilities was anchored in a family proud of its cultural heritage and good to both its sons and its daughters.

I'M OF ITALIAN EXTRACTION; both my mother and father migrated or pioneered to this country from Italy. My father had come here when he was eighteen, and he went back over there after about a year, and when he did, he met my mother and married her. My father had two brothers in Haverhill; they set up the Fantini Baking Company. He left Italy [because] he didn't feel that he could do as well there as he could in this country. I was born in Lawrence, Massachusetts, in 1914.

My father was a landowner in Italy, and he wanted to be a landowner in America. So he sold his shares in the bakery so that he could buy a farm, and at age one I moved to Tewksbury, Massachusetts. I had two older brothers and was the oldest of five sisters. I went to the Tewksbury schools until the age of thirteen, and of course those days were not days of plenty, so we all had to work. The only way you could get work was to go into the city of Lowell to get work in the factories.

First I went and worked in a shoe shop for a summer or so, but I didn't like it. There was a family nearby that had some girls who worked at the Newmarket Manufacturing Company on Market Street. They made silk cloth. At that time if you didn't have somebody that you knew that could train you, they wouldn't bother to hire you. They didn't have any training programs. But it wasn't difficult to find somebody to train you because everybody knew someone. So one of the older girls who lived around the corner trained me as a weaver. The woman who trained me was about five years older than me. She had older sisters and the sisters who were maybe ten, fifteen years older than she was. [They] were in there ahead of her. In fact, she was the baby of the family.

I was the first one [of my family] into the mills. One of my brothers went back to Italy, and the other worked at a dairy farm, doing boy's work, mechanic stuff like that. We did farm too! What spare time we had between the mill work, we farmed. In 1928 they only used to run six looms per person. They trained you for two or three weeks, and then she'd give you a loom to work just as long as you could go. Then I went on to two looms. And three and four, till I could get up to six after about six months. The supervisors would take their information from the person that was training you, and you did not get paid for training. And the person that trained you didn't get paid either. You were ready when the person who trained you felt that you were ready. She would submit your name to the supervisor. When they did bring you in to train you, you were pretty certain of getting work there.

It's very hard to work in silk. The silk reacts to the weather; if it's damp and wet, too wet, it reacts to that. If it's dry, it's like when you comb your hair, it flies and balloons out. They had what they called a humidifying system that sprayed water to get a relative humidity of about fifty-seven to sixty [percent] so those threads would lay right without any problems. My first week I made a lot of seconds, and if you did make seconds, they used to penalize you. They'd give you what you call a pink slip and charge you so much. So they took back all the pay I made that week. My first week's pay was four pennies! Four pennies.

That was a disgrace, but I brought them home anyway. The politicians finally passed a law against the penalties, and some people saved their pink slips and got all that back money. Every bit of it.

We ran Jacquard looms with four shuttles to weave silk plaid. The dyed threads of green, red, white, and black would be wound onto the warp beam. But you got to be very, very careful that you have the same amount of ends each time, because if you don't, your material becomes a second. You have to always be careful because the loom stops by itself through what they call a feeler. And that feeler has to be set so that when there's no thread in the shuttle, it touches the wooden part of the bobbin, and it stops the loom automatically. And you got to be sure to put the shuttle back in the same place, and you got to be sure what color you want. Because if you don't, you'll have to stop your loom and you have to pick off the threads that are wrong, and you have to start it all over again. And if you don't start it right, you're gonna make a mark, a starting mark of some kind, and you will make a second. A cut of cloth was about a hundred yards, and you were allowed not any more than a half dozen imperfections, and then after that it becomes a second.

When you ran a Jacquard, you really had to know it; if you didn't, the Jacquard was very, very hard. But I liked weaving. I was in silk weaving for about twenty-five years. It was intriguing; you had to give it a lot of attention and if you liked it, you could do it well. And if you didn't like it, it was a hard job. Many people never became weavers. I taught I don't know how many weavers.

Even good weavers had seconds. Like in the spring when the weather begins to change, you could be the best weaver in the block, and you'd still have seconds. Not as many because you would learn these little tricks that would help you. Spray it with water, but you can't spray too much because then it marks your cloth. A lot of people used to spit in the shuttle so the thread wouldn't balloon. The machinery would stop more often in that weather, and the mills would get out less work. You would make less money on piecework. They tried to update the condition of the weave room all the time to get a perfect combination of heat and humidity.

We started out weaving on six looms, and they had what they called a pick clock. It's like a little meter, and it has shift number 1, shift number 2, and shift number 3. On shift number 1, you turn the pointer of the pick clock to number 1 to register the picks, or each time the shuttle crosses the loom. That's how they made up the pay. Office girls would go around on Saturday morning to read all these meters and set your pay by that. If you were making a plain taffeta, very simple and very fast, that was [so much money]. But if you were making the heavy taffeta or satin that they used to use in wedding gowns, you didn't [end up earning] as much because it was really hard [work], a lot of picks per inch like a hundred and some per inch. When the National Recovery Act [NRA] came during the Roosevelt days, people started to speak up, and awful dissatisfaction started to surface. So the mills compensated people by paying so much for this style and so much for that style. If you had harder material to make, you were compensated for that; you were given more money per hundred picks. This is how we started getting a little recognition.

They were making satin, which is a very delicate product, very, very delicate, and at the same time they speeded up the looms. The newer looms came with different speeds and new gears. Then they replaced the belts and pulleys with electric motors. Then they gave us more than six looms, right up to twenty-seven. And then they used double shuttle looms. A bobbin that is filled with rayon or silk would last you twenty-five minutes. If you had two bobbins [and two shuttles], they would last you forty, fifty minutes easy, and you could operate more looms. As the work load increased, it had to be accepted if you wanted to work. You couldn't just say no, because if you said no, they'd just tell you to go home.

During the Roosevelt days and the National Recovery Act, they wanted to get the union in, and the mills refused to bring it in, and we had to go on strike. Anyone that belonged to the NRA all got these white capes with red linings, and Market Street in front of the mill was like a rug of white capes and red linings. And we wore the capes like a nurse's cape almost. You'd take one side of it and throw it over your shoulder so that the red would show. And I'm telling you, that strike was really something. They broke every window in that mill! I was right out there with them! After they made me work hard and they give me four pennies the first week, now I'm gonna break a window too! The strikers wanted better working conditions and better supervision. It was all right if you had a half-way human person, but in supervision you don't always find that. It was just demands all the time. The working conditions were bad, and they'd give you more and more work. No benefits, no vacations or sick time. After I got started as a weaver, I made around fourteen, fifteen dollars a week.

I moved around. I started at the Newmarket Manufacturing Company, and I worked there for about two or three years. It was a large

Uniformed NRA marchers at the Merrimack Manufacturing Company, 1934. *Courtesy of Lowell National Historical Park.*

place with hundreds of people in there. It was always harder to work for a place with many people because the competition among people was much greater. And if you weren't in the know with the foreman or supervisor, you never got the chance you really deserved, you know. And so for some reason or another, I was always going. One time I went to work on Jackson Street where Wolf's Manufacturing made jackets, and I was in the inspection department there for a while. So one morning I rode the elevator with these other people, and I thought to myself, I hear looms. And I could see them through a crack in the door. And I said, Oh gosh, I'm gonna find out if I can get in there. Somebody came by, and I asked him were they looking for help; I'm a weaver. So the next morning I went to work for Alan Larter, who was just starting out. He asked me if I knew other weavers, and I told him, Yes I do. I had two other sisters who were weavers; I had trained them. I trained many weavers for Alan Larter, and he paid me two extra dollars a week each time I was training a weaver.

It is a job that you had to like. I liked it because it was very difficult. You have to like it in order to want to do it. There are ways of looking at cloth so you can pick up imperfections just like that. You don't even have to have a good eye if you know how to do it, if you know how to walk at it and shade it, you can see anything. You can see the difference in a shade, even whites, you can see all the differences. I liked it, and I did it well.

I finally became what they call a weave room inspector, and I did that for many years. You walk around the weave room, and as you walk around you have to have a light with you, a strong light. Weaving is funny. The higher the building the worse for a loom. There's a certain give to a building. When a lot of machinery, especially looms, is banging back and forth, going this way and that way at the same time, they begin to synchronize. And when the looms are synchronized, you get what they call bars in the cloth. And when that happens you're going to have to stop a few looms, you know. So I'd start them [up] over again so that they won't synchronize, and sometimes they'd go for quite a few hours before they start synchronizing again. I could feel it happening.

The pattern for the cloth is set up in your headings, in the harness by the drawing-in girl. And then it naturally follows into the weave. It can be a cross pattern, or it could be dots and dashes; it could be little rows; it could be almost anything. They don't shut your loom down too long to change it. The loom fixers would have the harnesses already all drawn-in, and all they have to do is just take out what runs out and put that one right in again, because they like to do that as fast as possible because they want to get the yardage out. They do not want to lose any time. But they used to have layoffs. And if they didn't have any orders and they had layoffs, they would let one or two stay until all the looms run out.

A lot of times, two shuttles would meet in a loom and rip the whole thing outright. The weaver doesn't have time to fix that. So they had what they called a smash, and the smash-piecers, usually other women, were the ones that take care of that for us. Weaving was done by women in the daytime, but at one time it was against the law to work women nights. So the night shift was always a man's job. I think the only time the law was changed was during the Second World War. A woman could work the third shift because all the men were taken away. We even took over in the slashing, which always was a man's job. That's when they take the warp threads and put a sizing or starch on them and then dry them. It was heavy work, it was hard, and it was done by a slasher machine, which is very, very hot. Then the warp is wound onto the big beam and into the loom.

You can learn how to do some things to keep your machinery going rather than stop. They never wanted to see a loom stop, because once you stop a loom you're gonna make a bad mark, you know. But if it's making a bad second, you have to stop it. Say if your filling in the shuttle is loopy, you have to stop it 'cause it leaves little loops. You can adjust your own shuttle sometimes because it has a little screw and a little spring and sometimes it might get loose. You can if you know. A lot of people did not attempt it; a lot of people never became weavers. I've taught a lot of people, and I know some that never could have become weavers. They just didn't have it. It's quite a combination. You must have seen looms run. You've got the harnesses that go up and down, and you have the threads coming in this way, then you have the reed that goes back and forth, then you have your picker-sticks on the side that send your shuttle back and forth, then you have your gears that are picking up, and your material coming down. So you've got a lot of things going at one time, and it confuses a lot of people. They just couldn't synchronize with it.

While I was teaching weavers, I could tell who was gonna be good and who wasn't. The first thing to do is to teach them one thing until they got that one thing down pat, so pat they're sure of themselves, they can do it with their eyes closed. That first lesson is to change your shuttles. The hardest thing that people had in weaving was breaking of the thread ends on the warp side. The breaking of the ends in your shuttle was not that bad. You can find the place and fix it. But the breaking of the ends on the warp side, you have to put your hands in the hole and get the hooks and bring them through. Whenever I had anyone that I knew wasn't going to be a weaver, I thought it was best for them to know. If you knew how to tell them, it didn't bother them because they could go on to something else. They could do drop-wiring or drawing-in. I know a girl who couldn't become a weaver because she was too small, but she made a great draw-in girl. Too short and too small, but she was a great drop-wire girl.

The weave room was a good large room with four or five hundred looms. We were penalized if we were late to work. As long as you punched in by six, and, Boy, many times we made it it was just six! They only allowed you fifteen minutes for the week. After they gave us twenty-five looms apiece, our communication was mostly done with our hands. And of course when we got close enough to one another, we talked to one another. Most weavers kinda talk loud because that's the way they did it. If you have twenty-five looms, you have a [filling] thread in each that's only gonna last about twenty-four minutes, and then a lot of times the thread would break. That means you had to keep going all the time. There was always something stopped and you couldn't let them stop too long; if you did, your material would be a second. If you let a loom stop too long, you get a bar, a starting line in the cloth. So we used to have our money in our pocket for coffee before we even started in the morning, and one person used to go out and get it in a small place near us. While that person went out, all the other people stayed and had to pitch in and run that person's looms. We got up to where I could make eighty dollars a week before the war. That was good money. That is why a lot of people were attracted to weaving.

It wasn't really dangerous, but they didn't want small children in the weave shed. They didn't want anyone walking through the weave room unless they belonged there. Sometimes those shuttles fly out and they can hit you, and if they hit you they can hurt you. I had a shuttle glance me once in a while, but I never really got hurt.

We had to buy our own scissors with rounded tips so when you'd put your scissors on the cloth they would slide and wouldn't cut anything. You had to have a heddle hook and a reed hook, and that's about all you really needed. Sometimes we used a little comb so that we could comb the fur inside the shuttle. And then you had a pick made of ivory for a malfunction in the material or when the harness broke to pick out the threads. And when you did that, you had to be careful because you'd pull everything apart.

The loom really depends on your loom fixer. Some were brilliant loom fixers, and some were not. I was an inspector for many years, and then I got married in 1945 and I stayed home 'cause I had my son. Then Alan Larter called me up and wanted to talk to me. And he said to me, You know, Cheza, my seconds are goin' up to 20 percent. That's bad, and I don't understand what it's all about. So I went back in, and this time I straddled two shifts, the first and the second. There are some people fabulous for certain kinds of loom fixing, and everyone had a special thing that he could do better than the next one. So I gave each his duty, but I didn't tell any of them. It was all to their benefit because they were all producing and making good money.

To get along as a weave room inspector you had to like people. Second, you have to use your own head. You're not going to use it to tell a person that they can't do it right. That ain't gonna get you nowhere, you know. It was of no benefit to nobody, and everybody was in there to work, and everybody was in there to make as much as they possibly can. As an inspector I didn't supervise the loom fixers, I tagged the machines: the looms that weren't doing the right work. And they had to honor whatever the tagging was. When I made my rounds, I would tag a machine that needed to be corrected but was not making seconds yet. I wouldn't stop it. I'd tag it. And naturally the weavers were happy because the machines weren't stopped, and the loom fixer was happy because the looms weren't stopped with a lot of work backing up. So everybody was happy. And everybody was making money. The owner was happy; he was making money.

The union never got into Wannalancit Textile. Because whatever the union did, Alan Larter always raised the pay one or two cents more per hundred picks than the other mills. He gave us two weeks' vacation with pay and set up a bonus system. He didn't want to be bothered with the union because there was a lot of paperwork. So he always said that to him it was worth it to keep the union and the paperwork out. He was a very proud man, and one year gave back the money that had been raised to buy him a Christmas gift. He said to me he had everything he wanted, and he thought that the people deserved the money more than he, and he made me give it all back. He was a good man. He gave us wonderful Christmas parties. It was a really good place to work in; the feeling was good among the employees.

There was a smash-piecer in every room. When there was no work for them, they would walk around and whatever was wrong, if a loom was stopped, they used to start it. And the loom fixers did the same thing. Some of them didn't, and some of them did; most all of them did. If there was something stopped, they would start it. So that there was a feeling with people that was different than it is today.

Everyone knew that everyone had to work; there was no question about it. Because things weren't that easy in them days. I think it was more or less family oriented. Most anyone that worked in the mill was more than one from each family. So we were family oriented and that spilled over into our work. Today you can't find that at all hardly. Three of us sisters were weavers, and my sister Florence was a drop-wire girl. You take all of these people bringing that kind of money into one family, and it all pulled in. So it gave us a good living. It gave us a good start; it allowed us to own property. And I enjoyed doing it because the feeling was a very close feeling, like one big happy family.

I never got laid off but once, at the Lowell Silk Mill. That was during the depression years; then I went to work on wool. If you wanted to work, you could find work then too. But you had to want to work. You had to have the attitude that when you went to work you were not the boss. You had a boss over you. You had to work because if you didn't work they wouldn't keep you. If you were strong and healthy and could move around, you had a better chance of being kept on than the person that wasn't as strong and as fast and as on time.

When it came to mill work, I don't think employment had much to do with your nationality. You had French, you had Polish, you had Portuguese, and Italian. But there were other areas of employment that if you were Italian, you couldn't break into. Like the town jobs in Tewksbury and the Tewksbury [State] Hospital. I wanted to become a nurse, but I was Italian, and it was so hard to break in there. So I had to take another way. But the English people and the Irish people, they would be the first to get the supervisory jobs in the mills. Very few Italians or French ever got them. The Italian people always got the working jobs 'cause they all were workhorses. The Portuguese people were the same. They were always workhorses. I remember the supervisors, Charlie Lovitt, that don't sound like an Italian name, does it? Joe Roy. I mean these are all English and Irish people. But I always found the English much better to work for than the Irish.

I always got along. I got along with them real well, all the time. I was the type of person that always minded my own business. I did what I had to do. I knew my job and I knew my place. And that's how I was brought up. If you knew your job and you knew your place, you ain't got no worries, right? The only thing that I objected to was if I got into kind of a fight. Oh, there were sometimes when a supervisor might come along, there were a lot of times—I don't know how these people got into supervision—but there were a lot of times they knew less than the people that they were supervising. That's the thing I objected to. Of course when you start objecting, then it is time to move on. The supervisor is supervisor. So when that time came, well, I figured it was time for me to move on.

Most any man that went into weaving always went into weaving with the idea of going up higher than a weaver. He always wanted to end up loom fixing or going into slashing or into the machine shop. That was their stepping stone to something else. It was almost like a career ladder, up the ladder, you know. That was what was in the back of their minds when they took that job. Women didn't have anywhere to go. The only thing that women could have done was inspecting. Women didn't have much of an opportunity in the mill. I trained both men and women as weavers. Men had more rugged hands, and weaving is like crocheting and knitting and stuff like that. Women could do that. There are some men who are good at it, but they went into other jobs.

I was brought up by a wonderful, wonderful man, my father. He was very firm, very kind, and very lovable. My mother was a hard-working lady. She was a good housekeeper, a good cook, a good mother, and a good woman. But my father was a sweetheart. My father brought my brothers up like he brought up his girls. I remember one time my brother had a difficult time with him because he didn't want to marry a girl who thought she was pregnant. And my father said, I'll break every bone in your body; if the child is yours, you'll marry her. He said as far as he knew there was never going to be a Fantini without their rightful name. When it came to making the daughters worldly-wise, he let my mother do it. He was way ahead of his times. He always used to say, never be afraid of a smart woman. He used to say that a man who is a man is never going to be afraid of a smart woman. Because together they can be fantastic.

I didn't have a chance to go to school like I would have liked. But I think all the experience, the practical experience I got, broadened my knowledge. And it didn't make me bitter and I love life, and I like people. I wonder sometimes if I hadn't seen the best of America.

I Never Had a Job That I Sat Down

Mabel Delehanty Mangan
SPINNER

The discipline and self-denial that she learned in a poor Irish Catholic family and in an overcrowded parochial school prepared Mabel Delehanty to accept the hard-working life of a mill worker. Taken into a mill where other family members were employed, she briefly worked as a velvet cutter, one of the few skilled jobs available to young women workers. Then as the mills declined in the 1920s and 1930s, she worked off and on wherever she could for fifty years.

Mangan especially remembered her mother as one of the strong, capable women in the Irish-American neighborhood where she grew up. The authority of Irish community values began in the family and continued in the school and on the neighborhood doorsteps. Cultural divisions among mill workers undercut that sense of community and made Mabel Mangan feel excluded and uneasy. Managers deliberately used language and skill differences among mill workers to divide them.

Mangan understood that she had to work: "it's got to be." But resignation did not mean she ignored the bad working conditions and low pay or that she accepted injustice. She knew, like many other mill workers in Lowell, that resistance to harsh treatment was impossible without dependable union organization and good leadership.

I WAS BORN in the Irish neighborhood called the "Holy Acre," on March 20, 1901. I lived in Lowell all my life. There were nine of us, [and] we had a strict upbringing. What Mother and Father said was law. Our teachers, too. You didn't answer back; you didn't dare. I went to St. Patrick's School and to Notre Dame Academy. We had the nuns, of course, in the parochial school, and they gave us a thorough training, believe me! They didn't have any accelerated programs. If I was brighter than you, I was sent to take care of you and help you. There were so many of us that in the third grade we had three in a seat in those days. One of the little ones did something wrong one day, and the nun intervened, and me being on the end of the seat, I fell off and hit my head. When I came home and told my mother, what did my mother say? If you didn't deserve it, you would not get it! The nuns and the priests were supreme in those days. You were sent to school, and that nun was supposed to discipline you. And whatever she did, it was never questioned. It was right.

I graduated from St. Patrick's grammar school, and I went two years to Notre Dame Catholic High School for Girls. I had got a scholarship. That's as far as I got because my father was taken sick, and in the old mill days, the pays were small. My father was working as an oiler in the Merrimack mills for $10.50 a week. He worked from six in the morning to six at night, and the same on Saturday to noon.

But my mother was very clever. When my father went into the Merrimack Print Works to work for Mr. Wadleigh, he used to give my father the soiled pieces of cloth, you know, [just] a little oil or something. And with five girls, my mother made clothes for us. She made all her own clothes, and then she was the midwife for the neighborhood. She picked up a few extra dollars here and there by making clothes for the neighbors. She ran a boardinghouse to feed the professional men of the city for a while, until she had her fifth child, then that was too much. We had good food. Our mothers knew how to cook well and give us nourishing food, and we had warm clothes and a warm house. But outside of that, it was tough.

So I went into the mills to help out. We had no choice, like [when] we had our children. We had no choice; we had them or else. I started in the Merrimack mills when I was fifteen. I went into the velvet room, collecting the piece-rate checks [that measured the amount of production] and taking them to the office. I had an older sister in the velvet room who was a velvet cutter. So in the meantime, I learned velvet cutting. The velvet cutters were the elite of the mill workers in the city. We made ten dollars a week when the others was only making six. The real clever girls, the very smart ones, they could get off four pieces [or bolts of velvet] for thirteen dollars a week. So they used to call the velvet cutters the "400" of Lowell. Caesar Misch [a local clothing retailer] had a sale on fur coats; most of us went and bought one for a dollar down and a dollar a week. That's how we got the name, the "400" of Lowell. We could get a little bit of clothes; we were somebody.

Everybody worked so hard in those days. Your working hours took up mostly all your time. And Sunday was Mass and Benediction, you know. But on Sundays as we girls got older we would walk around the city. And we'd have the boys trailing after us, of course. We were decent boys and girls. We had fun. We'd sit on the benches and talk. There were dances on Saturday night at the Hibernian Hall, Irish dances and jigs and eight-hands-round. And then evenings, we'd sit on the doorsteps and sing or talk or tell ghost stories. It was mostly with the Irish.

One of my friends, her mother was real Irish. Oh, she was the wittiest lady. And she came out with her broom, and she sat on the top of the steps, and then she'd say, Time to go home. We'd all scurry every way, and she'd wave her broom. Mrs. Lafferty, oh, she was so funny! And she'd tell us what to do and what not to do. Like when I was almost sixteen, I'd have my time [menstrual period]. And all my mother said to me was, Take care of yourself! Guard your honor! Till the day I was married I didn't know what my honor was, but I knew I had to guard something! My mother was real strict; you couldn't get away with anything with her. She watched you like a hawk. If you dared to oppose her authority, your valise was outside the door. If you can do better someplace else—here, go!

She was a good mother. And she either killed you or cured you; never a doctor. Only if it got beyond her. I had typhoid fever once. I took my sister and myself up on Broadway one hot day, and we spent the afternoon in the horses' trough. And we both got typhoid fever. I was really bad with it, but that was the only time I remember a doctor. Anybody was sick, they'd go to Mrs. Delehanty, and she'd have a remedy. These Irish women brought the remedies from the old country. Over there, doctors and nurses were scarce, and the doctor would come a certain time of the year and leave these instructions in case he couldn't get back or they couldn't get to him. I had an Armenian woman once and, believe me, she was next door to being a doctor. She said they had to do these things because there was no doctors. That woman, she could put her finger right on what was wrong and tell them what to do.

We were all poor people. We had no money in the bank. We had no money [at all]. We were living from hand-to-mouth. There was no paid holidays. You lost a day, you lost your pay. And then if they cut [the piece rate], what could we do? We went hungry. So you see, we had no alternative. My father was too quiet a man to get involved in strikes, but I remember a strike at the Merrimack. We got nowhere. There was no organization. Lawrence was far ahead of us in fighting these things, but Lowell didn't have the know-how. No leadership. Half a loaf is better than none; that was their attitude.

Every morning at quarter of six, every door in the Acre would open,

Adams Street in the Acre, 1939. *Courtesy of the Lowell Housing Authority and the Center for Lowell History.*

and we'd all troop out, down to the Merrimack, the Prescott, the Boott, or the Tremont and Suffolk. We'd all be going down Merrimack Street in those days in the early morning. It was crowded with the mill workers going to work. No people in cars. There was no cars, and the streets were lined with people. And we'd be laughing and singing, going along. Some of us. And some of us were very upset at getting up and figuring there wasn't much to look forward to. But, so what, some of us looked at it this way. It's got to be. What else are you going to do? You can't stay home; your mother won't let you. You've got to go to work. On the Holy Days of Obligation, the Catholic girls and boys, we'd have to get up at half-past four in the morning to be at Mass at five [before work at six]. And with the old Irish mothers, you were there. Definitely!

I married when I was twenty. George worked in the Lowell Bleachery where you bleached the cloth. I had four children, a daughter and three sons. We both worked and struggled and helped the children whenever we could. We started at six, and we had two shifts. We worked from six to two-thirty, and then the two-thirty shift would work until eleven. I usually took the two-thirty to eleven shift when the children were growing up, because I could get them out to school in the morning, get their breakfast, and get their lunch ready. And my husband used to come home at lunch, and then I left the supper all ready for them. My husband was home at two-thirty then with the children. So between the two of us, we never had baby-sitters. We never left them alone; we were both with them. Always there for them. There was a day nursery, but most got baby-sitters, someone to sit. Most had grandmothers or mothers. But my mother was ninety.

They were very good children. They did for themselves; they helped themselves too. My boys got the G.I. bill, and my daughter graduated from state teachers' college and was a school teacher. I have a boy who is a scientist and worked at the Department of the Interior in Washington. He has a Ph.D. from Georgetown University. He has so many letters after his name, it's like an alphabet. My other boy, he travels a lot, and my youngest is an accountant.

Two of my sons worked in the mills during the summer vacation, but they didn't like it. They said, Mother, how ever did you stay in those places? They were dirty and noisy; the machines were going all the time. And we had cockroaches. One of the toolers in the velvet room that used to sharpen the [velvet-cutting] knives for us got hold of one of those cockroaches and put a string on his leg. That was his pet. He used to feed the darn thing. I forget what he used to call him. Then there were the rats. We had a bench where we used to sit and change to our old shoes. We'd take them out from under, and the rats would hop out. The sanitation wasn't good there. There was no ladies' room; they called them toilets, and they had no drinking water, only canal water. They weren't ladies' rooms, they were just toilets, and oh, the less said, the better! You brought your own lunch. And we got a fifteen-minute break. We started at six, and at ten o'clock, we'd have a fifteen-minute break.

There were no benefits in the mills. [If] you were sick, you were sick, and that was it. You took your vacation *if* you could afford it, usually a couple of weekends. Before the Depression there was no unemployment; there was plenty of work in the mills. The mills were running full-blast. Anyone that wanted to work, had work. World War I, that was when things changed for the better in the mills. They started paying a little more because they needed the help. The price of things went up, but the wages went up. During the Depression they weren't getting the orders. They kept running but they started laying off. My husband got laid off. The Bleachery, it moved South. That's when the mills started to move away. They gradually started going down and down and down till finally they couldn't compete with the South or whatever.

During the Depression, I worked in The Crax [Megowan-Educator Biscuit Company]. That's the cookies, you know. And I went in there because my husband was laid off, and we were trying to survive. I worked on the assembly line. The cookies came down the line, and we were supposed to pick out the broken ones and put them in a basket. This supervisor said to us, I don't want to see any cookies but broken ones in this basket. And she'd come along, and she said to me, Faster! I said, Well, I'm going as fast as I can. She said, Here you start fast and get faster. I used to come home at night, and you could wring my clothes out. So after about three weeks, I was down to eighty-nine pounds, and my husband said, Listen, you can't do this. We can't get along without you. We're in this together; we'll stay together. So I went back to The Crax, and I said [to the supervisor], Listen, lady, Lincoln freed the slaves, and I said, I don't intend to go back to those days! So I said, You can take your job, and you know what you can do with it!

Then I got work up to the Ames Worsted, and from then on, I was in the mills. I was in every mill in the city until it folded up. The last one was the Synthetic Yarns. I did winding, twisting, doffing. Most of it was piecework, but you were supposed to reach a certain quota. We had fun; the workers had fun. We were all in the same position. We knew we had to work for a living. We got along, and I worked with every nationality.

The only ones that were trouble sometimes were the French. The majority of them were very nice, but most places where I worked they talked in French. They'd say, Listen, she doesn't understand English, I'm going to say this to her in French. Then they'd tell me after. Or if I was in a group talking French, I'd say, Listen, I'll have to excuse myself, I don't understand what you're saying. And I'd walk away. But the majority of them were very, very nice. They just didn't have no desire to learn the English language or it was too difficult for them. They spoke French in the home, and then they sent the children to the French schools. In those days, they didn't teach them English. Now it's the law. Of course we had the jump on them. The English did us a favor in a way when they took our book [of Gaelic] away. When our fathers and mothers came here, they didn't have that language barrier. Both my parents and all my aunts and uncles came to America from Ireland.

My mother was ninety-two when she died. She was the first woman who got a pension from the Merrimack because she worked until she was eighty-five. My father wanted her to stop, and she would not. So my father said to Mr. Wadleigh, Fire her, please. He said, Yes, but I'm going to give her a pension. He gave her five dollars a month and told her, Mrs. Delehanty, you take it easy for a while. She was so proud; she told everybody.

We depended on the mills and the shoe shops and the dress shops. Those were our main things we did then. I only worked in the mills. I didn't work in the shoe shops or the dress shops because I wasn't very talented at sewing. A workhorse. I think that's what I'd call myself, a workhorse. Some people just liked spooling or twisting; they'd prefer that kind of work because they thought they were more efficient at it. Whichever you learned first, you usually stuck to it. My aunts were weavers, and I used to go in with them. But the noise would drive you out of your mind. When one department had a lull, they'd send you over to another department. That's how I learned different things. I worked in the Boott on the towels and sheets. That was good, quiet work, folding the towels. Then synthetic yarns came in, and we had to find out how to handle those. We had expediters, and they taught us not to mix the synthetic yarns. If you mixed them, that whole batch was no good, and that meant you—out!

Once when I was in the Ames Worsted, I was training a youngster, and I had her trained and everything. So one day, I was looking, and the whole sides of her spinning frames were down, doing nothing. I went into the ladies' room, and [there] she was, smoking. I said, Look, dear, I said, you won't make any money sitting in here. I said, All your frames are down; he won't like that. She said, I know it. She said, There's a better way than this to make a living. She said, You must have been nuts; you must have been nuts to do this! She said, I'm quitting! That's why they're down; I'm quitting, and she walked out.

I worked in the mills almost fifty years, off and on. I never had a job that I sat down. That's why I'm eighty-three years old [in 1984]. And I kept my figure. Whenever I came home, I had the housework and the kids to take care of. When I hit my pillow, I slept.

We Had to Take What Come

Diane Ouellette
TWISTER

Although they often began to work at fourteen, many women worked in the mills for only a short period, until they married and got out. Marrying a man who was not a mill worker was crucial to escaping lifelong work. The first pregnancy was usually the occasion for leaving. However brief their involvement, women mill workers had vivid memories of their experiences.

Diane Ouellette, a widow's daughter, went into the mills with her mother as soon as she could. All her pay went to support the family, but she had the energy to work the long hours of a second weekend job for her own money. This denied her the most pleasurable social activity of working-class female adolescents, dancing on Saturday night. Her marriage permitted her to leave the spinning room, but the death of a young mill worker very much like herself bothered her.

I WAS BORN in the Province of Quebec in 1898. My father died when I was five years old. My youngest brother, he was only two years old when my father died. When my mother was working in Canada, he was in an orphanage. I was brought up in an orphanage too. After I was old enough, she wanted me to pick up English because I would be miserable without English. In a year I could speak pretty well. I had to speak English in the mill. I was twelve years old when I came to Lowell with my mother and two brothers, one older and one younger. Her sister used to mind my youngest brother. I went to parochial school here until I reached fourteen in 1912. They wouldn't take you in the mills unless you were fourteen.

My mother worked in the United [States] Bunting company for over twenty years. They used to make American flags. She was a weaver. My mother couldn't hardly talk English because there were a lot of French women from Canada weaving. When I was fourteen, I got a job there in that place as a doffer. I was working with the spinning and winding and twisting in another building. A doffer takes bobbins that's full of yarn and takes them off the machine that winds wool on spools. You had to work fast. Though doffing wasn't piecework, you had to keep up with the work. I used to do some spinning too and winding. My mother was in a different department but in the same mill.

They were on strike when I was [first in the mill in 1912.]* A big strike, a three-month strike. But our little woolen mill wasn't on strike. It was mostly cotton mills that were on strike then. It was a lot of hardship, but I wasn't in it. I thought they should get a little more of a break. They wasn't giving them a break. Three or four months, that was a hardship then, but I didn't go through that.

I worked one time on the weaving for about eight months with my mother, but I didn't like it so I went back on twisting. I was so used to the other work that I thought that weaving was too much responsibility. I used to get discouraged when the thread would break. The weaving was louder than your doffing and spinning, and those shuttles used to make me nervous. It was kind of hard. So I went back to my old work.

When I was doffing, they used to pay you for five days and a half, $2.50 a week. That's what I was getting for doffing and for winding. The spinning frame was loud, and you had to be careful. We had to pull our braids up off our backs because they'd get tangled into the wheels; those wheels weren't covered up. So we had to be careful. Four times a day we had to doff 108 spindles. Every two hours we had to take all these spindles and fill them up again. We had to take what come. We had to pay attention to our work or else you'd lose your job, and you didn't want to lose it.

When I went to twisting on the ring twister, then we were on piecework. I could make as much as $7.00 or $7.50 a week. The first years that I worked there, we used to start at quarter of seven in the morning and finish at quarter of six with an hour for lunch. I used to leave my work for an hour, and I'd go and meet my mother at her looms. We didn't take many rest breaks because we were on piecework. We could have little breaks if we worked quick enough, but I was pretty good at it. You got used to it. We were tough.

I have only one bad memory of the mills. A girl that used to work with me, she went to Boston, and she committed suicide. That was a big blow for us because we used to like that girl so much, but it seemed like she was kind of discouraged. She used to work with me, doing the same

*Immediately after the Bread and Roses strike in Lawrence, another successful strike organized by the Industrial Workers of the World was held in Lowell.

work as I. And the first thing we knew, she had committed suicide. That was bad because she was well liked.

I left the Bunting sometimes when they had slack seasons, and I went to work as a winder in the Hamilton and the Appleton mills and in the Lawrence Hosiery. But I'd always go back to the Bunting. They had nice English bosses. Mine was English, and he was nice. As long as you do your work, you're all set. I worked in the mill for fourteen years until 1926. I used to like it; of course that was the only way you could earn your living. There was no way of going on relief those days. My mother was a widow, and I helped her out.

I used to work for Bass' Clothing Store on Central Street. I worked there for four years on Friday night and on Saturdays, all day. I used to get four dollars for a day and a half. I thought it was good. That was my spending money. Saturdays I worked until ten o'clock so I stayed home, but we used to have a lot of friends. I learned to play the piano, and we used to get together and sing. I never went to dances.

I left the mill because I got married. I worked a year after I was married, and I didn't go back to work because I raised three children. I met my husband through a family that my mother knew well. We got to know each other, and we got married. He worked as a printer for the Boston and Maine Railroad. My mother just passed fifty-three when she left the mill. She wasn't well. I took her into my home. He was working, and we all got along pretty well. She died at sixty. That's how I earned my living in the mills.

I Went There Just to See What It's Like

Dori Nelson

QUILLER

Some working-class families did not have a pressing need for their children's wages. Men with railroad jobs, telephone linemen, or self-employed small builders could do without the pay envelopes of their fourteen-year-old sons and daughters. After high school or trade school, however, their daughters entered a local job market that offered various kinds of low-paid, unskilled work that promised little training and no future to young unmarried women.

Although quilling paid little, Dori Nelson enjoyed working with the colorful silk thread and admired the beauty of the cloth that the mill produced—an appreciation shared by many women in silk work. Like Diane Ouellette, she remembered others who were not so lucky as she was: the serious, the overworked, and the discouraged.

I WAS BORN in Lowell and attended the public schools and two years at the Lowell Trade School. I took up sewing and hairdressing, but I didn't do either of them afterward. My father was a contractor. After trade school, I took jobs here and there with my girlfriends. Like shoe shops, box shops, Waltham Watch. I didn't give my pay to my mother, but I did used to always hand her five dollars every week. I didn't have to but I did, and the rest was mine. But money went a long way in those days. My dad's money was tied up in his houses, in his paints and wallpaper, and things that he had to get to fix the houses up with.

I worked in a printing place until I had to quit. My hands were all paper cuts from the paper. My sister could stand that better than I could. My hands were a mess. They were all cut up. You know when you shuffle papers like that and try to get them in piles? So I quit that before she did, but she quit the mill, and I stayed on. I liked trying different jobs. I liked working for the watch factory, the Waltham Watch. I loved that. But the fellow that drove back and forth in a passenger car took sick and couldn't go no more, and I had hard work trying to get a ride. So that's why I left that job.

I took a job in the Newmarket mills in 1937, and I worked four years until 1941. Then I gave my two-weeks' notice because I was going to be married. I worked in the quilling room at a very interesting job. In fact, I really liked it very much. I didn't like the heat of the mill, but I could stand it because I liked the people I was working with, and I liked the job. We made beautiful silk cloth. It was very pretty, and some was striped. I ran four machines with eight sides. I filled the bobbins with the silk thread to be woven into cloth by the weavers. I'd take an empty bobbin, and I'd put it on a spindle, press the lever down, and you'd keep going right along, get all the machine sides going. And they'd be filling up with this nice silk thread. And you kind of watch and as the last one that you run is slowing down, you have to try to get back to that one in time to keep them all going.

And then you had the stand with the pin board on it. The bobbins were hollow so when the bobbins were all filled with thread, you'd take them and put them by colors in rows on this pin board [arranged] to make the stripes. The pin board had stems. And you'd put them in a row until the pinboard was all filled. The pin boys would come in and take them into the weave room. Of course I got a look at the machines all going in the weave room once in a while, but I don't really understand anything about weaving. They'd take our work from the quilling room, and then they'd weave it into cloth, and in the end it would be brought downstairs to be inspected, which my sister did. I was getting fourteen dollars a week. I learned the job from one of the girls that worked on it. The boss told her to show me how.

I met my husband at the free movies for young people at the South Common. I got introduced to him there by somebody who knew him. He worked at the Boston and Maine Railroad at the time, and after that at the New England Telephone as a lineman. We both played the piano, and we used to spend a lot of time that way. It seems as though we liked that so well we didn't get into anything else. Before I went steady with him, I used to be at the dances almost every Saturday night. I loved dancing. I was well taken care of, so everything was all right. When the dance was over, I got taken back home. So everything was all right that way. My mother was very, very careful that way.

I might have stayed at the Newmarket mills longer if it wasn't that my husband wanted me to be at home. He worked at the Telephone and at that time the money was good, and he didn't want me in the mills, but I really enjoyed it. Some people worked in the mill, and they didn't have it very easy at home or anything, and I used to feel sorry for them because they used to work so hard. They'd take everything so serious, because if things aren't going right you take things more serious. Then when they got home, they had all this work they knew that they had to do no matter how tired they were. There was a young girl, she was a friend of mine, a Greek girl. She was such a nice kid, and when she got home, she had about four brothers, and she had to wash and iron their shirts and clean the house. She had a big family, and she worked very hard.

I went in there just to see what it's like and try it out, and then in the end I liked the job and kept it. And we used to have a lot of fun at lunchtime. Three of us kind of chummed together, and we'd eat out once before we got our pay and we'd eat out once after we got our pay. And then we'd go easy. I had a good life.

On Drawing-in,
You Have to Be Dedicated

Leona Bacon Pray

DRAWING-IN GIRL

In contrast to her difficult, hard-working adult life, Leona Pray remem-
bered her childhood as a beautiful dream. She was an ambitious young
woman who learned drawing-in, one of the few skilled jobs for women
mill workers. But then the Depression of the 1930s undermined the woolen
industry in Lawrence and forced Leona Pray and many others to seek any
job available in the cotton mills of other textile cities. Anything would do.

Her versatility, energy, and resourcefulness were born of desperate times
and personal responsibilities. Like her mother, she was dedicated to her
job. She worked in the mills for forty-nine years and saw most if not all of
the textile operations in the Lowell area close. The memories of her son,
Ronald Bacon, are recounted in the last section on the children of the last
generation.

I WAS BORN in Lawrence, Massachusetts, in 1906. My father and
mother, Henry and Alma Pouliot, were born in New England. Their
mothers knew each other. His mother came from Manchester [New
Hampshire] to Lawrence to work, and my grandmother was already in
Lawrence. They met in the mill, and for a while they were working
together in Lowell at the Merrimack mills. My mother's mother was a
weaver, and my father's mother was a spinner. After my mother got
married, she didn't work. My father made her stay home. My father
worked on the Boston and Maine in the winter and was a carpenter in
the summer. They had seven children; four lived, and three died when
they were children.

My childhood was beautiful! I'd go and live it all over again. I would!
We had Grandma and Grandpa with us. Grandpa worked the third
shift, and we'd play outside while he was asleep. There were seven
rooms in the cottage and a long, long porch. My grandmother had a big
garden, and at the end of the property there was a big stone wall. The
Boston and Maine Railroad line from Boston to Portland was up there.

At night after they had gathered all the freights around Boston, they'd be riding by towards Portland, and my father—he was a great one—he'd be on top of the car, and he'd swing his lantern. My uncle was a conductor on the freight.

We used to plant little radishes and scallions and, of course, eat what we'd planted. Grandmother used to grow corn, potatoes, cucumbers, tomatoes. She had the biggest plants you can imagine. We had apple trees and pear trees. We used to go and gather blueberries with my grandmother. We'd spend the whole day in the summer and bring a lunch and a bottle of water. It wasn't built up much then.

Those winters were great! We'd slide our sleds; there were no cars or anything. And my mother made our stockings, our mittens, our hats, our scarves and sweaters. She knitted them. You'd come home, and you'd smell the fresh bread. Ma was making bread. [Or] we'd smell cookies. It was always my mother baking. On Sundays my mother always made a big roast, sometimes beef, sometimes pork. Pa would come and eat with us after Sunday Mass. After Mama died, I used to darn his socks, 'cause Ma was very dedicated. I was two-months pregnant when she passed away.

I graduated from the Sacred Heart in 1920 and from the commercial college [but her father wouldn't let her get a job away from home]. I never minded working in the mill. Some people complained about it, but to me it was a job. I liked the people I worked with. I liked my job. I learned drawing-in. Our work when it's completed goes into the loom. Drawers-in have a stand to work on and a frame called a harness strung with wires or heddles with holes in the middle. And you have these patterns for herringbone or plaids to arrange within maybe twelve harnesses. To some people it was a hard job, but to me it was like second nature. On drawing-in, you have to be dedicated.

When the Depression hit in Lawrence, I went first to live in my uncle's house in Lowell. I got a job in 1930 or 1931 at the Lawrence Manufacturing Company, spinning. That's the only job open was spinning. All kinds of spinning, but I'd rather do drawing-in. I've been drawing-in through my life, but when there was no work and I got laid off, I did other jobs. Whenever I needed work and there was nothing I could get on woolen, I'd go see the nurse at the Boott mill, Doris Mitchell. She used to do the hiring; she talked to you. I used to go see Miss Mitchell. She'd always hire me, and she'd say to me, Leona when your [woolen] mill calls you, call me up and let me know one way or another, and go. If you need work, come back. You are in the versatile class. That's what she used to say to me.

Then I got a chance in 1933, there was an ad in the paper, they wanted drawing-in girls at the Uxbridge Worsted. They had two and a half floors. I went in there as a drawing-in girl. Off and on, we'd have a layoff. Then I'd go see Miss Mitchell at the Boott, and she'd give me work. Other times I'd go to the U.S. Bunting. I worked there [at the Uxbridge] on and off probably about seven years. I walked in one morning, and the boss was sitting at his desk. His back was turned. I see William J. Entwistle. Good morning, Mr. Entwistle! How are you? I'm looking for a job. I can do a lot of different things. Sit down, he says. Now nobody ever did that! Nobody would dare to go in there! I knew that but I was going to sell myself. And I did. He didn't need any drawing-in girls, but he needed somebody to make up those harnesses. Put the wires on them. Count them. So many on each for a certain pattern. I did that job. So I fitted right in. And when there was an opening on drawing-in, I was there.

They put me on drawing-in, but I also did battery hands in the weave room. The shuttle goes back and forth [in the loom]. Inside the shuttle there's a bobbin full of yarn, and when it's empty, a full bobbin would jump right into the shuttle. It's automatic. So I'd fill up the batteries. Wasn't hard. Gotta be on your toes. You had so many batteries to fill. You couldn't let them [become] empty. 'Cause if they went empty, your loom would stop. There was money lost for the company and the man that was running the loom. There was this poor old Armenian. I swear he was ninety, if he was a day. And he had a hard time, working. He shouldn't have been working. And he was a weaver. We had an hour for lunch. So I'd go over to him, and I'd say, Look, you sit down, you eat. I'll take care of your looms. Most of the time I was his battery hand when I was on batteries. Poor old man. I'd go over there, and I'd take care of his looms, and he was so glad. He'd eat his dinner. I did batteries, and everything else except mending. I started learning mending too, before the mill closed down.

We had mice in the mill and cockroaches too. I'd pack a lunch and take it with me. Beef or roast pork or pork scraps. I'd make a sandwich of that with lots of onion in it. I love onions. On one job at the Boott, I had my dinner on the window, these big window sills. I found a cock-roach in the bag; that was the end of it. I took one of those shafts from the harnesses in the drawing-in room. I bent each end. One end I swung

Drawing-in girl.
Courtesy of MATH.

over the [steam] pipes, and I hung my lunch bag. So they never got in there anymore. It's too high up.

Then I got laid off for quite a while. And I went to do housework and minding kids for this lady. And she used to make beer [during Prohibition]. And she'd have a party every Saturday night. So anyways I met my husband there; he was her cousin. The first thing I knew, we went out together for two years, and we got married [in 1933]. He was half Greek with a French mother. After my boy was born—he wasn't quite seven months old—we got left. I nursed my boy until one night I discovered my husband was running around. That killed everything. He took off in 1942. I lost everything. We had to put him to the bottle. I brought his clothes, his diapers, and his milk next door to a lady who had six children. I went back to work. When I married Mr. Pray, I was getting ready to retire.

During the war, there wasn't too, too much doing at the Uxbridge Worsted, and I went to work for General Electric. General Electric was making suits for the fliers. Those suits were heated. They had all little wires sewed in them. And a lining and a cover over the lining like a shell. I was an inspector. Now it's hard to see a little thin wire that's been sewed up. Your needles was not supposed to hit that wire at all. And I was on inspection. I used to try them out for heat. And then the war ended, and they closed up. I worked on and off, in and out, at the Boott, then my woolen mill called me; I'd go back. Then at the Merrimack; I was working third shift. They were on their way out. They were on their way out, and I could see it.

Then I worked at J. P. Stevens woolen mill in Dracut until 1971 when they closed down. On the board at the unemployment, they have [notices] of so many jobs opened. Drawing-in girl wanted. My sister calls me; I was asleep. She says, Lee, get in your car and go to the unemployment. They're looking for a drawing-in girl somewhere. So I went over there and was sent to Dracut. I made a hit with the boss. I told him the jobs I did and everything. He says, Come in Monday to work. So I went in, and I did different jobs there too. Dropping wires. The head girl who dropped wires used to scare everybody away. She got the best work and everything. When I went to work with her, I said, Look, Stella, I'm gonna be working here with you. Everybody quits or dies. Me, I'll be here a long time after you're gone. We worked together side by side, but I did tell her that. I'm here to work. And don't you try to take any work away from me.

The Boys Used to Get Away with Murder!

Emma Skehan

COMBER

As the oldest daughter in a working-class family, Emma Skehan filled-in at home for her working mother and lost her childhood. Her parents' aspirations to higher standards of conduct and taste for their children contrasted sharply with the realities of the mill where young women faced both mechanical dangers and sexual harassment. Hostile bosses rebuffed complaints and discouraged questions.

Like many other women workers, Emma Skehan waited for her chance to escape into better-paying war work in the early 1940s. Her legacy to her hard-working daughters was that of dignity achieved through intense effort.

MY MOTHER WAS BORN in this country, but my father was born in Quebec. I was born in Lowell in 1925, the oldest child with one brother and two sisters. [Her father] worked in the Sacred Heart School and at the Chelmsford granite quarries. My mother worked at that place where they made surgical stockings [Shaw Hosiery in Lowell]. She had to work. She worked until three or four in the afternoon, and then she came home and took care of the house. But in the meantime, it was me. After school, taking care of the house and taking care of my brother, it was me. My chore was to come home and make sure the children changed their clothes, get the potatoes started, clean the house, and make the beds. I didn't have no time for myself to go out and play.

As a child I loved to go to church. My father and I used to go to Mass together. He taught me when I was eight, whenever you're walking with a gentleman when you grow up, always make sure you are on the inside. And never swear, always be a perfect lady, and you'll never regret it. I loved my father immensely. He told us it was beautiful up there in Quebec. He was an artist, and I was too. He used to take me hunting and fishing. He showed me how to cook, and he showed me how to draw. I was very close to him. He was a very generous person and a perfection-ist.

My mother was a very sensitive person and very kind, very, very kind. She always taught us to be ladies. How to conduct ourselves and not give anybody anything to talk about. She taught us not to talk about anybody. If anybody was having trouble, not to talk. If you can't talk good, don't talk at all. At the supper table we always said grace, and there was no talking during the meal. We had white linen tablecloths, and everything was beautiful.

I remember the Depression, and it was very, very sad. That is when I had to quit school and go to work in 1940, going into seventh grade. My first job was at Insulated Wire. I used to take the threads that go around the wires and make sure they didn't break. That's what I was. It was hard because going home and having to eat supper and get your clothes ready for the next day and rushing up the street to meet the bus, it was rough. I stayed there for one and a half years. Then it was the Boott mills.

The little girl across the street told me. She was already working there, and I said to myself, I think I'll look into it, so I went down and applied. I was hired. They put me in the combers. It was very dangerous work because once those knives [nippers on the combing machine] came cutting, you had to watch your fingers.

And the boys used to horse around in there. Oh, the boys used to get away with murder! They would not work. They would be coming up our aisles and squeezing us, and oh, you could not concentrate. One would have the sweeping job and was supposed to sweep in the aisles and at the same time he would be, you know. . . . So one day I got very mad at him. I told him I didn't like that. You know, he used to squeeze me. He didn't care. The boys used to get kept on by the boss even though they wouldn't pick up our containers where the cotton went in. That was heavy work; sometimes we had to [move] it ourselves. One [boss] in particular was a tyrant, and he was a terror.

And it was hot. Even in the winter, it was real hot. You'd start off in the morning and leave the house, dressed up warm, and you'd get to the Boott mill and it was sweltering hot. And those old shoes we wore, walking in there, and the floors were oily, and you'd be breathing that lint. Your eyelashes would be all full of cotton. But we knew we had to make a week's pay in order to survive. And it was gloomy. I think they had twenty-five-watt [bulbs]. And the machines, the same thing over and over, and at lunchtime everybody used to rush to the old sinks, washed up in cold water, no hot water. There were about two to three hundred people in the room. Other girls would be sweeping; our hair would be covered with the cotton. We would have to go home and take a bath in galvanized tubs—no plumbing at the time—just the washbowl and that's it. And the outhouses until my father got a toilet put in. I remember coming home with our lunch pails and sleeping in those old beds of ours. Galvanized beds.

We used to hand in practically our whole pay. I remember me saving for a pair of patent leather shoes, and when I finally got them, I used to keep them in the closet and cover them so my sisters wouldn't take them on me. That's how hard it was. We used to try to save and go to the movies on Saturday at the Strand Theatre; that was a big thing then. And then take the bus and help Mom on Saturday or Sunday, help her make bread. She wasn't feeling very good; she had a heart condition. She died at forty-eight, so you can see, she worked hard, and I worked hard, and my father did painting. He worked on houses, ceilings, wallpapering, and things like that. It was always me that had to round up the gang [of kids] and make sure the little one was washed. So really I didn't have a chance to have a life until the [Second World] war broke out, and then I started going out with the boys. I got introduced to the USO [United Services Organizations], and I was a USO hostess.

When the parachute [operation] came in, we got wind of it, but they weren't hiring, so we stayed at the Boott mill. Roughly two years, until we knew definitely, and then we gave our notice and proceeded to go up to the parachute. I sewed on the parachute; we strung them and boxed them. It took quite a few girls to pack them and everything, and there were both camouflage and nylon ones, so it was quite a job. It was nice and clean up there and better pay. You were able to buy something for yourself on the weekend. At the Boott mill regular pay plus overtime would be about $20.45 a week for a workday of seven to three. At the parachute mill, it was 6:30 A.M. to 2:30 P.M., and I started off with $42, and it went up. Then [the textile conglomerate] Textron came in, and we worked there also. I worked at the parachute until I got married. My husband started off gardening, then he went to school and started plumbing.

Then I worked at Textron for about one year and a half after I got married. I did stitching on shower curtains. My grandmother had taught me how to stitch when I was seven or eight. So I knew how to stitch, and then I also went to trade school at Lowell vocational for sewing, housekeeping, home nursing, textiles, the works. There were roughly fifty to sixty people in one room at Textron, and of course there were different floors. Some of the workers were middle-aged, but they hired mostly the youngsters, teenagers. It was very interesting work. You concentrated, and it gave you a sense of accomplishment plus contentment. You could be independent a little bit. The floor lady used to go around, and she was very nice. If we had any kinds of complaints, we'd go to her, and she would show us. I enjoyed it, because it gave us a little bit of self-dignity. It was mostly women except for the boys who came and got the boxes and the men down in the cafeteria at the parachute. Some were from the Acre. I worked with a lot of Irish girls and Swedish.

At the Boott mill there was a lot of backbiting among the workers. Going up to the boss and squealing instead of coming right to you and telling you something. The boss was very hard. You couldn't feel free to go up and talk to the boss because sometimes he used to say, Well, if you don't like it, you can leave. So we just kind of swallowed and continued with our work. I don't know what it was or how much they were producing [in the early 1940s], but I do know we were awfully busy, awfully busy. I don't know where it was being shipped because we didn't have that much time to inquire about things. There was never any posters on the wall or nothing. By the time we got out of there, it was wash and woosh! Right out the door!

I always worked the first shift. If I took a day off [at the Boott], most of the time I'd call up or I'd tell the little girl across the street, but you could tell the next day when you went in that the boss wasn't too pleased. Sometimes I would cover for other people. It was a battle because you had to leave your machine and make sure your cotton was going down straight and make sure that the can wasn't full, and then make a beeline to the next one. When I kept that one going, I'd turn around and take the other one so all in all I had two machines to watch. You couldn't smoke. We weren't smoking at the time anyway; couldn't afford it. We had a fifteen-minute lunch break at 11:30. If you needed the ladies' room, you had to leave your machine, and make a beeline and come right out. But the next girl, she'd be watching.

At the parachute mill, they allowed you to smoke. I was smoking then, and you could go in and have a fast smoke and come out and go right back to your machine. And a half hour for lunch. I was sewing the double seams on parachutes. Then they transfer you to inspecting or boxing, and each job you had to pay attention to our work. But we all got along. There was no horsing around. If we got through with our boxing, then we had time to talk a little bit more, and ask where we were going that night and what you were going to wear. At Textron, there was half an hour for lunch. I used to bring a half a sandwich, and we'd be talking about different things. It was gay, beautiful; the girls were nice; everybody used to share. If you were short on change and you wanted to get a Coke, everybody used to share. That was the nicest place. I was stitching shower curtains and a girl put the rings in; we both were on a quota. Then I got a job at Raytheon as a solderer.

I have two daughers that are working at Wang Laboratories. One has three girls, and the other has two with another on the way. I help my girls a lot; I try to help them a lot. I taught them how to be a woman. To stand up for your own, and that when you have to struggle, it makes you a better person. I see them struggling, but I won't always help them because once they learn, it's going to make them a better person when they get the goal they were looking for. Instead of being handed it. What good is that, if you don't work for it?

So the Help Got Cocky,
We All Got Cocky

Yvonne Hoar
CLOTH ROOM WORKER

In contrast to the stereotype of French Canadian women as passive and docile, Yvonne Hoar was a vital young woman, an unpredictable "spit-fire" to her floor boss. She experienced years of barely suppressed outrage over the injustices inflicted on workers by the Merrimack management.

Yvonne Hoar's father had the job of connecting textile machinery together to facilitate the "stretch-out," a means of doubling and tripling work assignments. Hoar knew what the stretch-out meant to her co-workers, and she had to defy her father to become a union organizer. As a shop steward she witnessed and denounced the religious and ethnic discrimination that kept the mill workers divided among themselves.

But Yvonne Hoar refused to force her female coworkers to join the union. Without a union contract that specified a closed shop, she would not substitute union coercion for coercion by the boss. Nor could she forget the "poor souls," the unemployed or those unjustly fired from their jobs or bilked by local merchants. Her memories of life and work recapture the mood of a textile city in decline.*

I WAS BORN in North Adams, Massachusetts, December 27, 1908. Within a year and a half, we moved to Lowell. My father worked in the mills in North Adams, and his boss moved to Lowell, so he asked him to come with him. My father was a machinist. He always worked in the Merrimack mills for forty years. He worked on all kinds of machinery, any type of machinery that broke down. In later years he'd assemble them. Instead of running one machine, they added two machines together. A little later when they saw that went good, well, they added three machines together. That took the work of three girls; one girl

---

*Yvonne Hoar's reminiscences of mill work are reprinted courtesy of the Lowell Museum. They first appeared in a slightly longer version in Mary H. Blewett, ed., *Surviving Hard Times: The Working People of Lowell* (Lowell: Lowell Museum, 1982), pp. 125–40.

could run the three whole machines. All kinds of machines; he'd done the repairing on them.

My father, when he first came to Lowell, was getting twenty-five cents an hour, that was his wages then. The wages were not too, too good, but he worked day and night. He used to work, I remember, when we were kids. For seven years he never wore a white collar. He wore dark shirts, those dark gray shirts, like the iceman used to wear then. Just the laborers used to wear them, just the dark clothes, the dark gray shirts. Nothing fancy because he'd be all grease, and of course when he got into them, he'd wear overalls over them. He worked every Sunday of his life. He'd have to go back to work, then he'd work till ten or twelve o'clock at night in the mill. And I remember the year my brother Raymond was born, he came home, and he'd brought his pay. He'd made a hundred dollars. That was clear, of course; there was no income tax in them days. He had a hundred dollars, and that was a great thing. He thought that was the biggest money. They never thought they'd see a hundred dollars in their hands, and that was the biggest pay he'd ever made.

When he first came to Lowell, we lived in the corporation houses. They were dismal and dreary looking. They were dark. You'd have to have the lights on all day 'cause you couldn't see. It was all lamps in them days, kerosene and gas lamps. It was all one length from the street light to a back alley; the rooms were one right after another like stalls. My mother was petrified; she wouldn't leave us out of the house. We stayed there about three days till they found a place over a grocery store.

Sometimes there was trouble between the French and the Irish. The Irish were instigators. They were up across the common, the North Common. If you went up on the common, they had swings and teeters and all that. There'd always be a fight between the French and the Irish. The Irish would come up, Are you French? They'd knock the stuffings out of ya. And the Greek kids would be recognized because they'd go to the Greek school, and they'd wear sort of a blue pinafore uniform. That's how you could distinguish them from other nationalities. So they got hell kicked out of them too by the Irish. But don't worry; the Irish got theirs too. On Saturdays when they'd come down to Hart's Bakery for their beans, many a beanpot was spilled and broken for the wallops we took during the week. There were more Irish than us.

I graduated from grammar school, and I never went to high school or anything else 'cause I got a job then [she was fifteen]. Just before graduation I took this job minding five kids, five dollars a week. It was just a couple of streets up from us so I thought that was wonderful. I just wanted to get to work and make some money. I took the job, and I've been working ever since. The people I worked for were French. He was a painter, and she worked in a mill. I think it was the Massachusetts that she worked in, and she had five small children. I took care of the five small kids for about a year or so. Then I worked in a Boston hospital cafeteria with my sister for a year in 1923.

We weren't rich, and we weren't poor. My father worked all the time. We never wanted for anything, but we never had any luxuries, that's for sure. Just the necessities, three squares a day, and my mother was a very handy person. She made all our clothes, and she done all the sewing for us. She used to buy odd stockings that the bargain basement stores would get [in bulk] from the hosieries, and they'd pick them over and then sold them for a penny. She'd pick them over. Then she'd take them home and sew them, try to match them as best she could and sew them together. Then when you wore your long johns in the winter with those black stockings over them, you'd be bow-legged, lumpy—what a mess! That used to irritate me more than anything in my life. I used to cry every time I put them on in the morning; in fact we all did.

In 1924 I came home and went into the mill. I worked at the Merrimack. I went into the weave room where they were gonna teach me, in them days they called it battery girls. They had big wide machines [looms], and they had great big reels at the end of them, and they put the bobbins in there. And you'd thread it on the side. I only stayed one day in the weave room. It was the noisiest room you could ever be in. There's the machines going, and the shuttles going back and forth, and sometimes they'd fly off. They were pointed things and if they ever hit you, Boy, you'd know it! Those flying shuttles, they're dangerous. In fact, my mother got struck by one in the leg. Then the thing in between [the harness of the loom] with all the wires hanging off, it pushes the threads up [into a shed] and [the reed] keeps plopping back and forth. It's very, very noisy. In fact, the whole place vibrates. When I come out of there at night I was shaking; I was still in the mill. It's a place you have to get used to. Then I told my father I didn't like it, and he said. Well, you weren't getting paid for it anyways. You were just in there to learn to see if you liked it. I didn't get paid for the whole's day's work. They were just teaching me.

So then they put me up in the finishing room where I worked for Peter Burroughs. He was an old man then, and he had both of his legs cut off. He had sugar diabetes, and they had cut both his legs off, and he was in a wheelchair, but he was still the boss there. And that's where those machines were, one by one, when they started putting two together, then three together. They were doubling up all the machines so it made that much more work and less help to go by. In the finishing room I used to run these silent pegs, they called them. They'd put a load of velvet which was all cut by then in the back and a big iron wheel would run through the pegs. They had these great big reels that used to run the velvet through them. You'd have to thread the cloth in through the back. They'd go through these pegs and be hit by another piece of iron.* With one machine, sometimes you'd have to run them two or three times, but with the three machines together I'd only have to do it once. It saved a lot of time. Sometimes it'd have to go through six times, then it'd go to a brush machine, then to a folder. I'd run them folders; all you'd do is sit back and let it fold, back and forth.

I got married in 1927. My first home was very nice and quiet and much too big for us. We had a living room and a dining room, the kitchen and the bedroom, and there's two other rooms besides, and a washroom. We had steam heat. I bought a gas stove. No brains, you know, when you first get married, you think you're going to live there the rest of your life. We paid seven dollars a week. That was a good rent for that time. We moved around and then back to Lowell. I stayed home for several years, and the boy was three years old when I decided I was going back to work. The Depression was starting, and things were getting pretty slack. There was no work or anything. So I went back to work in the famous cloth works all over again. That was before all this looney stuff [about the union] started.

The baby was three years old; he worked and I worked. He'd take the baby up to his mother's, and I'd go to work. Then at night I'd get out of work and go to his mother's and pick him up. He was starting to get rambunctious. Grammy was having a hard time chasing after him. So, there was [the Lowell] day nursery. And I went in one day and found out how they went about it. How you brought the children in and how much it cost. She said she would be glad to have George, and that it was a nice place with a yard with swings and teeters and everything. I gave him breakfast, and they had a light lunch in the morning. At noon, they had their dinner, then they had a light lunch in the afternoon. It cost seventy-five cents a week.

So then in the morning, it was the problem of getting George across

*The process of pegging gave gloss to the pile of cotton velvet through dry friction.

the Aiken Street Bridge. That was an operation, but it wasn't too bad, and then at night I'd pick him up on my way home. It was on my way home, of course; my husband would be working later. I didn't mind that at all, but I found the Depression hard to get through. It was nip and tuck all the time. Of course, things were cheap, dirt cheap, but your money was so small. We were fortunate because he got a job with the WPA [Works Progress Administration], and I still had my job in the Merrimack. But I was only getting nine dollars a week then. But out of the goodness of his heart, Whittier kept me; I was a good worker. He knew that I was married and that I had a baby then. My husband was out of work for a while, then he got on WPA, and I was working in the mill. We were fortunate then compared to some poor souls. There was some pretty bad off, and there were breadlines all over the place.

The poor souls had nothing. They'd rob Peter to pay Paul. But brazen we were. My husband had friends in business, we were brazen then. We'd bought a radio during the Depression and paid a dollar a week for it. Every week I'd give him a dollar, and he'd go down and pay on it. One day he was going down, and he saw this friend, and he said, Where are you going? and he says, I'm going down to pay on my radio. I owe two weeks on it. His friend says, Give the two dollars to me. I'll give it to you in a couple of days, as soon as business comes in. He says, Gee, I gotta pay on it. So [instead] he gives him the money. Then he got the two dollars in his business. He was a good guy, and he gave it back. They all helped one another and like that. People were very good to one another in them days. They shared a lot. If you didn't have something and they did, they'd give it to you. If you had neighbors and you didn't have anything to eat, they'd take you in and feed you. If they didn't have anything to eat, well, you fed them. They'd feed you, and you'd feed them. That's the way it was then.

[In the Merrimack in the 1930s] we got $13 a week. No matter who you are or where you were in the mill, you got $13 a week.* You might as well have taken a deck of cards and passed it out. You really didn't need names, 'cause everyone got $13 a week. The one with the easiest job and the one with the hardest job got the same money as the rest of them.

Wouldn't do you any good to complain; they'd never complain. They were so petrified for their jobs in them days, it was pitiful. If you were a

*After the passage of the National Recovery Act in 1933, textile workers received a minimum wage of $13 a week for a forty-hour week.

good worker, in with the boss, it was okay, you weren't scared. But the others, the least little thing and those snoopers would snoop on you and would tell the boss, and you'd be out. They talk about patronage these days; there was nothing [to compare with it] in the mill. That's what finally drove the Merrimack out of business; it had too much patronage. [Then there was] your color, creed or nationality. Your creed. If you were a Catholic, you didn't fit worth a darn. I remember [Gustavus] Fox [the superintendent] saying that a Catholic would never work in the office of the Merrimack.

So in the long run, year by year, people started getting a little smarter and started talking about forming a union. Louis Vergados [a union steward in a local shoe shop] is the one who started the union in the Merrimack. He sent out this pamphlet that said to come to a meeting 'cause we were going to start a union. It was 1938. They were passing out the pamphlets. I still have one. I had my name in one of them because I was one of the agitators. They were going to have this meeting, and they all kept talking about it. All the girls kept saying, Are you going? Are you going? and I said, Of course not. I asked my girlfriend, Are you going to go? She said, I'll go if you go, and I said, You won't go 'cause you're chicken. She said, All right we're going, we're going right after work tonight. And we went, and that's where I got implicated by shooting my big mouth off. Telling them all different things. How the bosses were unfair to the help, which they were, and how there was one clique which could do anything they wanted, and it didn't matter. Let the other poor fools do anything, they'd be bounced right out. I told Louis all about it. And he said, Why don't you come on the committee? And I said, No, I couldn't do that, but they persuaded me and I ended up becoming a shop steward. I didn't set out to become a mill steward.

But if you think I didn't catch it then. Well, they were going to throw me in the canal and everything else. The boss started getting real cocky. At night we went to ring out our cards, and there was a little clique going out ahead of time. They'd run and punch their cards first. And they'd walk out. If any of us did it, the boss would come down and say, Get back to work until five of. And no one would ever say it was after five of or they'd get bounced. They tried to bounce me a couple of times, but my father had worked there for so long, and he was the one who had gotten me the job.

I remember one day Peter Burroughs came by and piled a whole load of velvet in back of me. Well, I didn't have any work, and I was waiting for the boys to come and bring me some. So he comes around and says, Why didn't you do that work in the back? and I said, 'Cause it wasn't there! and he said, You liar, it was so there! Well, I was a cocky little bugger then, and I jumped up and said, Don't you call me a liar. You just now put that there, and I'm sitting here watching you do it. Don't you dare call me a liar or I'll bat you on the side of the head, you dirty Englishman! He took off, and I hollered, not so loud anymore, after him, And you know what you can do with your job!

Well, I walked down to the dressing room. It was a room with hooks in it where the girls used to hang their coats, and there was a curtain across the front of it. The men had one on the other side. So I put on my hat and coat. I knew I was going to get killed by my father when I got home. First of all for jacking up. I was going out the door, and Burroughs said, Don't be so hasty, don't be so hasty, get back to work. No, I won't, I said. Just then my father comes walking through, and he says to him, Joe, where'd you get that little spitfire? She has more darn nerve than anybody. I said, He just called me a liar, and I'm not a liar. My father said, Get back to work, get back to work. I said, I'm not going back to work for him. I had to get back to work because my father told me to. Then Burroughs says, You started it, you started it. So he comes in and starts to push things here and there. He wanted to get in good with me then. Anyways there was these windows in the Merrimack that were close to the door and opened out. He says, Push [the wheelchair] down the room, and I said, I'll push you down the room. I have a good mind to push you out the window! Get out of here, get out of here, leave me alone! he said. He never asked me to push him again.

After that I worked in the cloth room. That was a better job. But there was more patronage in there than in the other place. And they favored people of English background, and your bosses and supers and higher-ups were English. And if you were anything else, they looked at you like you were dirt. You were dirt, that's all, and I was getting the thirteen dollars a week. At that time there wasn't much work in the [velvet] finishing room and rather than lay me off, because of my father—not because I was a good worker, because they didn't like me that much— they put me in the cloth room. And I stayed there a few years. I got married while I was in the finishing room, then moved up to the cloth room. That's where we started the union, in the cloth room. That's when my father disowned me. He said, I never thought I'd see my daughter standing at the gate, talking to a union leader. He almost killed me. But he wouldn't join. He had been there too long, and I told him he was afraid for his job. But they got him out anyways; he was getting older, and they were replacing everybody with younger men.

As steward in the union, I had to take their complaints, and everyone had complaints. The least little thing, of course. It was a new union, and we had never been in a union before. Well, this guy from the state labor board in Boston came down. He wanted to ask some of the girls questions, one by one in the office. I guess it was all right, but I said, No, you don't; I'm gonna be in there too! He said, No, you aren't; this isn't any of your business. I'm head of the labor board, and this has nothing to do with your union. So I stayed out, and I called Louis. I said, He's in there questioning all the girls, and he won't let me in. He laughed and said, That's okay, Yvonne, you'll meet him after work. Come up because we're going to have a meeting up here. And he was there. He said, So, this is the little one who wanted to come in. And I said, Yes, but you wouldn't let me. He said, Listen, Yvonne, learn to crawl before you learn to walk.

Then things started to get so bad that they had to hire a personnel manager. Whittier was my boss then. And they were in the clique again, running to punch their cards, and he came down one night, and I was first at the clock. He says, It's not five of yet, Yvonne, and I says, Yes, it is, the green light's on. You're not supposed to have your hat and coat on yet, and I said, That's because I'm a little faster than them, so I have them on. He says, You're supposed to be at your bench. Wait a minute, Whittier, I says, Whenever anyone else is in line, it's all stiff and grins. They can punch [out] anytime they want to. I was shop steward at the time. You're not going to make flesh of one and fish of another, the way this place has been run all their lives. Well, you're not going to do it no more. So the help got cocky, we all got cocky. They're not going to push it down our throats like before. They got their rights. They know what they could do and what they couldn't do. They weren't going to infringe on their rights. They'd come over, Hey, Yvonne, look what they're trying to make me do. And Boy, the fellas, they were the worst! They'd push me on. They agitated me more than anybody. They'd come down and say, Hey, they done this to me. So of course, I'd have to go into the office and squawk.

There was this floor lady, Mrs. Camp; she was English too. She was a snip if there ever was one. And she was always trying to rub it in to one girl or the other, so finally I got her in the office one day with the super, and he starts talking about what the girls were doing. And I says, It's no more than right; the other girls are doing it, why can't she do it? And she says, Well, Yvonne, you're a pretty good talker, but, she says, things aren't right. They haven't been right since the union started. I says, If it weren't for you, and people like you and the likes of you, there never would have been a union in this place. But it was the likes of you that brought the unions in, I says. If there wasn't so much partiality for one to another, I says, and that's the whole thing in a nutshell.

One day, I don't know what it was over, they all went on strike, the whole mill. So they had to go get the personnel manager. They went and got the personnel, and he says, I'm firing your leader, meaning me. And they said, You're gonna what? and they all rushed him. I was petrified. I thought sure to God they were gonna kill him! They all raced to the door after him. Boy, did he go running! He ran out of that room so fast, and then, of course, the whole kit and caboodle stopped.

And of course they all got their raises, even the ones that didn't want to join the union. Louis said, Talk 'em into it or fire them. No, Louis, I says, I'm not going to talk 'em into it. If they don't want to join, they don't want to join. This isn't a closed shop or anything. They're not bothering anybody. I says, Leave 'em alone. He says, Jesus, those broads! I says, They're not broads, Louis, they're girls, they're young ladies. He says, Since when? They're old maids. Nonetheless, I says, they're girls who have been here a good many years, and I'm not having them lose their jobs over the union, I says. I admit if they weren't doing their work or something, but we got things we want now, we've got our rights now and everything else. So let it stand at that. That's the way it stood for quite a while.

Our union dues weren't very high, about a quarter a month, and the benefits were better working conditions, you weren't getting fired, you weren't afraid of turning your head and getting fired for it, you could speak up about lies. Certain ones would go in the main office and everything and lie about the help, and some poor soul would get bounced for no reason at all. With the union they could go in and fight for their cause. So they'd go and fight, and we fought plenty. But it got so bad that after a while they didn't want to give in to the union; they didn't want the help to run the place either. Finally it went from bad to worse, and the mill went down, and they sold out. [Jacob] Ziskind bought the whole place. They'd [the independent union] be putting in overtime for men, and they weren't even there. When they got paid, they'd have to split it up with the bosses, and when they finally caught up with them, they called it the Teapot Dome thing. A whole bunch of them got fired because of it. It was bigger than the Teapot Dome thing.

Even in the beginning, they'd bring help in from Canada, and—the poor souls—the bosses would take part of their pay for getting them jobs. They'd take so much of their pay every week for a certain length of time. If they bought furniture or anything. I saw your furniture men in Lowell get rich; they'd sell them furniture. They'd repossess it if the poor souls lost their jobs. They'd take back the furniture and make them buy it back from them again.

They hired all sorts of cheap labor: Greeks, Italians, French. Not the English. All the English got the good jobs. All us foreigners got the poor jobs. But I got my end in anyways when I went in the office there, when I was on the committee with Louis Vergados. Fox was telling us how good he was to us, how he done this for us and how he hadn't done that for us. So I said to him, You yourself said there'd never be a Catholic working in the office. Is there a Catholic working in the office? He said, Well, there must be. I said, There ain't a damn one in there, and you know it. There ain't one Catholic in that whole office, not in the main office, the mill office or anywhere else! They were all Protestants, not that they weren't nice girls, they were lovely girls. But just to show you how narrow-minded and black-hearted they were, very, very narrow-minded.

And the poor Greek fellows that worked in the dye house. The poor fellas would come in wearing only pants and drawers in the vats there. They'd go in and their arms would be bare because they'd have to drag the cloth out of the vats. Their stomachs would be blue, green, purple, whatever the color happened to be at the time. It was hot; they'd sweat. It was wicked. You wouldn't put a human being to work in a place like that. They were afraid for their jobs. They were meek. They were brow-beaten. There was so little around, although you heard a little of wealth. They were too proud. They'd work for their money at no matter how degrading a job rather than go on welfare. There was very little welfare then. You very seldom heard of it.

During World War II, I left the Merrimack and went to the Remington [Arms] for two years. They were making bullets and everything for the war. Gee, I got good money there. A dollar and a quarter or a dollar and a half an hour. I think I got $1.75. That was good money then. I inspected bullets. They'd have big conveyors. They'd have the conveyors in front of you and a big case of bullets. You'd inspect them and then put so many in a box and put them on a conveyor. It was a good little job. You'd have to work change-shifts, nights and days. That was the hardest part of it; getting used to that, but outside of that it was a pretty good little job. Once I left the Merrimack, I was done with the union. I wasn't as cocky then. I was calming down. They were paying better money at the Remington, and the Merrimack wasn't doing so hot then. It was starting to go down; they weren't doing too, too good. Most all mills weren't doing too good then, because they didn't have the help. They were all flocking to Remington for the better money.

I stayed out of work for a while but then I went to the Wannalancit, and I learned spooling. For all the years I had been in a mill I hadn't learned spooling. I had seen it done when I was a kid doing doffing on short hours. After the yarn was all wound on spools, I'd take it off and they'd weigh it. Then they'd get as much yarn as would be twirled all around the spool. Spooling is similar to that. So I started spooling. When I went into the Wannalancit, they asked, What did you do in the mill? and I says, I was a battery girl. He says, You're dating yourself, Yvonne. Battery girls went out a long time ago! But I had been out of the mill a long time.

Before that I went to the shoe shops. I did almost everything! I put the polish on them. Then from dressing, I went to packing, I went to floor girl: you'd have to pick up the shoes, the defects, and you'd take them down to get repaired. If it was a heel, you'd take it to the heeler; if it was the vamp, you'd bring it over to the vamper. Then you'd take it to the repair girls. They'd grain it over, then they'd bring it back, and I'd have to pack them. That was a good little job too. You couldn't stop for a minute though without somebody yelling, I need this, I need that. It was after I quit there that I went to the Wannalancit. I liked it there. I was spooling, and I was working nights which I had never done except when I worked at Remington. So I could sleep in the morning. I always got up at five-thirty in the morning, and I always said I'm going to get a job where I can sleep in the mornings. That's the only job I miss out of all of them, the Wannalancit.

They Used to Say, If You
Married a Mender, You Were Rich

Evelyn Cassidy Winters

MENDER

Too small at fourteen to do the same work as her mother, a winder, Evelyn Cassidy became a burler with a chance to learn mending, a valuable trade. Only a real friend or perhaps a compassionate woman who understood the difficulties of mill life would take the time away from her own piecework to teach this painstaking job to another.

Having a trade made Evelyn Winters feel different and better than other mill workers, but growing up in a large, poor family during the Depression left its mark on her. She was glad just to have a job. To be a mender was something special. Still, she envied those with better chances.

Memories of the closeness and richness of neighborhood life when she was a child kept her from leaving the street where she was born and raised. Although the community around her changed, her continued residence in her old neighborhood seemed somehow to keep the past and its values alive.

MY MOTHER WAS BORN in Lawrence, and my father was born in Lowell. My mother's father, my grandfather, worked in the coal yards, and there were more coal yards in Lowell than there was in Lawrence. That's how they came up here. My grandfather used to fill the coal truck, and then they'd come to your home and open your cellar window and put [the coal down] a chute into your coal bin. My father was a barber, and my mother worked at the Hamilton mills as a spinner, and she used to have to pass the barber shop. He used to wink at her, and that's how they met. My father was nine years older than my mother; I think she was nineteen when they got married.

She had nine children; I was the fifth one down. She brought up nine children for a good many years. When my last brother was born and he was nine months old, she started her work again. I was out of grammar school, so I took care of him. It was during the Depression. She was a winder in the Bunting mill. I tried winding, but I was too short to handle the spindles and the machine itself. She was the one that was teaching me how, until she found out that my arms couldn't reach both up and down at the same time to bring your thread together to tie it in a knot. I couldn't make the knot. I was too short, so I had to give it up.

It wasn't a question of your parents approving or disapproving of you working. You had to. You had to help out. I had four older sisters and myself. We all did it and thought nothing of it. We didn't [come home] and say, Well, here's five bucks. We'd come home and give our envelopes in, and you were lucky if you got the change out of it. Or, if you needed something to wear, you got it from them. As far as spending money goes, you had to go ask your mother. My mother was the boss in the house. If you'd say, Gee, I'd love to go to the show; if she had it, she'd give it to you. But don't forget, when you have nine mouths to feed— nine, ten, eleven mouths to feed—in them days you were lucky if you got five cents at the end of the week to have an ice cream cone. The kids today have a lot more than we had. We had to make our own fun, and these kids have got money for cars, and they can do whatever they want.

I didn't get through high school, but my sisters did. As far as college went, you wouldn't even give that a thought, in my family anyway. I don't think that kids coming out of college know what the hell they're doing because all they're doing is book learning. They're not really learning anything through experience. They don't want to start at the bottom rung like we had to and work up. They want to start at the top and go higher. They can sit and read and read and read, but you ask them, How do you thread a needle? They don't know.

I started in 1941 up on the fourth floor of the Bunting. I went in as a burler. When the [woolen] cloth was raw from the looms, we used to put it on a table and rub our hands over it, looking for knots. And we used to have to put tweezers in the knot and push it through onto the back, so it could be shaved off. Burling was hard on the eyes. You have eighty-five yards of cloth in one roll, and it might be forty-five or forty-eight inches wide. You have just a table, and you're rubbing your hands over every bit of it, looking for knots. And there were quite a few knots. In the same room, that's where the mending was done. If you could find somebody that liked you well enough, they would teach you how to mend. Mending is a trade, and not too many of them wanted to teach. But we got some that taught us.

The older menders, when they'd see younger girls come in, they resented it because they figured, Well, maybe she'll take my job away from me. We were on piecework, and a lot of them didn't want to give up their time to teach us because that's how they made their money. The woman that taught me, she was more or less a friend, so she took the time. But I'll bet she lost quite a bit of money teaching me, because I wasn't an easy girl to teach. If there was a thread out of the pattern, we'd have to sew that thread in, and we'd have to pick up the pattern of that stitch. We always sat by the daylight to see. We always worked days, not nights. Believe me, it wasn't any easy job because you had your needle in this hand and your scissors in the same hand. And if that thread was way out, you had to pick up the stitches [and reconstruct the weave pattern] all the way. It was a trade, good paying.

This was in 1941. And then we got a thirty-five-cent raise because we were getting government work. We were getting gabardine for the air force, and we were getting what they called indigo blue for the navy. When we got a bale of indigo blue, they would come to you, and they would say, This is for you, Evelyn, and drop it. That would give you three dollars even before you touched it. And that was a lot easier to work with, because it wasn't so close a weave as the gabardine.

We had boys that carried our work to us and away from us. We didn't have any lifting to do. Just pulling. We had one boss and one second hand. The second hand used to keep us in line, take attendance, and if they saw you—we used to sneak to the ladies' room—he'd knock on the wall because [the ladies' room] had an open door, just a frame. One end of the room had a ladies' and a men's room, and so did the other end of the room. So if you were in the middle, you had your choice of going either way. We always went to the one farthest from the office. And when you're nineteen and twenty, you think you can do anything and get away with it.

We didn't have a union. We never got a raise every year. We were just thankful that we had a job and was getting money to live on. When the American Woolen [in Lawrence] gave a raise, we usually got it. Maybe not the same amount, but we used to get some of it anyway. And that way, it kept the union out. We'd have different fellows standing at the gate with the union things, but we'd just pass by them. We wouldn't have anything to do with the union. They were afraid to get into it because the Bunting stressed no union. If you did start a rumpus, you'd get put out because they didn't take any guff. There were too many people looking for work to start a commotion like that. In 1941 several times they'd be at the gate, but we'd just walk by and ignore them. We wouldn't even take their flyers.

We didn't dare be late in the mill. We'd be ten minutes early. We

Mending and inspecting. *Courtesy of MATH.*

didn't have to punch [a time clock], but we had to be right in our seat when that bell rang for one o'clock. I used to go home for my lunch because all I did was live two streets down from the mill. We have one girl [where I work now]; she gets away with murder. [In the mills] she would have been out on her ear so fast that she wouldn't know what struck her. Because they would never put up with that when I was growing up. No way! But she's doing it and she's not the only one. We call them "the deadwood," [the] older people, you know. We don't say anything to them because they'd harass you so bad it wouldn't be worth it.

The mill was hard. Believe me, when you went in there, like on a June day, we were up on the fourth floor, and the sun beaming on a flat roof and just them little windows. No air-conditioning, no fan. With all that cloth on top of us, believe me, we sweat ourselves to death. Never had a weight problem. Never. And in the wintertime, the mortar between the bricks would be so rotted out that you'd have to take pieces of the cloth and stuff it in there to keep warm. Or the square panes [in the windows], bring pieces of cardboard to put in. They never fixed it up. But it was a job, and you had to go to it. You had a wooden chair and a table that had a peg in the middle of it so that you could tip it or make it flat. You were lucky to have that. You had a window sill; we used to bring a piece of oilcloth to make it clean and put our tool bag on it. Our pincushions, we used to have to pin on us.

You wouldn't dare look out the window because if the boss came by, he'd say, Is that all you've got to do? I'll give you more. Always being watched. There were windows on both sides of the room. The burlers were in the middle, and the menders were on the windows. Each window had a table. There were maybe thirty or thirty-five menders and maybe sixty, sixty-five in that one room, plus the fellows that carried the cloth. Then there was one girl at a sewing machine that used to sew the numbers on the cloth before we got it, certain numbers that they would match up. Each piece that come off the weave room had to have a certain number, and the girl in the mending room would sew them on.

We bought our own mending tools. We had to pay for our needles and everything. The only thing we didn't have to pay for was the thread because we got it from the end of the cloth that was given to us. There was no waste, very little. I was never injured on the job, but I saw a woman take a heart attack in the mill. She was quite elderly; in them days everybody looked old. She never came back. We separated ourselves from the other workers. If you were a mender, you were higher paid than the burlers. We're too good to be associated with the burlers. But nine times out of ten, it might have been maybe a dollar more that the menders were making than the burlers. We never associated with each other out of the mill. We went home, and you went home to your house, and I went home to mine, and that's the way they did.

I met my husband at a dance at the Commodore Ballroom, a beautiful dance hall in them days. It was my first time at the Commodore, and my husband was a very good dancer. So that's how we met. I didn't go every week. I had a strict mother. She always wanted you in hearing distance. So my [future] husband used to come down and sit in the yard or in the parlor, and that would be it. And then of course, with my brothers and sisters, I'd always have one of them that I had to watch while my mother was doing something. So I really didn't get out too much from around the house.

I stayed at the Bunting until it closed in 1950. I went from there to Raytheon in Waltham, and then I was out of work for three years. I had a new baby. Then I was collecting unemployment, and they sent us to the Talbot mills [in Billerica] for over a week, and we lasted eleven years out there. There were three women that was collecting, and the three of us were menders. If we didn't go out to the Talbot mills, we wouldn't have been able to collect unemployment. So we went out for the eight days [required]. We met out there, when we were waiting for the boss to put us in our place, and each one of us said the same thing, it was the unemployment office that made us come out here for eight days. Eleven years we lasted, and [then] that place closed down. I saw that place close. I'm a great one for shutting down the places that I work. Now [1985] I'm at Wang, and we just had a real sad layoff. I didn't get it, but believe me, it hurt when I saw the different ones that were being ushered out by the guards. But they're being picked up in other places.

I was born and brought up around here in this neighborhood. I think in all my lifetime, I've moved four times, and it was always either across the street or right around here somewhere. We had Irish. We had French. We had Italians. We had Polish, Armenians, and a colored family. And I didn't think they were any different than I was. We knew they were Polish, but, hey, so what, you know? Or Portuguese, Greek. We had all nationalities. In them days, you could say, Well, I think I'll go out and get some air in the summer. And you might take a walk up the street, and you'd stop at this one and talk with her for a few minutes or the one across the street. Not today! I don't think there's three of us old neighbors left living in this neighborhood. I can remember my mother used to make corned beef and cabbage, and the Italian man across the street used to smell my mother's corned beef and cabbage, and his wife would be making spaghetti and meat sauce. And he'd holler over, Mrs. Cassidy, I'll swap with you. So my mother'd give him a bowl of corned beef and cabbage, and they'd send over a batch of spaghetti and meatballs. But you don't see that today. You say good morning or good night, but that's it. It's not like the old neighborhood. There's no reason; it just happens.

In my neighborhood, different ones bought houses out in Dracut or out in Tewksbury, and they've moved away. And the new ones that come in, they seem afraid to mix in. Somebody said to me, Oh, I've got to get out of this neighborhood. I can't stand this neighborhood, because of this or that. I was born and brought up in this neighborhood, and I haven't gotten out of it, and I never intend to. Now I can be in the country where my daughter lives in Dracut. I can be in the country until four o'clock, but then I want to come home to the city. I just could never live out in the country. I would die. I would die.

I'm Not an Old Greek.
I Don't Eat Bread and Oil!

Jean Rouses
SPINNER

Although Jean Rouses could not avoid work in the mills, by 1947 things had changed. Union contracts negotiated during the economic boom of World War II improved working conditions, introduced benefits, and increased wages in those few mills that continued operations into the 1940s and 1950s. Jean Rouses was proud of the role that her mother had played in helping to bring about those changes and, like her, she "spoke her mind."

Her fascination with the machinery that she ran and her commitment to her job made her a valued employee. As a spinner, she faced the peculiar limits on what women could do in the mill. She could not touch the mechanism that drove the frame nor could she readily name the machine parts, yet female spinners manipulated the timing of the process, lifted heavy boxes, and sometimes worked in tandem with male spinners to earn more money.

As one of the youngest spinners at the Merrimack before it began to close in 1956, she missed the chance to teach others what she had been taught. When the mill shut down and the spinning frames fell silent, Jean Rouses, like many of the younger members of the last generation, had to seek new work.

I GRADUATED HIGH SCHOOL in 1947. I had very good marks but I couldn't get a job at office work. I couldn't even buy a job then. I went to the [employment] agency to buy a job, and I couldn't buy one, so I ended up going to the mill. My mother, Soultana Gogou Rouses, worked in the mill, and my sister Bessie. And my sister talked me into going into it too, until I got an office job. But I didn't until later on, when I left the mill.

I used to visit them at the Boott mill. We weren't allowed to go all the way through the mill, but she brought me into her area. And then I was mostly in the office where my sister Mary worked.* My mother was a spinner and a doffer but mostly she spinned. She was the one that took care of probably twenty frames at a whack. And then they put her on samples to determine the type of yarn they needed. Bess Tsoumas, she taught me to spin. I had to take care of two frames. When the bobbins filled up, I would stop the machine and doff them. The idea was when you started it up again not to have too many breaks, because then you clogged up the frame, and you had to take this little hook and pull out all the yarn that was coming in as roving. It was this thick cotton; it looked like a string only it was cotton called roving. They would feed right through the machine to a point that they'd spin [out] so thin and then [they] would go onto the bobbin as thread. If you didn't break too many of those when you'd pump the frame, you were lucky. I learned to start it just perfectly.

It took me less than six months to learn how to do that. I was good at it because I cared. I mean, I took the time; I'm like that. If I'm going to do a job, I'm going to do it right. I always was a competitive girl. I guess I got that from my mother. Anyway, I had a good teacher, but I only had a couple of people come in that I taught. And then, I got so good that this man decided that we both should work together. He had his two frames aside of me, and when he stopped his frame, I would help him doff one side, and he would doff the other because we were both very fast. I have big hands, large enough to hold the bobbins [easily]. I was quick at it, and that way we both made more boxes [of full bobbins] and more money. We both got good at it. The bosses didn't mind as long as we got the work out. Later on I was given a job of handling a whole section of fifteen frames.

We also had to clean our frames. That was very intricate because if you got loose cotton into the bobbin, the thread would make a lot of what they call burrs. We cleaned our frames a couple of times a day depending on how thick the thread was. There was a plate on top of the frame and these steel caps, and the cotton roving would pick up all this cotton so that it would not go through into the bobbin and spindle. If it fouled up, we had this hook that we'd use. As a matter of fact, I've got a few scars on my hands from it. We would have to clean out the roll, but I got pretty good at it.

*For Jean's sister Mary, see Mary Rouses Karafelis in the last section on the children of the last generation.

Ring spinner.
Courtesy of MATH.

The machinery was modern, up-to-date, pretty good. They kept it clean. The crew of girls would shut down the frames and remove the roving and clean and oil the frames once every two months. We had breakdowns, and when they broke down they fixed the machine. It was a pretty intricate mechanism, and there were quite a few mechanics, a special one in each section, to fix them. It depended on the job whether it would require more or less time, but usually he worked as fast as he could. We weren't allowed to touch anything mechanical. But there were these little things that spun around the ring to bring the thread up. It was just a little bit of a thing; I don't know the name of it.* We would have to put them on the ring if that came off or new ones were needed. Then there were pigtails [yarn guides, see fig. D] that would feed the thread right through onto the bobbin. They sometimes broke off; then you had to wait until the maintenance men fixed those.

After doffing, we had these carts, really like a little go-cart, and in front there was a box full of the empty bobbins and in back we would throw in the filled-up ones. We had to lift those heavy boxes and pile them up on the cart. I mean women, you know, had to lift them up. Then

*She is referring to a traveler, which is on the ring and gives twist to the yarn being spun.

we'd take another box. We did all this. No one helped us really. We did it ourselves.

The spinning room was huge and noisy. Not as noisy as the weave room; it would bust your eardrums. I would never work in the weaving department, but it was interesting watching it. I enjoyed spinning, I really did. But you still had to holler. We had pretty good supervisors and mechanics. We all got along. There were the old-timers, and of course my mother, but she was put in a special room to do the sampling. They had twenty frames in there, and she was either on the first shift or second shift, depending on when they needed her. Mostly first shift. When I first started, I had to work on the second shift, one-thirty to ten, then I moved to the first. But I liked the second shift because it was easy to dress up and go out afterwards. We took a half-hour break and ate on the job which wasn't too bad. We took care of one another. Sometimes you'd say, Would you watch my frame? And you'd take off. They'd watch it. It was pretty good. It was very interesting just watching those machines roll. Very, very interesting to take out the bobbin and then put another one in. Snap it right in. It was all in the changing of the filled bobbins and putting in an empty one and starting up that frame. That was the most important thing, to start it and not have breakdowns.

The time went along pretty good. It was just a regular job. I wasn't bored, I mean you couldn't be bored. You had to keep walking around to make sure you didn't have breakage. If one broke and started filling up with cotton on the roller, then it could break two or three more; a long time, you'd be in trouble. Sometimes it got so bad that you'd have to shut your machine off and clean that all out. Most of the time we walked around and walked around. The floors were a little slippery with the grease that was used on the enormous belts and dripped down, and we had to watch out for that. They were safety conscious then. The supervisors always walked around and watched you. And then we had an overseer, and we would go in to him if we had a big problem. We had our stewards because we had a union. But the supervisor, the one I worked for, was very, very gracious. His name was Ernie Wilson, a very, very nice man. We had our mechanics, and we got along very, very good. But compared to the old times, the long hours they put in, five in the morning to five at night, it was really something. But with us, the eight hours, and we had our unions. They fought for us.

I was put on samples, and they gave me new bobbins to work with because I was fast with my hands on doffing. Those bobbins were tough. My hands would swell up so much that I had to stop. It got real bad. I tried to tell them that my hands had swollen to the maximum. I had to cry myself off the job. They wouldn't take me off because I was good at it. It was my mother who talked them into stopping, Look at my daughter's hands! This was their way of sampling new bobbins and new machinery and a new type of cotton roving. We had different ways of feeding [piecing up] a broken thread into the machine because sometimes if you just held it and fed it into the machine, you would make a burr. But I used to twist it right into the [ribbon of] cotton that was coming out [of the front rolls], and I'd spin it right in. I was taught that by my teacher, and I got pretty good at that. It was a challenge, really. Then I got a different type job cleaning the frames. You had to clean under all the roving that was being fed because it would mass up. It got real dusty. I had to clean forty of them, two, three times a day, and they would fill up and fill up [with cotton].

I worked with the old-timers. I was one of the youngest; there were very few young spinners. There was all kinds of nationalities, all kinds. On my floor, an awful lot of Greeks, a lot of Frenchmen, and there was some Polish. Still mostly Greek and French. I did not go out with them unless we went to a union party or something like that. I had my own set of Greek friends, and after work we would go out. My mother and I worked the same floor, but she worked on one end and I worked on the other end. My sister worked in the same department. We were all friendly, and we all got along except for some squabbling but not real fighting. We were too busy to have celebrations or special occasions except maybe to chip in and buy a gift, but we never had a cake or anything.

I nearly became a shop steward, but I didn't because my mother had been through all that, and she said, No, it's too much, too many problems for me to get involved. But if you had a problem, you went right in to the overseer. You talked to him, and he would help you out. But if you had a problem concerning your machine or your floor, and you told your supervisor a couple of times, he would get out-of-sorts. You'd say, Well, I'm going to see Charlie [the overseer]. Well, go ahead, he'd say. Go right ahead and do that. I never went over his head, Mr. Wilson's head, unless I had to. Or sometimes Charlie would call you into the office and ask you how you're doing and things like that. The squabbling was just nothing; they were too busy working, keeping up their frames. If they had a fight, it was because their frame was shut down, and they were losing money. The spinners were on piecework and got paid by the box—so many boxes we got out and the more the better.

I had short hair so I didn't have to worry about the belts, but we had to walk between those big wheels with the belting. Actually we didn't have to but that was the only way to get through. We wore these blue aprons with big patch pockets, and we'd put the cotton [waste] in there. We had our hook, the real heavy brass type, tied to our belt. If you made the hook real sharp, it worked better on your roll; you could pull out over an inch of cotton that was wrapping around the roll. The mechanics gave us the hooks, and they would even sharpen them for you. Some people had smaller ones; I had a large one. It was quite interesting, but it was also quite dusty in there. The lint would get you.

I wore loafers, kind of a rubber type that didn't slip. Some of the girls, the young kids in their twenties that cleaned the rolls, wore dungarees. Most wore cotton dresses; my mother made me some pretty ones. We had a large locker room with our own lockers and good facilities when I went in the place. But it was hard work, you can't say it wasn't. Mill work was hard. You had to keep going all the time, and you didn't care whether you ate after a while just as long as you did your work. And lifting those heavy boxes [of bobbins]. I saw one woman, this poor woman, she was putting hers a little too high [on the cart], and it hit her in the head. It was her fault, a crazy accident.

My mother saw an awful lot of changes. She worked at the Boott and at the Merrimack. She averted a strike at one time. She spoke English, and she got them all together and talked them out of striking. She explained they were only going to hurt themselves because they had no union at that time, and they would only hurt themselves. They wouldn't have any money coming in, but that she would tell the boss what their problem was and he would fix it. Which he did. My mother had a way with her about speaking. She was quite the philosopher. She told the head one what the problems were, why these people want to strike, and it got a little better after that. It took awhile, but they did what was asked. She was pretty proud of that.

My mother fought if there was a problem. They picked her for sampling because she could speak English. A lot of Greeks refused to learn the language. They spoke broken English but they didn't understand. She bothered to learn English and become an American citizen. She wore her little flag till the day she died. She couldn't wait to get those papers. I asked her, What if we went to war with Greece? She said, I would worry about my people, but I am an American right now. She wanted to learn, and she did. That's why she could speak to these bosses. She learned with us kids. And if there was a problem, she just went right in there and told them at the union, this and that, blah, blah, blah, and they got it. She had a way with them.

She was just fourteen when she came over, and she brought her sister's papers. At the last minute her sister didn't want to come over, so she took her sister's papers. She was considered sixteen, so they took her into the mill. And she worked there all her life. She went to the Green School, nights, to learn her ABC's.* While my sister was learning, my mother was learning too. She really taught herself, because she wanted to be an American so bad. I mean Greek-American, because she loved her Greek. She made sure that we spoke Greek. She would ask us a question in English, but we had to answer in Greek. She believed in education, but she was from the old school and believed that the boys should go to college. My mother would have been a schoolteacher; she knew how to go in and talk. And a lot of these older Greek women were very jealous of her. They thought that naturally she's got something going with the boss, but she didn't. She just spoke her mind, and that was it. Her name was Sally; and it was Sally, I want you to do this; Sally, I want you to do that.

I was in the building where they made the velvet. We were allowed to buy it at a certain price. We got the most beautiful velvet. It was really gorgeous and all colors. My mother and my sisters made beautiful clothes out of it. But I had a sour note in my building. One boss tried to change me onto another job, and I said, No, I wouldn't do it. And he told me that I was fired. Well, I went right to the main office and talked to Frank Maria [director of industrial relations], and I told him. I said to him, I'm not an old Greek. I don't eat bread and oil! That was just an expression. I told him that this overseer opened my locker, packed my stuff with my paycheck, and sent it down to the main office. Which he had no right to do; supposing my check was lost?

Frank set up a meeting for the following Monday, and we had a big to-do about it. And I just spoke my mind, and I told them I didn't deserve that menial job. It was like sweeping floors compared to spinning and doffing. I got back an apology, and that was about it. [She went back to spinning]. My mother told me I shouldn't have done that, that I should have gone to see her. But in a way it put him in his place because he had second thoughts about doing that again. In fact, he got a calling-down for it. He should not have done it that way, which goes to show you

*On the Green School, see p. 71.

a little of how the higher-ups can be. That was towards the end, before the place closed down.

It was sad. A lot of people worked hard but they enjoyed their work. It was a kind of job that you took pride in. As a young person I wanted an office job, but I still would have enjoyed staying there. The word went around that [the Merrimack] was just going to close down and that's all there was to it. Mr. Ziskind had died; maybe he would have kept it open. The rumor was that they were going down South for cheaper labor. That hurt a lot of us, and a lot of us spoke our minds. After the mills closed, the mechanics got mechanics' jobs, and most of the women went into stitching.

We had very, very good bosses. Mr. Ziskind who owned the Merrimack mills was very good to us. Gave us a bonus at Christmas plus a big can of cookies. And we had a first-aid clinic there if you needed it, and a credit union. It wasn't bad at all when I went there in 1947. By that time they had hammered out of the mill what these poor souls like my mother had done in the early 1900s. After the Merrimack closed, she and my sister went into stitching, and I got a couple of menial jobs, cutting threads because I was not a machine stitcher. Then in 1956 one of my girlfriends got me an office job at the Raytheon Company and I stayed there for twenty-two and a half years. To tell you the truth, I missed the work in the mill. I really enjoyed it. It wasn't just do something and forget it. I used to be ashamed to say I worked in the mill, but then I wasn't because it was a job that you did and you had pride in it.

The Men

Introduction

MANY SONS of mill workers in Lowell went to work as soon as their sisters did, but being boys meant that their lives and work would be different. While sons and daughters were raised in the same world of crowded tenements and ethnic culture, the imperatives of being male led to differing expectations and behavior. Boys faced lifelong employment, something not expected for girls if they were lucky. It seemed more important for families to provide a son with as much education as possible, or, even better, with access to a skill or trade, than to worry about a daughter's training. Chores and play introduced boys early to the streets and byways of the city where sisters usually did not follow. From these experiences, young males moved into public activities that seemed to be naturally theirs. The divided worlds of manhood and womanhood developed out of childhood circumstances and family expectations.

When they were fourteen, boys could apply for the unskilled mill jobs: sweeping floors, cleaning bobbins, and delivering materials. Those who delayed their first mill work by staying in high school for a year or longer tended to come from families well settled in the city and able to protect at least some of their children from being forced to meet the immediate needs of the family. But poverty and large numbers of sisters and brothers proved something of an equalizer, and on their fourteenth birthdays, boys often showed up at the mill doors, eager for work of any kind.

Like girls in working-class families, boys grew up in a variety of circumstances. Some had working mothers; others had homebound mothers with many children to care for. Fathers who were mill workers routinely worked the long hours of two jobs, but others were absent, sick, or dead. Some families had a miscellany of boys and girls. Others had one adored brother and many sisters or a baby girl with many older brothers. Sometimes a widow raised an only son. Sisters could be difficult if they were older and assumed the right to be like a mother and boss the younger children. Brothers knew whom they had to obey and occasionally treated older sisters to the rough and tumble of sibling fights to even the score.

Some wives and mothers worked after marriage until the husband

and father got a job that provided an adequate income, but they also worked if the man earned little, drank, or deserted his family. Widows were compelled to work at jobs outside the home. Then the children were cared for on a daily basis by grandmothers or baby-sitting neighbors. When both parents worked, as one Polish weaver remembered, "the kids took care of the kids," often with help from neighbors or relatives. A dissolute or absent father caused the oldest son to take his place, close to his mother. Assuming this adult role prematurely, a son might continue as head of the family until his own marriage or even later.

While they were still in school, young mill workers had learned the interconnecting patterns of manhood and womanhood. Working mothers did duty both as mill workers and as housekeepers. Fathers also did double duty by moonlighting at two jobs or at least by engaging in some sort of money-making on the side. It was more often the father who was absent from the house, preferring to work the second or third shift for an extra fifteen cents an hour, but sometimes he had no choice. A mother who stayed home signified a successful man at the head of the family. As one mill worker approvingly described his hard-working but homebound mother: "She never was in any factory." Mothers might take mill jobs to help out when necessary, but most male workers tried to shield their wives from factory work. Later, as adults, boys would use their parents' experiences as models for the proper roles for themselves and their wives and daughters.

The mix of boys and girls in the family usually determined what kinds and how much domestic work each contributed. Both boys and girls did chores, but boys were responsible for more physical and public kinds. In families with many sons and few daughters, boys dried dishes and washed clothes on washboards. Those who did this work remembered not minding having to help their exhausted mothers. One man remembered the sympathetic laughter of a school officer who came looking for the truant and found him in the yard at the washtub. Both sons and daughters ran home from school at noontime to light the fire for dinner if two parents worked or to deliver their mother's freshly cooked food in a dinner pail to their father at the mill. Sons who did this sometimes got special rewards from their fathers: movies and candy on Saturday afternoons. The boys alone were expected to haul coal and wood from the cellar up the tenement backstairs after they had helped their fathers chop up the wood into stove-length pieces. If there were no sons in the

Working-class boyhood. Exterior of Acre housing, 1939. *Courtesy of the Lowell Housing Authority and the Center for Lowell History.*

family or they were too young, the father did this chore after his own day's work.

Carrying coal up three or four flights daily and twice on Saturday in preparation for Sunday was inescapable and hated by many boys, but it was fun to scavenge for extra fuel. Gangs of young boys, usually of the same nationality but more mixed in ethnic character by the 1930s, roamed the streets and railroad tracks for cast-off coal. Coke from the yard of the gas company and trees fallen in parks and waysides were fair game as long as you didn't get caught. A rough justice excused petty stealing on the grounds of family need in the depression years.

Sons took great delight in the treats their mothers provided like homemade ice cream and special dishes, holidays, and songs and good times. One son recalled his mother fondly as a "good living woman" in contrast to his reprobate father. These were the kinds of women they hoped to marry one day. Sons appreciated their mothers' hard physical work giving them delicious meals, keeping a tenement scrupulously clean, and taking good care of them, although they did not regard housework as a real job. It was women's work and brought in no money.

Even before a youth reached fourteen, his parents made it clear that "it would be nice if you had a job." Girls helped out at home before they became fourteen; boys got "little" jobs like delivering groceries up flights of tenement stairs or shining shoes. Sons could earn some cash by selling newspapers for a half-cent profit on each copy. Newsboys learned to negotiate the corridors of city hall to get their newsseller's license and stood on street corners in all kinds of weather hawking their papers. If they lived outside the central city, boys might work during the summers, haying and weeding for local farmers. Even better, for the fun of it, was collecting junk to sell. Adventuresome lads would build rafts to float on the Merrimack River to areas where the river bottom was littered with metal junk from the mills. During Prohibition in the 1920s, young hustlers gathered old bottles from the city dump and washed them out for neighborhood bootleggers who paid them a penny apiece.

It was safer for boys on the streets if they were in a gang. Battles were fought over control of public spaces like the North Commons or even over the right to use a certain sidewalk in a neighborhood. Shifting coalitions of new immigrant children formed and reformed to fight the long-established Irish kids whose families were being slowly displaced in the Acre by Greeks and Poles. Even the Irish policeman on the beat might resent young "foreigners" and take it out on boys with his night-stick. Schoolboy violence reflected prejudices learned from adults.

With school days and odd jobs over, the young fourteen-year-old approached the mill wearing long work pants or overalls like his father. There he was sized up by the boss. Being judged fit to work conferred a pleasing sense of worthwhile manliness. One loom fixer proudly recalled being picked for a job out of a crowd of unemployed after showing his hands. Some boys looking for work could name the parts of the loom, know-how taught around the family supper table to impress the boss.

The offer of a job, even if it was on short hours and only sweeping up cotton lint, meant entering the adult world of male workers. The wage earner's first pay envelope was given to his parents with great solemnity and pride. That money represented the earnings of a young man. This almost inevitable entry into mill work represented the way that working-class families controlled their children's chances and then took most of their wages for family needs. Some mill workers wondered years later about that inevitability. Had mill work been the only possibility or might they have gotten something else?

For many parents without better options for their children, the best way to help a young son survive in the mills was to get a skill by using all the influence the family might muster. Then fathers and brothers could watch over the young man's progress up the job ladder toward the most desirable kinds of work. Frequently this involved actual instruction by family members in how to weave, how to slash, or how to fix. The ideal of the family labor system was to have all male relatives—young and old alike—working for the same mill, in the same section, and on the same machinery. The family labor system became indispensable to Lowell's ethnic communities. A few paternalistic mills also offered men a chance to join in organized sports on company teams, and this opportunity meant a lot to young athletes with enough energy after their shift to play baseball or soccer. This commitment to the family and this dependence on the good will of the bosses was tested whenever coworkers clamored for union organization.

Young men without family members or ethnic ties to help them faced real difficulties in getting out of the unskilled, low-paying jobs of bobbin-boy or sweeper. One Irish-American mill worker received a small tip each week from the carpet weaver whom he helped, but he got no chance to learn the skill. As the mills declined in the 1930s, some fathers refused to teach their sons their skills as mill workers, hoping that they would seek other work elsewhere. Other fathers were unable to help out. They had never worked in the mills or had failed to get skilled work for themselves. Getting a chance to learn to weave—at no extra pay for either the teacher or the learner—often meant ending up on the late shift. The on-the-job teaching took place in snatches. A weaver might quickly show a bobbin-boy how to make a weaver's knot, "You do that, see?"

Nonetheless, the male camaraderie of the mill floor with its scurrying bobbin-boys, weavers, fixers, and bosses created a world where older men sometimes assumed a measure of responsibility, with the permission of the overseer, for teaching young men who were not of their own families or ethnic groups. One Portuguese weaver was taught loom fixing by an elderly fixer who had never had a son and wished to leave his tools and knowledge to some young man who could take "his place." One of the pleasures of teaching a younger man to fix was that it reaffirmed how essential a man's mechanical judgments were to mill operations. An observant and dependable roving boy caught the eye of a sympathetic mule spinner and was given a chance to grasp and run the complicated spinning mechanism. If they could, young men attended the free night classes at the Lowell Textile School where they learned the principles and practicalities of machinery, fabric construction, and production standards.

The memories of these workers reflected the experience of individuals caught up in some phase of the process of immigration and adjustment to the industrial urban world of Lowell in the early twentieth century. Some of them were emigrants from Poland and Portugal: ambitious young men escaping military conscription or seeking dollars to send home to their families. Men seemed to spearhead the act of crossing the Atlantic as adventuring brothers, as newly-wed husbands, or as fathers and sons making way for mothers and younger children to follow. New arrivals depended on their countrymen to find them a place in the mills. Still, the world of the single young immigrant male without a family in Lowell could be a depressing round of unheated boarding-houses, cheap restaurants, and hot showers taken in barber shops. During the early twentieth century, Greeks, Portuguese, and French Canadians returned periodically to their native lands to reconsider their choices or to touch base with families and country.

Most mill workers of the last generation were American-born children with immigrant parents whose memories formed much of the lore of family life. Many knew their relatives and the homeland only from family stories. At home, the mother and father spoke in their native tongue, taught morality and religious ritual, and told tales of the old country and of family still there. Children learned the language and customs to please their parents, but, once instructed in French, Greek or Yiddish, boys and girls ran out to play with their English-speaking schoolmates. The inroads made by school, the streets and playgrounds, radio in the 1930s, military service, and, after World War II, intermarriage and television began to undermine and dissipate the cultural purity of ethnic families and neighborhoods.

Although the father represented formal authority, young mill workers watched both their mothers and their fathers engage in chasing the kids and teaching them the old language and customs. But to mothers, religion seemed to signify piety and moral rules, whereas fathers were more likely to practice religion in public ways that involved cultural values and homeland politics. Immigrant husbands often learned English before their homebound wives, who might also remain illiterate even in their native language and thus doubly cut off from newspapers and public life. Greek men re-created the male bonds of village life in the coffee houses on Market Street in the Acre, where puppet shows and old-country newspapers sparked discussions of homeland politics. French Canadian, Polish, and Portuguese men formed mutual aid and benevolent societies and, with the help of their mothers, wives, and sisters, organized parties, shows, and festivals with music, dancing, and homeland foods. The gangs of boys who had collected junk and battled each other over neighborhood turf grew up to shape ethnic public life as adult men.

Before marriage, groups of young men used their weekends to carouse freely and explore the wonders of Saturday nights in the local ballrooms, poolhalls, bowling alleys, barrooms, cafés, and nickel lunches. After a grueling work week that extended through Saturday morning, they always went out. Even if he were almost broke, a young man could hang around downtown cafés and bars that provided free cheese and pretzels and cheap beer on Saturday nights. The best times in the 1930s were at the Commodore Ballroom where dressed-up mill workers danced to swing music. At amusement parks, men had to buy a set of tickets to dance and the price of the ticket varied with the popularity of the dance band. On the weekends, young male workers crammed in as many exhausting hours as possible, drinking beer with friends, going to the beach, dancing, playing cards, going to Mass, more

Greek coffee house patrons in the Acre, 1914. *Courtesy of the Lowell Museum.*

beach and card playing, and finally collapsing into bed for a little sleep before work on the Monday shift.

At some point in this world of weekend leisure or in the mills, a few young workers developed contacts with women from other ethnic communities that parents could not censor. Intermarriage with all its cultural tensions became more common for the generation born in the twenties and tested in World War II, but before 1940, most men workers married women from their own ethnic communities. Courtships were often closely controlled by the girl's family. One young loom fixer saved enough money to buy a used car, but then found it almost impossible to persuade girls from his community to go for rides with him. Mothers influenced their sons' choices through arranged marriages or by quickly vetoing girls with unfamiliar last names. Tightly organized ethnic communities both protected their members and fostered suspicions of outsiders. When a man married, things became different. He controlled his own paycheck at last, but having a wife and children required a man to find a steady job at good money. When women married, they began to juggle home and work; when men married, their work outside the home intensified.

Whether through family connections or ethnic ties, getting a chance to learn a skill was crucial. Most skilled male workers remembered examples of the failed men in the mills: a drunken father who always remained a "filling boy," a sweeper who died with his lunch in his mouth and whose corpse was dragged out roughly, and other men with no alternatives to the dirtiest of work or outdoor pick-and-shovel jobs. To learn a skill was to achieve a respectable manhood.

Many of the less-skilled jobs for men in the mills were extremely dangerous. Working in the dye house or the card room, moving heavy warp beams around, even sweeping out around elevators, threatened serious, sometimes fatal, injury if a man was distracted by fatigue or boredom. The personal vigilance required to keep a worker from getting hurt caused both anxiety and exhaustion. Workers and some bosses carried scars as badges of their experiences. Many mill workers, recognizing their lack of options, stoically accepted the conditions of work as matters of fate: "I didn't stop and think about it too much or you go crazy in a sense."

Men wore clothing in the mill that disguised the oily dirt and helped them with their jobs. Fixers put on dark gray shirts that hid grease marks and stains and overalls that had convenient pockets and places for wrenches and tools. When they had to crawl under the looms, they braved filth and spit. Carders wore dark-colored, tight-fitting jerseys and dungarees (which no woman dared to show up in) to minimize the dangers of getting a sleeve caught in the machinery. A hat kept out some of the linty grime, and work shoes maintained a grip on floors slippery from the grease that dripped off machines and belts. Dye house workers labored in tee shirts or stripped to the waist, wearing pants and boots wrapped up in scraps of cloth to keep the acids and dyes from penetrating to their skin. These work clothes were stored on nails in the mill rooms or in dressing rooms or lockers. Mill workers who left work after their shift noticeably greasy and dirty were commonly referred to as mill rats.

The job ladder for men could lead from bobbin-boy and filling hand up to skilled work such as fixing, slashing, and mule spinning. These jobs were for men only, and nationality was often crucial. Lancashire English and Irish-American workers got the best chances at moving up to foremen. Franco-Americans dominated loom fixing, while a few became supervisors.* Many Greek-American men ended up in the dye house. Slashers endured intense heat, a mule spinner needed "good legs," and fixers relied on mechanical ability not expected from girls. Work in the dye house and carding room was regarded as much too dangerous for women. To many men, the women who worked in the mills during World War II as slashers or for the first time on the night shift seemed a degraded and unsavory group.

Tensions between women and men in the mill took many forms. Male workers sometimes sexually harassed young women, knowing that the boss would look the other way. Men watched women workers cry openly in anguish over defective work or the contents of their pay envelope. Nevertheless, one loom fixer refused to submit his injury to a notoriously tough company nurse at the Newmarket who favored women workers. Another remembered ducking a necessary confrontation with a tobacco-chewing woman weaver. Managers sometimes exploited the tensions between men and women workers from different communities.

Female workers were used in various ways by the mills to run new machines and replace skilled men, to lower wage rates, and to break strikes called by men's unions. During one strike in the early 1930s, strikebreaking men took women on each arm as they violated the picket line of union mule spinners, knowing that they would not use "rough-stuff" against women workers. Women who joined in strike activities were welcome but considered unreliable. Female activists usually stuck to organizing other women workers in the spinning or cloth rooms. These distinctions in labor activity reflected the different job ladders for men and women.

A mule spinner operated complicated, dangerous, moving equipment; women ring spinners tended stationary frames where the machine parts did the work. As these machines undermined the skills of mule spinners, those men who remained in the woolen mills to work on ring spinning frames usually operated by women found they just couldn't "handle it." A loom fixer might begin as a battery hand and work with girls, then advance to weaving, which he often learned from a woman weaver. Men regarded weaving as a chance to learn the causes of mechanical breakdowns; most women weavers, who were not per-

*Franco-American was a term adopted in the late nineteenth century by the French Canadian community in Lowell to emphasize that many had become naturalized citizens; it is used here to indicate American-born second- or third-generation people of French Canadian cultural background.

mitted to be fixers, saw trouble-prone looms as obstacles to making money. When a young man became a fixer, he left behind female coworkers, potential fines for defective work, piece rates, and the overt speed-up. Fixers acted together as a group of skilled men to resist extra work and to define the proper pace of effort. Many loom fixers took care to wash off the grease and change their clothes when their shift was over. Fixers were given deference and respect as "big shots in the mill." The sexual division of labor and the superiority of men's work seemed both natural and logical.

The most successful, long-term organization among mill workers was the independent loom fixers' union. In a special sense, loom fixers regarded their work as a self-directed job that they did alone. But it was also a job like mule spinning, which often involved asking for help and advice from others in the trade. Fixers worked as partners on opposite shifts to anticipate major overhauls and keep the machinery functioning. Good partners were "decent" men, "quick fixers," but they did not control conditions in the mill. They felt incessant pressures for their attention from the impatient weavers who were trying to make some money off their balky, usually worn-out looms. Inexperienced or arrogant managers might decide to ignore the advice of "good fixers" and undermine capable foremen. With the labor shortages of World War II, loom fixers faced added work, a redefinition of the job, and paycuts for returning veterans.

For the few who got the chance, supervision meant more money and the enviable position of simply giving out the work, watching it run, and responding to occasional problems. Every fixer wanted to be the head man, the boss fixer, who was usually careful to be seen doing small jobs while he gave orders for the big jobs to his men. A boss fixer might become the boss of a weave room, then a second hand or foreman; he might even dream of becoming an overseer. A man's attitude toward workers and unions shifted when he supervised or kept track of production. A supervisor could be persuaded that the longer the machines ran without intervention, the more competition among the work force, and the clearer the lines of authority, the better for management. But supervising others marked you as a company man, ineligible for union membership, likely to be shunned at social clubs, and sworn at openly or ignored by other mill workers. Sympathetic men who became personnel managers often got an earful about the darkest side of workers' lives: physical abuse, abortions, infidelity, drunkenness, and despair.

The few skilled male workers who caught the boss's eye might get

Loom fixer at the
Wannalancit, 1980.
*Courtesy of the Lowell
National Historical Park.*

promoted but most mill workers learned to be suspicious when a "friendly" boss asked them to do something or called them "a good worker." Whatever the request, it was likely to be difficult or dangerous, or, if refused, mean no job at all. A hard worker might be used as a measure to reduce the piece rate, and workers kept secret from time-study or efficiency men the shortcuts they devised for various jobs. Good ideas about improvements often received little recognition and no reward. Male workers were well aware of the sexual harrassment of women by supervisors, which was one good reason to see to it that wives or daughters never entered the mill. Bosses practiced little rackets or "clips" to get kickbacks from mill workers. Pro-union workers often cited abuses of authority as well as low wages and dangerous working conditions as major reasons for organizing.

Ethnic identity did not seem to determine labor activism among men. Brothers from Lancashire disagreed over the merits of organization, while the American-born children of French Canadian immigrants were divided, some trusting in family loyalty to the mill or personal fatalism rather than unions. Despite their reputation for deserting labor-management conflicts to seek other jobs, Franco-Americans ran the loom fixers' union that cooperated with the CIO in organizing the Boott and the Newmarket in the 1940s. Many Polish-American workers supported unions as an extension of homeland politics, but others became bosses, notorious for their slavish commitment to the mill owners. Greek-American union leaders fought over the future of the organization at the Merrimack after World War II. Some Portuguese and Polish immigrants wanted more than anything else to abandon industrial work and return to farming.

To those critical of union policy, including some who were union members, each increase in wages meant that the machinery ran faster and the worker sweated more. One carder experienced such increasing levels of exhaustion as a result of the vigilance required to keep from getting hurt that he became desperately sick. The faster the work went, the more stoppages disrupted production. Machine malfunctions and breakdowns required a lot of cooperation among workers, but if the boss caught the fixer doing the oiler's job, both could be fired. Production was the name of the game, but the rules were getting crazier. Union objectives such as higher wages and better conditions failed to address needed improvements in the production process that might have helped the mills stay in operation. Some workers who had grown up with a punishing work ethic resisted too many paid holidays as unsound policy that eroded the workers' standard of living.

Much pro-union activity was a response to the behavior of managers. Those who knew the business and could do the work on many of the operations were respected. But those supervisors' sons and college boys who ignored the basic requirements of turning out good cloth and who undermined the judgment and authority of experienced mill workers earned silent contempt and barely concealed anger. When irresponsible managers who were unfamiliar with the work misused foremen, all male authority seemed to be undercut. The reaction was outraged impotence. Petty tyrants and former mill hands who behaved like they "owned the mill" created hard feelings and prompted retaliation. If a boss did not value a skilled worker or his work, he took a walk to another mill or to another mill town. Unskilled workers or those with few options ground their teeth and stayed on.

Anger had to be carefully concealed during the hard times of the depression years when even unskilled mill work seemed better than outdoor work: pick-and-shovel jobs or cleaning streets. The unemployed sat in the waiting rooms of the mills on the chance of getting "the word": some work as a spare hand. If a man was not seen there in the waiting room, day after day, he would not be hired. Being out of work for extended periods became frightening, and skilled men often became migratory workers who got access to somebody's car and went on the road seeking a few days' or a few weeks' work as spare hands. On these jobs, they confronted strange bosses, unfamiliar machinery, new work rules, and resentful coworkers.

The depression years directed the political interests of mill workers away from their parents' homeland politics and their token voting in municipal elections taught in Americanization classes. Irish-American men and women had been galvanized into local political activity as a result of the presidential candidacy of Al Smith in 1928. The collapse of the economy in 1929 only intensified the misery of an already depressed textile industry in New England. Many mill workers, both men and women, idolized Franklin Delano Roosevelt and the Democratic party and became avid supporters and precinct workers. The National Recovery Act had increased the wages of textile workers, the unemployed found jobs on local WPA projects, and the Wagner Act created electoral procedures and government regulations that encouraged unions. But others found the Democratic party too conservative and sought inspiration in radical ideas critical of the New Deal. Some of the newest immigrants preferred labor politics linked with European socialism to mainstream American political parties.

The mill owners and their representatives grumbled about popular New Deal programs but they sought to intimidate labor organizers, radicals, and Socialists in the late thirties. Many mill workers believed that the bosses and their community supporters used the World War II draft system to rid Lowell of labor agitators and "Communists." Troublemakers ended up in the army, while the threat of a change in their draft status kept others from seeking better jobs or causing problems. Leadership in the independent union organized in 1939 at the Merrimack fell into the hands of women and men past the draft age. Bosses reassigned and reorganized work long before the veterans returned, and many who did return refused to go back to the mills.

The war itself worked a change on the draftees. Those lucky enough to escape death or injury during the war, returned home with a different perspective on their lives in Lowell. Ethnic differences and jobs in the mills no longer seemed important. As one loom fixer put it after his own service in World War I, when you get out, "you want to ramble."

Veterans of World War II came back from the service wanting more money for work that they quickly saw managers had redesigned. When they were refused, they quit. Some came back with grievances against bosses who had cheated them out of their last paycheck before induction. Others, having tested their physical courage at war, could face old fears. In comparison, the war era offered less challenging experiences to women workers. As they had during the depression years, they remained in Lowell. The war work came to them.

World War II seemed the turning point for mill workers in Lowell. The war stimulated union organization and changed work in the mills. Men returned to jobs that women had performed during their absence. After the war, unions in the remaining textile operations became stronger, and wages and working conditions improved. As a result, the family labor system and the bonds of ethnic life in the workplace began to dissolve. However, the surviving textile operations faced fatal challenges from postwar domestic and foreign competitors. Just as things began to get a little better, the world of the last generation fell apart.

As the few surviving Lowell mills declined in the late 1940s, many men in the mills faced retirement or needed some kind of a new job. Some farsighted men had worked second jobs for the city or county government, but for lifetime mill workers, being old usually meant no pension or any payment from the mill. As one mule spinner remembered it: "Out! You were on your own; you get nothing." Many others were afraid that they were too old for any sort of job or that the assessing look of the personnel manager as he scanned their applications meant they were useless. Old skills and years of experience were irrelevant to new jobs in electronics or assembly-line work. Many who did locate work in the electronics industry were pleased with the higher wages and decent conditions, but, to a skilled man, working as a janitor or putting together parts of computers that were tested by somebody else only filled time and put food on the table until retirement. Like the women workers, the men placed their hopes for the future in their children and grandchildren.

That's What They Used to Call Them: Mill Rats

Harry Dickenson
LOOM FIXER

For a child born to working-class parents in Blackburn, England, life was "all mill," and as a boy Harry Dickenson accepted textile work as a matter of course. Dickenson immigrated to the United States when he was ten, as his family hauled itself across the Atlantic in stages, by ones and twos. Being a boy from Lancashire immediately opened doors leading to skilled work and later to supervisory jobs.

His father was troublesome and an embarrassment, and Harry became his mother's favorite son, taking on special responsibilities. After experiencing years of satisfying work at the Boott, Dickenson watched major deterioration set in. In the 1930s, the Harvard-educated sons of the owner were put in charge of production and ignored knowledgeable and seasoned foremen.

For years, Harry Dickenson observed abuses of authority by supervisors that only union grievance procedures could block. But when the union leaders at the Boott ignored the quality of production, they seemed as wrong-headed as the bosses. When the Boott closed in 1954, Dickenson faced what many other mill workers did: assembly-line jobs in local light industry at low wages.

I WAS BORN in 1895 in a place called Blackburn in Lancashire, England. I came to this country when I was ten years old. My oldest brother was already here. After a while he wrote, and my father and I came [in 1905]. The year after, we sent for the rest of the family to come to Lisbon, Maine. My uncle, aunt, and cousin were also there. That's where I graduated from school, in Lisbon, a small place.

When I went to school in England, they were strict as hell. If you did anything wrong the master used to have a cane. You used to put your hand out, and he would whack you. I remember one time, I was walking in to go to our seats, and as I was going to my seat I saw a book on the floor, an arithmetic book. Naturally I picked it up and put it on the desk. I got called out in the center of the room and whack! We can't say nothing, not in England. They're the boss.

In Maine it was more sociable. We used to go to school in snow up to our necks. Then when we got to the school, [we'd] take our shoes and stockings off and dry them in front of the stove. When I went to school, I'd have to run home at noontime and get the dinner on the table so when they came home from work for one hour at noon, they would have their dinner and go back. Mother would prepare the things, and I would run home from school, put it on the stove, and have it ready for them when they came. I used to look after chopping the wood for the stove, and my sisters used to clean the house and had their routine. Mother would make them do it.

After graduation I got a job in the mill for fifty cents a day. It was the custom for English people when you get a certain age. If they were good enough to work in the mill, you're supposed to work in the mill. It was always that way. That's why you never had an idea of changing or anything. You talked mill, morning, noon, and night. You were supposed to be in the mill. What was good for your mother and your sisters, you were supposed to be. That's the worst part of it, I think. That is the worst part of any family. You don't give the kids a chance to get interested in anything else. You have to be a mill rat. That's what they called them: mill rats.

I started in Lisbon in the spinning room, doffing. After a while my brother, he had a foreman's job in a mill in Lewistown, Maine, so he brought me up there. Up there I was a filling boy, and after a while I got started weaving and went on to learn fixing.

In 1918 I became a foreman there when I was twenty-three years old in the Androscoggin Mill in Lewiston, Maine. When I went to war, they told me that when I came back I would have my job, but when I came back I didn't have my job. I did have my job, but I didn't have my pay that I was getting when I went to war. The boss had gone away, and the superintendent had taken over. I asked him about my pay, and he got kind of nasty. I said, All I want from you is my [back pay] check. I settled up right there.

When you come out of the army, you want to ramble. I had a sister down near Pawtucket, Rhode Island, so I went down there for a while. My family had gone to Lowell. They kept after me so much to go back into the mill. So, like a damn fool, I went back. My brother, he was a boss in the Boott mill, and he got me in there, fixing. I was there from around 1922 until they quit in 1954.

From fixing, I had a foremanship. The manager, a good friend of mine, was an English fellow. One day there was a job come vacant so I took it. At that time I was getting $32 per week, fixing. I said, I won't take it unless I get a raise, so he gave me $36 with the chance that if I made good I was going to get more. The man that left the job was getting $59 per week.

I came to Lowell and lived with my parents. I had charge of the family up to about twenty-nine years old until I got married. I had two sisters and three brothers. Of course I came from an English family, and the rule was if your mother worked in the mill, you were supposed to do the same thing, and all the children went to the mill. The same with my brother; he was all mill. He was good though; he knew his business.

In England my mother was a weaver. The way it was done there, she may have had four looms, sometimes six. It wasn't automatic. When the kids hit a certain age, they'd get them in the mill as tenders. The weaver got a [learner called a] tender. She is supposed to learn the girl. After a while the girl could do it, and they'd put her on two looms. Then if she progressed, she would go on four looms. That was the old style.

My mother was proud, and she looked after the kids. She was a good living woman; she was all right. But her married life—my dad, he used to go on the rampage once in a while and used to make it hard. The mother was good. I stayed with her; I was her favorite. I had the trouble of putting her away. She died at eighty-three, and my father at ninety-one. I looked after them.

She was a religious person. If we did anything wrong, we got told. When I came to this country, my uncle belonged to the Baptist church. Of course I was born Episcopalian [Church of England]. But when we came to this country, we all started going to the Baptist. After a while I got discouraged.

I had a brother-in-law who used to drink quite a lot, but I like him an awful lot. My sister in Pawtucket called me up in Lowell, and she asked me if I could get him a job in Lowell. I said, I'll try. I got him a job in the Bay State mill; he was a slasher. He stayed here quite awhile, and then he had a chance to go back and work in a mill in Pawtucket, so he went back. There had been a complete change in him. He stopped his drinking and he bought a house. He had three kids. Then in the mill, he stepped on a nail, and he got blood poisoning in his foot that started gangrene. The way we were brought up, if you do the right thing, you get your reward. When he died, I took it hard. I never went to church since. I got nothing against religion, but sometimes it don't seem fair.

My father used to drink like hell, and he used to make it hard for the family. That's why I got attached to my mother. Until he died, he was a problem. When my mother died, I had him and my younger brother. I tried to make life good for him, but every once in a while he'd go out, and he wasn't very nice when he came back. He was good in his way, but he had his faults.

He had a lot of jobs. In England he was working on the railroad where the trains come in. One time, there was a football game in London, and he wanted to go in the worst way so he asked a guy, would he cover for him? So he went. When he came back, he was out of a job. The guy never covered for him. Then he worked in some paper mill or something like that. When he came to this country, he started in the mill. I guess he was washing floors. All through his life he was a filling boy, picking up empty bobbins and things like that. In the Boott.

Some mills are run better than others on account of management. We used to go to work at the Boott [in the 1920s and the 1930s], and I'd rather go to work there than go to the show. Everyone was pleasant. Then the head of the mill, he started putting his sons in there. The head one was [Frederick A.] Flather. He had two sons, John [Rogers] and Frederick. Must have put them in there around 1940. It became altogether different. Before that they used to hire a man to run the mill that knew the business. Give them full charge, and they used to make good stuff. When they started putting the sons in there that had come out of college, it was a different story altogether. Instead of doing the right things, instead of working with your people in the mill that's been there twenty and thirty years such as their foremen, it changed. It started going down.

Frederick was the worst one. What he did was break down the standards of the foremanship. He'd take a man off a junk pile and put him in the mill as a foreman. He really ruined the mill. But John, he was older than Frederick, you could talk to him; he had more reason. Frederick seemed to take charge, and you couldn't do anything about it.

When I was foreman—in the mill you have got to have heat, warmth, and then you've got to have humidity and no drafts. Drafts in the weave room cause static electricity, and it dries everything up. When I was foreman, I was in the [weave] room there, and it used to be so cold that they couldn't keep the tension on the cloth, the corduroy. They had weights on the loom but they couldn't keep the tension on the fabric, and when the cloth was going through, it would kind of fray on the side and spoil it. So I had trouble there and kept asking for more heat, but all they did was laugh at me.

Some of the weavers were having a hard time, and there was a empty place there next to the weave room where every so often windows was open [and there were drafts]. The weavers couldn't do nothing. They'd work hard for nothing. So I spoke to another guy, I was fixing looms then. I said, Give me the right to close those windows. He came through and saw it. Ordered them all down but then the windows were open again. So you couldn't do nothing. I've seen [Frederick A. Flather] the father, if he had a room that was cold, and they was having a hard time, the father would come in there and get the carpenters to board that room all in, close it in. Then after that the work went along. Them weavers went to work in the morning and worked with their sweaters on and coats and rubbers on. Then you go down to the first-aid department and make a complaint of no heat [and get nothing]. The people couldn't quit; they had to work. The people was willing to do their work and produce if management would give them the necessary things to do it with, like humidity and keep the room warm which it should be. Any manufacturer will tell you that the mill has got to be warm. Toward the last of it, heat didn't mean a thing.

It didn't make no difference, [Frederick Flather] was going to have his way. He called all the bosses together; I'll show you what kind of a guy he is. You couldn't [just] sit him at a table. All the bosses was there, and you got a stand with a chair on top [for him]. I used to play the trumpet [in a dance band], and I used to say I'm going to take my trumpet and I'm going to blast it out; Here Comes the King! Anyway, there was another boss there, and I don't know what the hell went wrong, but [Frederick] was blasting him, gave him an awful blasting. Then he turned to me in the same department and he said, You heard what I said to him? I said, Yes. He said, That goes for you too. When I came out of the conference room, the nurse right next door says to me, What's the matter with you? [I said,] I've seen better miscarriages go down the sewer than that guy. Oh, she says. I mean it, I said.

Before the union, the bosses could do anything they wanted. Suppose you work for a boss. Now you're doing your work, but he's getting ideas. They'd discharge them or move them from one job to another just for spite. That's what I liked the union for. [They'd ask] what you was fired for? Was she doing the work? We could put the case right in front of arbitration. That's what I liked about it.

For instance, this girl—she was a lovely girl, you know what I mean? She was a battery hand. I guess the boss was trying to rigmarole, but she wouldn't come across. What he did, he took her off the job that she was used to and put her on another job. Finally she quit. There was a lot of that done. The boss taking advantage of a person like that. You either come across or nothing. You know what I mean? I never was that way.

My brother was all mill. When I got [to be] foreman, we had our arguments. Maybe some people don't belong in unions; I think it is a godsend. We used to have our arguments about that. What I liked about the union, it gave us the right if you had a case like that to take it up for arbitration, argue it out. Me and my brother used to argue on different things. He was against the union, but I was for the union for the protection of the workers.

When I was in the union, I was president of the union [CIO], we had other fights in there. We used to fight them down to the statehouse and everything. [At first] we fought for a raise in pay. Of course we had to take a vote on that. There is always two sides to everything. You need money to run a business, and you've got to have labor to get your profit. If both sides would compromise and be fair about it there is no trouble, but, just the same, management don't want to give you a raise. They tried to negotiate, and they didn't, so they came out on strike. Finally got it. If you fight for it well, the union comes in, and we got the union in [around 1945]. It was ten years before he closed up [in 1954].

I was the president. When anything came up [and] we had to go to arbitration or anything like that, I had a shop committee, one person from every department. Somebody that actually knew the work. Then we would have [arbitration] sessions in Boston at the statehouse be-tween their lawyer and the representative from the union. Oh we used to fight like hell. One time we was getting nowhere, so then I got mad. I said, Mr. Flather, are we going to settle this thing? All this man who is your lawyer can say is, It can't be done. The union official kicked my shin under the table; I shouldn't have spoken out. But right after that, the thing was settled. They took the lawyer out and came back. [They had] settled the thing outside.

The older son, John Rogers Flather, he knew my brother Bill. He told me I was fair. [He said], if we do wrong, we get it [from the arbitrator], and if he says the workers are wrong, he gives it to them. Which is the only right way of doing it. Some people think that because you're union, you can do anything you want, but you can't.

I was in there about eight years [as president of the union], and a bunch got together and had an election and got a new set of officers. It didn't last long. They had people on the shop committee that didn't know what it's all about. They ruined the thing. One meeting was so disgusting. Instead of talking on the subject concerning manufacturing stuff, they were bringing up the [condition of] the toilets. So foolish. Then they [told] management, we could run the mill better than you can. There was no sense to it. I went down to one meeting; I was disgusted.

The dues were thirty-five cents a week, and then the union wanted to put in fifty cents [dues]. So we put it on the [bulletin] board so that at the next meeting there would be a question of raising the dues. So I was down in the machine shop, and one of the members there, an electrician, he started blasting me out because of raising the dues. I said, What the hell are you talking about? The notice was up; why didn't you attend the meeting? People are not satisfied. Then another guy he didn't want to pay fifty cents, but he was covered by [union] insurance. When he went to the hospital, I looked up what it cost. I think it costs around $265. He was finding fault with fifty cents, but still when he went to the hospital, everything was paid.

After I got out of the Boott in 1954 [at sixty], there was some rumor going around that if you were forty-five years old you couldn't get a [mill] job. So I had a chance to work in the Merrimack, and I went down for an interview and the first thing he asked me, How old are you? When I told him, I said, Oh, oh; I'm all done. He said, Why do you say, oh, oh, for? I said I heard at forty-five you can't get a job; you're too old. He says, Listen if you can do the job, you can start the next day. So I got it.

I only worked there a little while, and then that [Merrimack] mill folded up. That was a good mill to work with. Everyone was surprised when that went out; that was a good running mill. I suppose competition from the South and them different countries, Japan and all that stuff coming in. They couldn't survive the competition from the South. A lot of mills moved down South on account of the benefits in the weather, cheaper labor. Saco-Lowell used to be a big machine shop here; they went down South. You can't blame them.

So I was out of work. Toward the last of it [in the mill] I was getting around $1.75 an hour. The only thing I could get was working with a plumber for just over a dollar [an hour]. Then that blew up. Then I started to get a job in Symphonic, making radios and things like that. I started there for a dollar an hour. Then that went out, and I was sixty-nine, so I retired.

You Had to Go to Work Early
and Get Some Money

Charles Costello
MULE SPINNER

After years of unskilled, physically demanding cotton mill jobs that led nowhere, Charles Costello, with the help of relatives, found work in a woolen mill. There he hoped to learn one of the skilled trades for men in the industry: mule spinning. Whether he got the chance depended solely on whether one of the mule spinners would let him try.

In cotton textiles, the replacement of mule spinning with ring spinning began at the turn of the century, while in wool the shift came later in the 1930s. Costello and his fellow union mule spinners relived the experience of those in cotton whose machines were smashed up in front of them and whose jobs were filled by lower-paid, non-union women.

During the depression years, Costello and many others went on the road, scrambling for a few weeks' work. As migratory industrial workers, they faced unfamiliar machinery and received no help from fellow spinners. When the Depression eased and jobs opened up, Charles Costello got on at a woolen mill as a steady spinner but was forced to witness the complete erosion of his trade.

BETWEEN 1915 and 1920, when we were kids, we lived on French Street near the Merrimack River. Our house had a big backyard and was only maybe a hundred yards away from it. There were five boys in the family, and my Uncle Tommy was only six months older than I was. [On Saturday afternoon the mills would drain the canals to clean them.] Every Sunday the water got low [enough] so we could go across the river [in the area] between the Merrimack mills and the Boott mills. There were rocks, but the water was way down low, and sometimes it was almost dry. And we'd pick up all the junk, the brass, the copper, whatever was there.

We built a raft maybe five feet wide and ten feet long. And we'd load it up with all that junk. We'd keep going back and forth across the river and pull that junk into our yard. We might get a ton or two tons of stuff before we'd stop by the end of Sunday. Every Monday morning, the junk man would come around, and he'd give my uncle a price for it.

It would be copper and old broken kinds of iron and steel they used in the shops that was thrown out the windows into the canal raceways [or into the river]. The water in the canals would push it all right down to the river. Some of it was [bronze travelers from twisting machines], little bits of things. You'd figure maybe a hundred or a hundred and fifty to a pound, but you'd pick them up by the handfuls anyway. You might put them into a can or bag. The junk man would come around, and he'd settle for it and take it away.

Then in the twenties after my mother and father died, we moved in with my relatives and lived there until 1933 when I got married, and then we lived there a little bit longer. I had started working [in 1915] at fourteen years old in the Lowell Carpet Mills. After my folks died, there was ten of us in my aunt and uncle's family. You had to go to work early and get some money.

I was what they called a creeler there. The carpet mill made rugs. I'd have to take care of the little spools with all different colors of yarn—red, blue, green—whatever, on them for the carpet looms. As they ran out, you had to put a full one in and make sure they always had enough yarn. I was a helper to a Jacquard weaver. The Jacquard loom would design the rug. It was all done automatically. My weaver, he used to give me a quarter a week. Just a tip from the weaver. I was making $3.15 a week. If you went up to sparehand [weaver], it was $3.90 a week. I stayed there until the carpet mill moved out [in 1917]. Then when I was sixteen, I went to the Boott mill.

I worked as a sweeper in the weave room, sweeping under the looms, going after the fuzz from the cotton yarn. Sweep up underneath, before they put the new warp in the looms. Clean up underneath and keep the place clean. You never knew how many warps were going to run out each day. You'd have to be around to clean it all up. The warps were small for dish towels; I've never seen the big ones. Boott mills made mostly all kitchen towels and gingham then. The warp was about the width of a towel, say about two feet.

Then [about 1918] up at the Hamilton mill, I took care of the magazines [batteries for the looms]. It's a round cylinder, and it might hold thirty bobbins. You had to keep them cylinders full [of bobbins]. I forget how many machines we had to take care of. It wouldn't take you long to learn. You'd get used to it and put them in like nobody's business. You'd go up and down and keep them filled. You'd go this way and come down that way and keep going around and around just to keep them filled up so that they wouldn't run out.

Each time the shuttle goes across, it takes so much yarn, and Boy, they used to go boom, boom, boom, boom, boom! They used to go like sixty, as fast as blazes, especially in the cotton. When the little finger or feeler in the shuttle don't feel the yarn any more, it automatically pushed that bobbin out of the shuttle and puts in another bobbin. So there's no stoppage; just keeps going back and forth. That's why you got to keep them filled all the time. I stayed at the Hamilton mills for about a year and a half.

Then a fellow from my neighborhood offered me a job on a lunch cart. I never done anything like that before, but I got a better wage. It was slow, very slow, getting business, starting business. Oh, it was always slow. Cripes, you would be sitting in the corner for half an hour at a time sometimes if you didn't get any customers. It was on Appleton Street right across from the telephone company. While I was there [around 1920], they had a strike, the telephone operators striking for higher wages. The girls used to come over. They used to come over and get a sandwich and coffee or something. And I used to give them free food. Not expensive stuff. You couldn't come over and order ten hamburgs. You'd get a light feed. I stayed there maybe a year. And when business come along pretty good and I figured I ought to get a little more money, he wouldn't give it to me. He wouldn't give me any more, so I quit.

My uncle worked out to the [American Woolen] mill in Collinsville, and he got me a job out there in the spinning department. So I went out there, and I was a roving carrier who carries the roving down from the card room and puts it behind the mules [mule spinning machines]. Your mule had 360 ends [of yarn to spin]. You brought that roving down to the spinner, and he'd piece it in, one by one. I worked maybe a year and a half, and then I got a job mule spinning.

It's a good job, but you had a lot of walking. You had to have pretty good legs. It's pretty heavy when you've got 360 ends there, and there's weights all the way around your mule at different intervals. You might have eight weights, two pounds a piece, and three others. That's to keep the tension when the mule backs off so it will wind nice and even on the bobbins. So there wouldn't be no kinks [in the yarn].

Once you get used to it, you could go right along. You needed more than one person to start a new lot. Once you got the [roving] ends in, the fixer'd be there, and he'd be helping you. You might have the fixer, and you might have two fixers. And yourself, and maybe your alley mate. You always had an alley mate, because your mule was coming back and forth, this way and that, and his mule was coming this way and that. You had a space about as wide as a table in between. He'd be watching his, and I'd be watching mine.

It took about a year and a half to learn. It all depends. Some guy will take a liking to you, and you'll take a liking to a certain spinner. You try to learn, try to piece up, and watch what they're doing. And then some guy'll have a little confidence [in you], and he'll say, try it. And you'll try it, but jeepers, cripes, you might give him a breakdown! I might give the guy a smash, and I'll lose all his [yarn] ends. Then you got to piece up 360 ends. It ain't funny! But after a while if you can get people that'll take a chance with you, some guy'll say, We'll try it. Now go easy, take your time. It isn't everybody'd let you do it.

There was no [mule spinners'] union there then, although other places around were unionized. They had trouble in Lawrence, Haverhill, and Andover [Massachusetts], and they'd come up [to Collinsville] and walk around our place but nobody'd make a move, never, nothing. Never could pull them out. We did finally get a spinners' union, [local] number 959, and we used to have meetings right over in the square. The only way you could get a good crowd was to have a barrel of beer. We'd have the meeting, and then after the meeting they could have the beer. The only trouble was it was so hard collecting dues. I was the secretary, like. My job was to go around the thirty-six buildings in the Collinsville mill and see if I could collect dues.

The union didn't last in Collinsville; it didn't last that long. [It was] out in Collinsville because the mules went out, and the [spinning] frames came in around [1934]. They put in the frames, and they had all women running the frames. It's on the same principle as the mules, only the frames was stationary, while the mules were moving back and forth. The frames just stood there and just the spindles moved. We got warning that the thirty-six mules were going out. McKittrick [owner of a textile machinery company] was the guy that done all the demolishing. He came in with a sledge hammer and give them a whack. Yes, they didn't want us [mule spinners] to get nowhere. But the Navy Yard [mill] in Dracut got a lot of the parts of the mules [from Collinsville].

At the Navy Yard in Dracut, the J. P. Stevens mill, there was no union there at all. They tried to unionize everyone in the shop, but it didn't work out. I think they had three walkouts to unionize, and they lost. But the women was the ones that killed it each time. Yes, the women folks

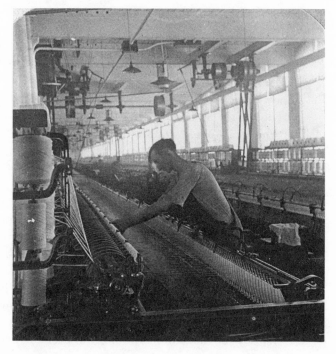

Mule spinner.
Courtesy of MATH.

were the ones that killed it each time. The last one we had out there, the different spinners and weavers [strikebreakers], they'd walk through the gate with a woman on each arm. There wasn't any throwing [things at them], but there was booing and yakking and stuff like that.

Before they took the mules out [in 1934], we got three pay cuts, 25 [percent], 25 [percent], and I think it was 15 [percent], all over about a year's time. Times were getting kind of tough. It was tough working. If you want to keep working, you'll have to take a cut. There were no other jobs available because hardly any plants were running. Nobody was buying. They couldn't buy a towel [from the Boott]. Even if they was working, they couldn't buy themselves a towel. There was no orders coming in.

I worked for the WPA and took care of forests and stuff like that for $13.50 a week. Nobody had any work. Cripes, there was thousands and thousands of people who had to go on them jobs. They had a commissary up on Jackson Street for food and stuff like that. You had to go up for that. If you knew the right person, you'd get mostly anything, and if you didn't know anybody, you'd get what they gave you. I didn't work for quite a while there one time. Then I got a job here and a job there, but I had to keep scrambling.

Some guy'd come along who had a car, and he'd say, Anything up there [in the woolen mills in Maine or in Haverhill or Maynard, Massachusetts]? I'd say, Sure. Two or three of us would go up there. You know, come in and don't know how long it'd last, might last two or three nights, might last a week, might last two weeks. You'd go up to Maynard or Maine. I worked up there maybe four or five times. It wouldn't be steady; you'd be in for two or three weeks and then be out again. Spinning.

[The plant in Haverhill] it was a big plant, an enormous plant that belonged to American Woolen. And we'd go up, and all the spinners that weren't steady [would] meet in a certain room. The boss spinner would come up to you and say, Charlie Costello, you go down to mule number sixteen or mule number four. That would be my machine. Well, I'd have to find out where number four was. So as you go along, you'd say, Hey, where's four? Where's four? You'd finally get there. Might take you five minutes; might take you ten minutes. Anyway, you'd go up and find your mule and start it. You'd never have the same mule every day. Every day you had a different mule for every night you went into work. Never got used to any of them.

Sometimes the mule would go like a bat out of hell and break all your ends and everything else. Might break parts of the mule sometimes, and what a job you'd have then, rethreading the whole goldarned thing. You'd be about fifteen or twenty minutes [at it]. Have to go through the whole rigmarole. In Collinsville and the Navy Yard, all the spinners down there'd leave their mules and come up, and they'd help you piece them up and in five minutes time you're going again. [At the end of the shift], you'd have to wipe [the mules] down every day before you left. You had to sweep up and clean off the top. You'd have to leave it clean for the next guy that came in, and he'd have to do the same thing. That job might last a week, two weeks or last two or three nights. I got a steady job out to the Navy Yard [in 1947]. It took a couple of years, because you always had to wait until somebody died or something to get a job [as a spinner].

A spinner would be out, and they'd say, somebody's sick. Why don't you come up and see? Maybe you might get a couple of days' work. So I did, and I finally got around to where he'd call me when he needed me. Somebody out sick or something like that. And finally came around there was a time when there was a steady job as a spinner. They built a new mill, and it had double mules operated by women. [I think it was] two women spinners on each mule, in pairs. They used to have to take care of both of them. One on one side and the other had to be on the other side. You had to take care of two mules, and there was 200 ends on each one. I was only there for maybe a couple of weeks. When I got the job there, I overslept. I was supposed to go in that morning, but I overslept. I didn't have no dough; couldn't hire a cab. So I asked one of the cabbies to take me up to the Navy Yard, so he took me up. I don't think he [ever] got paid. And the roving was indigo blue; it would get all over your arms.

I retired [from the Navy Yard in 1967] when I was sixty-six years old. I wouldn't have retired then only I got sick. I thought that [lung] operation would be the end of me, but I tried to keep working after I came out of the hospital. At the Navy Yard, they had that profit-sharing thing there. You had to be there, stay in, and work there for three years, steady. Each year went along, and you got a slip telling you how much you were in the profit-sharing. But you didn't get it in cash. You had to wait until you retire, and then you'd get it all at one time.

If you were there five years, ten years, after you retire, you might get a thousand dollars. I worked there steady for twenty years, and I got five hundred dollars. If I had stayed there until they closed, I would have had maybe fifteen hundred dollars. But where I was forced to retire on account of being sick, they gave me five hundred dollars. That was mandatory; if profit-sharing wasn't in there, I wouldn't get nothing. All the older people in them days, there was no profit-sharing, no pension, no nothing. Figure you were done—out. You're on your own. You get nothing.

I always was a mule spinner. Oh, I had the [ring spinning] frames for a while, but I just couldn't handle it. I don't know why, I just couldn't. I understood all about it, but it was too much. I met a lot of fine people [in the mill]. They were all one class, and cripes, there was no beating each other over the head for anything. They were all the same.

I Started from the Bottom
Like Everybody Else

Albert Parent

WEAVER, LOOM FIXER, SECOND HAND

The pinnacle of mill work for a man was to be a supervisor or second hand. Few made it there. Those who did benefited from being the right nationality, from family connections, and, in the case of Albert Parent, from hard work and wartime labor shortages.

Albert Parent's steady, diligent efforts as a weaver and loom fixer attracted the attention of his bosses. To his astonishment, they asked him one day to put on a white shirt and tie and join them as a second hand. Being a boss meant being a company man. Being a company man brought antagonism from union loom fixers and ostracism at his French Canadian social clubs.

Being a boss for a man who had "started from the bottom like everybody else," made Albert Parent tough but generous, "mean" but fair. One of his cherished memories was his first day as a mill worker in 1922, on his fourteenth birthday.

I REMEMBER the first day. I'm fourteen years old, and I weighed eighty-seven pounds. I was a little thing. I was like a tooth pick. So I'm looking for a pair of long pants. Of course, I used to wear short pants at that age. I'm looking for a pair of my father's khaki pants. I found a pair. So I got myself a big pin that they used on diapers or on horse blankets: the big, big pins. And I tried to make them about my size, the pants. Tied them up in the back here. So after I got in them, they were a little loose so I got a little tighter with the pin, and I'm wearing the long pants. 'Course I put a sweater on top. I must have had a lump in the back at work.

I'm fourteen years old that morning, and I went out looking for a job. My mother doesn't want to let me go looking for a job. I says, I'm going looking for a job. I go to the Tremont and Suffolk. To the weave shed on Suffolk Street. So I'm standing near the doorway, a bashful kid at that age, very bashful. I see a man, a red-headed guy, coming towards me. I almost ran away, but I waited.

He said, Little boy, are you looking for your dad? I says, No, I'm looking for a job. When I was fourteen, there was jobs [just] like that. There was plenty of work. [He says], You sure you're strong enough to work? I said, Bet your life I am. I says, I'm strong as a bull. I was [only] that big, you know. Come here, [he says], I want to show you something. He brings me to one of these looms, and there's a box with a stand with some bobbins in it, and on the loom there's a round battery, they call it. That's where you put the bobbins in and wind it on the end. He said, So you think you could do that? Sure! I really wanted that job. Okay, he says, you got a job.

So he came back about an hour later, and he says, You're going to have to go to city hall to get a working card. I says, I don't know where that is, but I'll go. He told me where to go, city hall. So I went there, and I came back with a card, and I gave it to him, and he says, You're all set. You're an employee. You work. I had one row of twenty or thirty looms.

We worked forty-eight hours a week and the first week, I didn't get no pay. You have to work one week without pay, and then your second week, you get your first [week's] pay. So about two weeks [after I started], I got my pay. I worked forty-eight hours, and my pay was $7.34. When I got my first pay, I was so glad to get it, when I got home I knew my father was going to come for supper at five o'clock. So I took his plate, I turned it upside down, and I put my pay under it.

So my father comes home, and I'm watching him. He goes to the sink, he washed his face and hands, and then he came and sat down. I used to sit on his left. He noticed his place turned upside down, so he just turned it over. He said, Oh. He looks on there, Albert Parent; my name was on the envelope. Why, he said, you got a pay, I see. Yes. So he opened it up, and he dumps it on his plate. There's a five and two ones, and there's thirty-four cents. He takes the thirty-four cents, and he says, Here, this is yours. I was a rich kid! Honest! Thirty-four cents; you could get anything for a nickel at the nickel lunch called Ouellettes. Piece of pie, a nickel. Hamburger, five cents. A plate of beans, five cents. A glass of milk, five cents. A plate of soup, five cents.

My father used to weave at the Lowell Weaving on Pawtucket Street. Over there they wove big, heavy canvas. Heavy, heavy. You couldn't tear it. And they had big, big looms there, and I used to go there. [While I was still in school], I used to bring my father his dinner. I used to take some bobbins that were almost empty, and I'd put them in my pocket because there was string on them and that string I used for my kite at the Aiken Street Park.

After a while, I got out of the Tremont and Suffolk, and I worked on the Boston and Maine Railroad. That's where I worked for summers, on the railroad. Heroux, the boss in the weave room at the Tremont and Suffolk, was a really good friend of my family. He always hired me for the winter. That's how I began to get interested in weaving.

I started in weaving only after I got married. It was slack everywhere. First of all, me and the wife were working in the shoe shop, and we were both laid off like that. We used to have our meals at my father's. My father says, You come here and have your meals. At night you go home and sleep. I used to live with my mother-in-law and my brother-in-law. That's when we were first married. I had a friend that I played checkers with. He says, You looking for a job, Albert? I says, Yes. He says, You come with me tomorrow morning. We'll go to the Newmarket employment office. I'm pretty sure I can get you a job.

There was a fellow hiring there. His name was Paul Whittier. He was six feet tall and as wide as a toothpick; he used to smoke a lot. Anyway, he gave me the job. He told me to come in the next morning to work in number one mill on Market Street. I got in there, and I started from the bottom like everybody else. Sweeping, cleaning looms when the warps ran out. Things like that. And in between, I used to learn how to make a [weaver's] knot and how to pass it through the reed. The weavers used to let me do it. They'd say, Come on, you do that, see? That's how I learned. So one day, the boss comes to me, and he says, Hey, would you like to learn to weave? I said, I know a little bit about it. He says, I have two or three openings on the third shift [ten to six in the morning]. Would you mind the third shift? I says, I don't care what shift as long as I have a job.

So he put me on the third shift with another fellow that was a weaver, and the other fellow showed me very good. Inside of a couple of months, I got my own set of looms. Four looms to work on, and we had to fill up our shuttle. A shuttle is what the bobbin goes into. You have to thread it. Every time the bobbin got empty in the loom, there was a feeler inside the box where the shuttle went in. And the feeler would go and [activate a stop action], and the loom would stop. That meant the bobbin was empty. You have to put in a full one, tie it up, pass it through or thread it, and then put it back in the loom. Start the loom. That was good for another ten minutes.

In the meantime, there was always one loom stopped, a broken thread, something like that. I had to go in back of the loom, and you had to be careful. Like me, I was very hairy on my hands and the [silk] thread used to wind around. If I take my hand [away] too fast, I'd break three or four of them. Then I had trouble; that's what they call a little smash. It took me awhile to get used to it.

On that kind of job, we used to make sixteen to eighteen dollars a week. That's all we made. And you had to work. There was no loafing around. There was always work to do on four looms. When you have to feed them [the bobbins] yourself, it's a lot of work. So I done that for quite a while, and then finally one day the boss asked me if I wanted to work in a special room downstairs where they got some new looms. He says, You've got four looms, here. Down there, you're going to have twenty-four. Twenty-four, and you won't work half as hard as you work on these four.

First of all, you won't even have to thread the bobbin. It goes in automatic. It was a round battery and when the bobbin got empty, there was a hammer that used to come down and push the full bobbin into the shuttle. It was doing all that while the loom was running. It would have to be done fast, a split second. Brrupt, that's it! And the loom would keep running, never stopped, and when I left the mill, the people had ninety looms. On each loom we had a flag. And every time the loom would stop for something, a broken end or something, the flag would go up and the weaver all the way down the other end [of the weave room] would say, Oh, I got one stopped down there. So he'd walk all the way down there, piece up whatever was broken there, start it up, turn around, and whoop! There's another one stopped over there.

Later on I got to know this boss. He was an Acadian, and we used to talk French with him. He says, Would you like to fix looms? I said, Oh, I don't know. I got a good job weaving. I used to make quite a bit of money weaving then. We had changed over from regular [silk] cloth to parachute cloth. That's around 1940, 1942. He says, You can make just as much as a spare fixer. I says, I won't be making less money? Because I have a budget made at home. No, no, he said. You're going to make maybe three or four dollars more a week. I says, Okay, I'll try that. Okay, he says, next Monday, buy yourself some wrenches. You'll come in as a loom fixer. You're going to be a spare loom fixer. I'll have someone with you to learn you a few tricks and all that. And that's how I started in the loom fixing business.

It didn't take very long. They put me on the section. I had ninety looms. If you see the flag up too long, it meant that the loom fixer has got to go there. There's a machine broke someplace there. Or sometimes the weaver would come and tell us herself. Say she had loom number twelve something, and it keeps banging and keeps doing something. And we go there and find the trouble and fix it and get it going. But we didn't want to keep them waiting too long because they were losing money and in those days, everybody was money-mad. Aw jeese! If they had to wait awhile, eh!

Sometimes [during the war] we had what they called a blackout. The whole mill would shut down. The women, they were going crazy; they lose the money. The union proposed to have the mill pay those people so much an hour when there's a blackout, but they didn't win. Whenever we had a big job [to fix], we could wait sometimes until the warp runs out, when there's nothing in the loom. See, it's easier to work. Sometimes you couldn't wait, you'd have to do it right away. You'd have to get under the loom, and you come out of there, you look like a rat, all grease and all. But I liked to fix looms.

So anyway, one day this boss, he says, Albert, you know what? I says, I know what, but I don't know what you're going to say. He says, I'm going to make you a boss. I says, You're crazy! Oh yes, I'm going to make you a boss. I've been looking at all your production there: weaving, fixing. All the time you've been working here, you're one hell of a good man, he says, and we want you. I says, I don't want that; I don't think I want that. Well, I'm going to make a suggestion to you, he says. I leave it up to you. Monday morning, next Monday morning, you come in on the first shift with a nice white shirt with a necktie on. You come in here, and he says, you're a boss.

I said, Hey, I don't think I'd want that. [He says,] You either be a boss on Monday or stay home. Just like that ! I knew he didn't mean it, but I didn't trust him. So well, [I says], I'll think it over. No thinking, he says. If you tell me no on Monday, don't come here no more. I start swearing in French. He says, Don't swear at me! I know people, and you're the one I want. Monday morning you come in all jazzed up, and you got a job as boss. That's how I started as a second hand.

You couldn't belong to the union if you were a boss. I belonged to the union before I was a boss. But the minute they made me a second hand, automatically I was out of the union. They cannot have a boss in the union. That's who they call a company man, a boss. I belonged to [some French Canadian social clubs] for a while, and then when I started being the big shot—they called me the big shot—that's when I stopped going over there. My overseer told me one time, he says, You know, Albert, he says, I think in the near future you have a good chance to be an overseer. An overseer. Hey, they were paying over a hundred dollars [a week] then. I was wishing I could get a job like that, but it never happened because the mills closed down after a while.

I was boss for three or four years then I started getting in trouble with the union, especially the president of the union. He worked in my department; his name was Romeo Tellier. So I fired him three, four, five times while he worked for me. I'd say, You get the hell home. I remember though one time he's not going home, and he kept on working. I'm going to get paid, he says. I says, Oh no, you don't. See this [time] card, see this here? Your time is right on here. You're all done. Yeh, yeh, yeh, he says, I'm going to hang around.

I gets in the office; I call the cruiser. They say, What's the matter? I say, I'm Mr. Parent; I'm the boss at the Newmarket mill, and I have trouble with the president of the union here. I just fired him. I told him to go home, and he doesn't want to get home. They said, We'll be there shortly. So I was waiting for them in the hallway, and finally the cruiser came. Five cops, five of them. All young guys, all big, strapping guys. Are you Mr. Parent? Yes, come with me upstairs. So there goes the [union] guy I had fired up the middle aisle, daring me. I says, I fired that guy. One of [the cops] takes off after him, a big guy. You ought to see that [union] guy get the hell out of that room, get in the toilet, and put on his other pants. Then he came out of there; Okay, I'll go home.

The trouble that I had with the union. . . . They were devils, the union. They hired him, the president of the union again; of course they had to take him. I was in number two mill, and they sent him to number one. Telephone rings, and I goes in the office. Albert, you son of a bitch, you sent me that goddamned president over here! He started raising hell with me. I said, Well, you do the same as I did. Don't take him. He says, They told me I have to. Well, I said, I wish you luck with him.

Many years later I'm working with my brother Roger at the store, and we have a truck that delivers newspapers early in the morning. Who comes in to deliver papers? Tellier. You want to see the look on him when he saw me. You work here? I says, Yes. He says, Well, you can't fire me on this job I've got. But I had fun with him; he didn't hold it against me. After the mill shut down and I'd meet him on the street, he'd say, Hi Al! He didn't call me Mr. Parent. In the mill he called me Mr. Parent, but outside he called me Albert. Oh, I had a lot of fun in there, by Jesus.

[In the mill,] I had what they called an experimenting room near the office. They had three looms in there: an old, old Draper loom, a Crompton and Knowles loom, and a Jacquard loom. A Jacquard is a loom that would weave flowers in casket cloth. And we had to know all about them. Whenever we had a [new] spare fixer, I'd bring him down there a couple of hours once in a while, and I'd say, I want to show you something. I used to be mean about it, but it helped them. I used to take a loom apart, piece by piece and line them all up. So the guy must have said to himself, That'll be easy. I'll take one piece after another. He was watching me, the way I was taking them out and after a while, I said, I'm going to leave you here two hours to put them all back. When you're all done, don't start the loom. Come and see me. I want to inspect it before. He says, Okay, I'll do that. And just before I'd leave, I'd mix [up] the goddamn things. The guy must have said, That son of a bitch!

So after a while, he'd come over and say, I'm kind of stuck. You better come and give me a couple of pointers. I done my best. I took out my book, and I says, You follow the book now. You start again over here; I'll be back in an hour. Don't sweat. Take your time; I'll be back. I come back after a while, and he had about three-quarters of it done. I checked what he had done, and I said, There's nothing wrong with this. This is perfect here. I'll be back in another hour. [Then] by God, he done it. He done the whole thing. Now, I says, this is not all. You're going to have to run that loom and make sure it is running okay. He would sweat gumballs. So that's how you learn. That's the way I learned too. But I had good bosses. Hey, they gave me a lot of breaks, and I gave a lot of my people a lot of breaks too in different things.

One time in the summertime, it's warm. My God! And in the weave room it was always damp. We had humidifiers hanging from the ceiling and throwing some of that dampness all the time over everything. You couldn't run a loom without that because the [silk] yarn would be too brittle and break. People were all wet. Ninety in there when you go in. After you get all wet, [then] it seems you feel okay. People got used to that. After you're all wet, it would keep you cool-like. Jeese, I had some guys, they'd swear in French: we're going to work in this goddamn weather! Well, I says, you have to; you'll be all right after you have a good sweat. Many of them, they went home. They'd say, The hell with this! I'll come back tomorrow if it's not so warm.

One time, it was during the war on the third shift we had a lot of women. It was a hard time to get men. I had one from Lawrence; she smelled like a drunk every night. So one night, the lunch man got off the elevator with his big truck, and he had all kinds of food on there. So I'm right in back of her when she's picking up her food. Oh, she ate like an elephant! And the last thing she says, Have you got any B. L. Tobacco? The guy said, Yes. She says, Give me a plug of that. She used to chew B. L. Tobacco!

[So] I got complaints that they showed brown spots on the cloth from a certain section of the mill. And of course, I didn't think it was my section. My overseer came over to me one day, Albert, you got a problem. You know those brown spots? They're in your department. They're in your looms. You find out who's doing that. Find out where that oil is coming from. They thought it was oil, [but I guessed what it was].

I got called in [to what was called] the "club room to go see movies." They had the cloth going over big rolls with a light in the back and every defect, we'd see it. Whoop, I see a brown spot. The roll went around a little while, whoop, another brown spot. It must be oil, I said.

The guy says, I'll tell you what we'll do. He took a razor blade and cut a square with the brown spot and took it to a room where they analyzed all that stuff and when he got through, he started to laugh. I said, What's the matter? He says, You know what that is? It's oil, I said, I'm sure. Don't be too sure; it's chewing tobacco. I says, Oh no! He says, Yes. Well, I says, I have two or three that I know chew. So the next day the office girl made me some slips that I gave to all the people working in that department to have some kind of a little box in their pocket, if they chew. Everytime they want to spit, spit in the can, close it, and put it in their pocket. You cannot spit on the floor no more; orders from the main office!

Like We Say a Big Shot in the Mill

John Falante

LOOM FIXER

As an eager and ambitious sixteen-year-old, John Falante left his widowed mother and family in Portugal and immigrated to Lowell where his sister got him a menial job in a cotton mill. An aging loom fixer who saw in John Falante the son he never had offered to teach him the trade dominated by French Canadians.

Falante always considered himself lucky, but he usually benefited from connections within the Portuguese community that got him jobs and chances to learn. His marriage took him out of the dingy, overcrowded world of boardinghouses and rented rooms for single men into the absorbing culture of the Portuguese family in Lowell.

The union loom fixers who changed their clothes before they left the mills at night were prideful men, "big shots." Although the decades he spent fixing looms in the crashing din of countless weave rooms destroyed his hearing, Falante had the pleasure of seeing his own children well educated and out of the mills.

I WAS BORN on Madeira Island, Portugal, in 1904, and in 1920 it took me seven days on a ship to get here to Boston. I never seen snow. In Madeira I used to see a little ice. When I got to Boston on January the twentieth, if I don't mistake [the date], the back of the ship was all snow. I never seen that before.

My father died, and my mother had seven kids and had no way to take care of them. I had a sister over here in Lowell, and when I get to be sixteen years old, my sister told me I could come over and get a job here and send little by little what I was making [back to my mother]. So I was lucky when I got here. I got a job in the Tremont mills. My sister used to work in the weave room. When everything shut down, she went [back] to the old country. In those days she had a few dollars, and she didn't want to spend it, so she buy a little farm, nice place, and get married.

As soon as I come to this country I was in night school, because I wanted to learn English pretty fast. I used to go to the Rialto [movie theater]. You used to pay ten cents, and those days was not talking movies. They used to show the pictures and write down [the words] on the board. I wanted to learn fast. I used to mind my own business, go to work, go to school. My ambition was to learn English as fast [as I could]. My father wanted me to go to school to learn to be an engineer. I used to love to go to school. When my father died, we couldn't afford it. When I was sixteen in the village, I says, Hey, I gotta do something. So I come over here.

I used to spin and doff filling for the weave room for four or five dollars a week. It was good money. I didn't care what kind of work as long as I had work to make a little money. In those days everybody the same. If they had a job, they would be happy. Today is different. You don't like your job, you look for another one. But those days, you got a job, you happy man. And no ask questions either. Never ask how much you're gonna get. You get a job, you happy.

When I first came over, I went in the boardinghouse because my sister didn't have no room [for me]. I didn't like it. It was pretty tough. I used to get to the table sometimes, there was not much left because everyone come first, first serve. The rooms, we didn't have one room a person. Sometimes two, three beds in one room, and two, three in bed. When I move to another boardinghouse, it was not so bad. They had two beds in one room; didn't cost me so much. I used to save a half a dollar; you save half a dollar it was something. A lady used to wait for me; I had my plate. It was nice, but the first boardinghouse was pretty tough.

The ladies that didn't go to work, they used to take care of the boardinghouse and of some babies. There was no bathroom [in the boardinghouse]. [If] I wanted to take bath, I had to go to the barber shop. They had showers there. I had to go over there and pay a quarter to take a bath. They had about three or four stalls in the barber shop and water as warm as you want. They give you new [clean] towels all the time. You're all done, put it in the basket. A lot of people had no baths and in these boardinghouses, no steam heat.

In the boardinghouse [when he first came to Lowell] they used a big bell; everybody got to get up. They give you pretty good food if you get a chance to eat. They give you steaks, pork chops, and sometimes a little Portuguese soup with cabbage leaves, especially in my boardinghouse. The Portuguese loved it; they put potatoes and a piece of meat and beans in there. At first this was a Portuguese boardinghouse.

The old people had violins, ukelele, and guitars and singing; they have their own parties with the old songs from the old country. They go from house to house at Christmas and New Year's. Now and then they used to make a little show at a nice little hall on Central Street. They had Portuguese show there. When they came across [from Portugal] they used to bring a guitar round their shoulders. They loved to play. When the mills closed down, all gone. Some they stay around, but the most went back to the old country. They didn't want to spend the few dollars that they had. They figured they had enough to go back. Some come back again, and some they don't. I figure someday I get married; my children can get something better [here]. I don't want to go back; I love this country.

So when I was nineteen, around 1924, the mills started to shut down and no job. I happened to be lucky enough to go to Newmarket, New Hampshire, and I got a job there. I used to know a fellow that worked there in the card room, and he told me there is a job in the spin room like you spin. You can come; they'll give you a job. I worked nights. Then the spinning room shut down even in Newmarket, New Hampshire. They used to ship filling [yarn] out, but they shut that down and didn't need no more filling. So I went in the weave room. When I got in the weave room I meet a fellow of my nationality, he's Portuguese and a supervisor there. He says, Learn how to weave, then stay long enough, and we'll give you a chance to learn how to fix looms.

When I went into the weave room to learn how to weave, I never forget an old man named Sinclair. He told me, he says, You look like my son. I want you to learn how to fix looms. He said he had two daughters that was two nuns and never had a son. So you're my son. He was a good, nice old man, Sinclair. He had a big tool box. He says, You take my job, and you take my tools. And I did that. I was a young fellow, nineteen years old; I says, I want to be a good fixer. He says, I want you to be a fixer like me. I am a good fixer, he says, I am seventy-five years old. I'm going to give up. I want you to take my place. Thank God for the old man. Then I learned fixing, and I was a boss fixer, and the old man, I never forget. He gave me a good start! He was like my father.

When I was in New Hampshire, all those English people [at the mill] there, they used to love to play soccer. I had a good time to play soccer. We had a big field, and we used to play soccer almost every night after work. Then when I came to Lowell the second time, I used to play. They had a Portuguese club soccer team.

I work for a few years there, and when they had a strike in Newmarket, New Hampshire, they moved [the mill] to Lowell. In New Hampshire we worked six to six. In Massachusetts, it's six to five. When

Roosevelt came in, they put it forty-eight hours. Those days if you was a loom fixer, you was like we say a big shot in the mill. Was a big guy; used to make a little more money, and everybody used to respect him because he was a loom fixer. You take the weave room. They had to like the loom fixer so the loom fixer come and fix their looms. Those days they had to work piecework. If you didn't get your machine fixed, you don't make no money. They were very nice to me.

When you're a loom fixer, we would bring nice clothes in, take the clothes off, and put on overalls. They had pockets where you put a wrench, screwdrivers, and everything. When we were all done work, they had a little sink with [cold] running water and some kind of soap or powder. Wash good, dress up, come out of work. The ladies didn't change much. They used to put on some kind of apron or dress over [their clothes]. The men they almost all of them used to change, especially in the weave room. We used to get our hands full of grease; we had to wash our hands.

Nineteen twenty-eight, 1929, 1930, very bad. No jobs, no work, nowheres. You couldn't get anything. No help from the city; you just suffer, that's all. Thank God I always had a job. I used to go from one place to another. I had bought a little Chevrolet in New Hampshire; it was pretty hard to get any place. [With no mill work] some of the Portuguese went [on] construction work. It is the only job they could get, pick and shovel. They worked [in the] open [on] streets, roads, here and there, pick and shovel. Like mosquitoes, so many people working there. Those days, 1930, 1931, 1932. People was like mosquitoes on the job 'cause everybody throw a little shovel here and there. Roosevelt put these people to work. Had to go to work, clean canals, brooks here and there, clean the streets.

I met my wife in 1932, and we got married in 1933. After work sometimes I used to go up Moody Street 'cause I used to have a room there when I come back to Lowell [after the Newmarket mill moved]. I had no family here so I had a room. There was a lot of Portuguese there on Moody Street. They had a [Portuguese] grocery store there. She used to work in the Hub Hosiery, and all the girls from there they lived downtown, and they used to go through Moody Street to go downtown. So I used to watch her, and say, Oh, that's my girl. Things happen.

I never used to shop at the Portuguese stores until I got married. In those days, I used to live in a room, and I used to buy a meal ticket for three dollars at the Laconia Restaurant. The restaurant used to sell them. If you paid cash, it was like three and half or four dollars. So the meal ticket saves you a dollar, but the restaurant liked that because it was sure we would eat there all week. They put the price on there for what we eat and then punched the tickets.

Everybody used to work those days even in 1933, 1934, 1935. I was lucky; [my wife] went to work and helped me out a little bit. When I got my children, I wanted to send them to school. The first girl is a nurse. My boy is an accountant. I figure my father always used to tell me, I don't leave you anything, but I want you to be well educated, and he tried. But after he died, he couldn't do no more. I had to come here. So I figured the same thing with my family. If I can give them school, I give.

When the [Newmarket] closed down in Lowell too, I had to go to the Wannalancit Mills. I work a few years there. I was not too satisfied. I used to help the overseer tell the fixers what to do; supervise it a little. Then Mr. Larter asked me to go and run a section there that was low. They wanted production out of this section, but he cut my pay. I was getting paid like a second hand [foreman], but [then] he cut me [to] loom fixer. I didn't like that. So I worked a few weeks. I didn't see nothing done, so I told him I was gonna quit, and I went to the United Elastic. They wanted to start up new looms, Draper looms, so they was glad to get me. I stayed in United Elastic for twelve years until the end.

I enjoyed work there. No bosses, nobody bother me. I do my work. If anything happen, they say, Boss, take care of John. You know him better than I. So I didn't have to worry about anybody [else] tell me to do this or that. I used to like my work anyway. They knew that, and I do the work well. Fixed right so the weavers could get a good running load.

They all used to love me, and I used to love them. No trouble when the weavers see me go and fix the looms, Hey, Johnny! Hey! The only thing sometimes we couldn't talk too good because the noise. We used to make signs. Sometimes the girls [clapped or banged their hands] telling me to fix the looms. Sometimes the fixers who used to work in the other section would say, Oh, the hell with them! I never had no trouble, no trouble at all.

The weave room was hot, I remember sweat, sweat, sweat, and they had these humidifers that spit water all over the place. Sick or no sick, people went to work. They got to work. Was afraid they stay out too much when they was sick, they put somebody else in your job. You're gone.

I still get trouble in my ears. I went to the doctor; I told him I can't hear too good. He ask me where I work. [When I told him], he says, Just forget it; that's from those noises all day. In the weave room especially, those looms used to bang, bang, bang, all day. Gets in your ears, but you can't take that out. The ear doctor told me ears is perfect, but can't do nothing.

I Learned It Myself
as I Went Along

Albert Cote
LOOM FIXER

An emigrant from Canada at just two weeks old, Albert Cote learned loom fixing from his father. French Canadian men controlled loom fixing in the Lowell mills, and Cote was a loyal member of the loom fixers' independent union at the Boott mills. Still, when the CIO and the loom fixers struck the mill in 1948, Cote followed a pattern common to French Canadian mill workers with large families in New England, preferring to leave the city, seek other work, and return when the strike was over.

When Cote invented a simple mechanism that helped the weavers avoid marks in the cloth from broken threads, all he got from management in return for his ingenuity was "a love tap on the back." He learned to volunteer nothing.

Fixing looms represented a clear example of the pooling of experience and mechanical ability of coworkers that facilitated production in the deteriorating mills and underlay the loyalty of the fixers to their union. The working relationship between the "good fixer" like Cote and the weavers was also essential.

In a declining industry, even good fixers lost their jobs, and Albert Cote, like many textile workers, turned to light industries and retail sales, but his expert mechanical judgment was virtually useless on an assembly line.

MY PARENTS came from Canada. Which place, I don't know. And they came to New Hampshire and settled in Dover. All my brothers and sisters were born in New Hampshire, but I was born in Canada which I only stayed there two weeks. I went to school in Dover, and all my brothers and sisters went there. My father was working in the mill. My mother didn't work. She stayed home. Once we got out of school, we all worked in the Pacific mill in Dover [a subsidiary of the Pacific Mills in Lawrence, Massachusetts]. That was about the only place you could work in. I started off as a bobbin-boy, a battery boy, a weaver, and then I went on to loom fixing.

All my brothers were weavers. When I got in the mill [in 1927], I was fifteen. You couldn't work before sixteen, so I forged my name as sixteen for the second shift. I worked to help my parents out. We were nine in the family, so that was a lot of mouths to feed.

My father was a loom fixer. When I first started I was on the floor doing a big job and when something we didn't know [came up], we used to ask the loom fixer that ran the section. And my father was one of them guys that had a section there. So that's the way I learned. And I learned as we were weaving, because you run your own loom, and you have an idea when it breaks down what's the cause of it. So right off, you tell the loom fixer what it done, and he'd go right there, right to the point and fix it right off. You put two bobbins on the loom for the loom fixer. Three bobbins would be for the smash-piecer, that's when they break a lot of ends on the warp. She would come over, and she would fix that up. And four bobbins is to take the roll of cloth off [the loom]. The roll was too big.

In the Pacific mill I played baseball. I played semipro. The mill would sponsor it, and every year from when I went to work in the Pacific mill, I'd play ball for them. At the end of the year, we'd play the Pacific Mills in Lawrence. One game at home and one game away at the end of the season. And then the mill would pay for all our trips, and then we'd go and see the Boston Red Sox which the mill paid for it. I taught Little League for twenty-three years, little League games from nine to twelve years old. I liked that very much. But you had to have patience with kids like that. So my social life was mostly tied into sports. I always did like sports.

When the Pacific mill closed down [in Dover] in 1941, then I got a job in Lowell. I went to the Boott mill and applied for a job. It just happened they had many loom fixers from New Bedford looking for jobs, and I says to myself, I'll never get a job here because them guys are more experienced than me. So the overseer called me in the office, and he asked me, What was your trade before you came here? I says, I was a loom fixer in the Pacific mill in Dover. So he asked me, You think you could learn to fix on dobbies [looms with multiple harnesses] or side-cam? I says, Well I don't know but I can learn. He says, Okay, you come in tomorrow morning with your tool box and go to work. I worked there for about seven years.

The Boott wasn't paying too much. The other mills were paying more, the woolen mills. But [if you were working], you couldn't quit. If you'd quit, they'd draft you right into the service. I had a deferment because I had a family, and I was skilled worker. That's the only way I got away from the draft. But at the end [of the war in 1945], I got a greeting from the president that I had to go pass my physical. I had three kids at the time. So I was supposed to leave a certain date that week, and then it was V-E [Victory in Europe] Day. They sent me a letter that my draft was cancelled.

I learned [loom fixing] myself as I went along. When I was stuck, I'd go and ask the other loom fixers to come over and show me how to set the loom, time it. That's the worst part of it is to get the timing. Once you get the timing of the loom, there's nothing to it, to fix it. Then after I timed the loom, I learned on the dobby head, and the first thing you know I had no trouble at all. I knew the darn thing inside out.

There was a lot of towels they were weaving down there at the Boott mill, and they had some dobbies, little dobbies that used to make letters in the middle of the cloth. Like "delivery room" or "operating room," and it weaves right in the middle of the towel. I had some little dobbies that [hadn't] been run for years, so they asked me if I could work on it and try to get it started again. So I did. I told my boss, I said, Put a man on my job, and I says, I'll see what I can do. I don't promise to fix it. They'd been stopped for years, and there might be a lot of rust in there. So what I did, I took it all apart, and I built it over again. Then I got it started. It had a skip, and I had a little trouble finding that skip, but I found it, and the darn thing, I ran it the rest of the night. Perfect.

I took a piece, I gave it to the boss, he looked at it, and, he says, It's very good. The next day [on the second shift] I came in, the darn thing was on the bum again. They worked on it [on the first shift], and they screwed it all up. So the boss came over to me again, and he says, You want to work on that again? He said, They was trying to run it today, and they couldn't do it. So I went over and looked at it. I says, Okay, I'll work on it. Put that guy back on my job, I says. I'm not going to let my job go for this. So he did. I worked eight hours on it the first day. The second day I worked about four and a half hours. Then I really got it started, and I ran it the rest of the night. So I told my boss, I said, Now I hope they don't touch it tomorrow because I want to run it another day to see if it will be all right. So they didn't run it the next day. I came in, in the afternoon, and I started it up and watched it all night. Perfect.

My section was a good section. I kept it up pretty good. No trouble. I had good weavers. I worked alone as a fixer; I had my own job. I had forty-eight to fifty looms to fix. Then when I worked at the Merrimack, they had some looms that were long, long looms. And they cut them down and made them smaller. So they set them up, and then I had the job of starting them up. Me and another guy.

Well, we finally got [those dobbies] going and after we got them going good there, I come out with a patent. Whenever the [yarn] end would break, it would make a mis-pick. You would have a full length of thread, and then you'd have a half a length with some missing, and it'll show up after you weave it in. Like a dropstitch in a cloth. So what I done, I took a piece of wood about eight inches long and made two holes on each end. I made a pedal and hooked it onto a gear lever. The weavers when they have a broken pick and they want to move the cloth back [on the loom], they'd have to use their hand to open that gear and then push it down. Well, I made it easier for them. I put a pedal there, and all they had to do was step on it, then push the gear back, get that broken pick, and start it up again. The weavers had to push this thing by hand, and naturally it gets sore in the middle of your hand after eight hours. So with this, all you had to do is just step on it, and that was it.

At the time, I told my head fixer about it. So the boss [of the weave room] he came over—his son was working [as a loom fixer] right aside of me—and he come over, he wanted me to do the same thing on his son's section. So I told my head fixer, and he says, Well, what did you tell him? I said, Well, I told him, I said, if I get the time, I'll go and do it. He [the head fixer] says, You done the right thing. So whenever I'd see the boss, I'd make believe working on my looms, so I wouldn't go over there and do it. They even asked my partner, the day fixer that worked on my job [on the first shift], to do the same thing. We done a little bit of it but not too much, so they had to ask somebody else to come over and do it. They didn't recognize it at all. I had stopped the overseer of the weave room and I told him; I showed how it worked. So all he done is give me a love tap on the back and that's about it. That's the furthest it went.

I worked there [at the Boott] for eight years, and I enjoyed it. I went on the floor [as boss fixer], and I had charge of the floor with guys which all we done is big jobs. Like if they have a cam shaft broken. And I came in, in the afternoon, and I'd go in the office and get my orders, and then I'd take my men. I'd tell them, You do this job here and you do that job. And whenever they had a big job that took them all night, I'd go around and I'd do all the small jobs to show that I did some work during the night.

I never had any problems. Sometimes you would get stuck, but you work it out. You'd have to think and start from what work you've done, and how you set it, and work your way up until you get to what the trouble is. Or you talk to one fixer, and he'll tell you, Did you try this?

Maybe try this; that might do it. That's the way we straightened out our problems because we worked together. One fixer was stuck, you'd go over and try to help him out. Or if he had a big job or he had a lot of work in his section and if our section was running good, we'd go and give him a hand. And vice versa. So that's why we got along pretty good.

When I was a loom fixer, we didn't belong in the CIO. We was on our own. We had our union, the Loom Fixers' Union, but they still had the CIO in there. The [fixers'] union was organized in the Boott mill, before I got in there [in 1941]. I helped to organize the CIO in the Boott mill, which we couldn't get in on account of we had our own union. But later on, we did have to get into that CIO. The supervisors didn't like it; you weren't supposed to try to organize the people in the mill; you were supposed to do it outside the mill. But they couldn't fire you or they would have. They'd have them up to the [National Labor] Relations Board right off. They couldn't fire you, but they'd make it hard for you because the mill didn't want no union in them days.

Once we had the union in there, and then we automatically got a raise right off the bat. Before, they wouldn't give us a raise; we had no union or nothing. And the loom fixers, we went on strike once for a raise, and still we didn't get it. So the loom fixers went on strike, and then the whole mill went on strike a second time [in 1948]. I think that strike was for more money.

[During the 1948 strike], I worked in Biddeford, Maine. My brother was working in the weave room, so I thought I'd go down [east] and see if they were hiring, and they hired me right off. I had a car to get there, [and] I stayed with him probably six months. After I heard the Boott mill settled, I came back and I went to my job. Then I worked a year or two in the Wood mill in Lawrence as a [woolen] weaver. Then from there, we got laid off. From there I got a job in the Merrimack mill.

If you don't get along with your weavers, you're going to have a hard time. Which happened to a few loom fixers and weavers too. You go there, and the weaver says, There's something wrong with that loom. You look at it, and you don't do nothing about it. You start it [back] up and go away and that would aggravate the weaver that you didn't fix it. [The weaver] still had to put two bobbins on the loom, which the loom fixer didn't like. He kept going back to this loom. But me, when I had a job on a loom, I would stay on that loom. If I didn't have much work to do, I would stay on that loom for about fifteen or twenty minutes. Look at it run, and if it's all right, I'd go away and do my other jobs, then I'd come back to it. You've got to find it, what causes the trouble.

I had one [young] guy that came down from the Lowell Textile Institute. He was surveying the weave room for a start, so the boss sent him over to me. He introduced himself, and I did myself. And then he asked about different things, about how to set the loom. The way it was in the book [at the institute], it would say, you set this part here, like a sweep, you set it eight inches. Which lots of time, an old loom, you can't set it at eight inches. You've got to set it at nine or nine and a half. So he wanted to know why you had to set that sweep so many inches more than what it said in the book. So I showed him why.

I said, Now, I'm going to set that sweep at eight inches as it says in the book, and you'll see what's going to happen. So I set it at eight inches, then I started the loom. The sweep's what pushes the shuttle from one end to the other, so when I started the loom, the sweep came and only pushed the shuttle half way across the cloth and the loom stopped right there. It just banged. I says, That's the reason why we got to set it because there are a lot of parts in there that are worn out and you've got to set it according to each loom and the way it was going to run.

When a part is worn out, you've got to move whatever it is up a little closer. But if the part would break, we had to put in a new part. Then you've got to adjust all that side all over again, according to that new part. But everything he had in the book, it was all right for a brand new loom. The guy was with me for eight hours. Well, not exactly eight hours. He'd quit about an hour before quitting time. That was on the second shift. I used to start at one-thirty to ten, and we had a half hour for lunch. So he stayed with me for seven hours. And then he told me, he says, You know, he says, I learned more with you than I did in the book.

If a guy would retire or something, and the overseer would think you'd make a good supervisor, he'd go over and talk to you and ask you if you'd be willing to take it. That was the only way you got the supervisor's job. What [the supervisor] had to do, when they came in, in the afternoon, he'd have to check and see that all the people was in. And if there's somebody was out sick, well, he's got to report it to the office, and the office would have some spare [hands], so they'd let them go to work. In them days, you go over there every day, if you're looking for a job. You go in every day, and if they need somebody, they take you from the floor and put you on the job. Today they'll call you up and tell you to come in a certain day. But them days, you had to be there to get the job.

I worked in the Merrimack mill and then that closed down [in 1956], and I worked in Uxbridge [Massachusetts] as a loom fixer and a weaver.

I didn't stay there too long. Then I went and I worked in a hardware store. I didn't care too much for [it]. At first I liked it, but [after a while] I was running the whole thing by myself. He was always gone. And I didn't like to work Saturdays. But I worked there eight years, and then he sold out the business. From there, I went one year in a hardware distributor plant in Nashua [New Hampshire]. It wasn't paying much, so I went to work for a company that built automatic pin-setting machines for bowling alleys. I worked there a year. I got laid off, and then I went to work for an electrical company that went bankrupt.

So from there I went to the Wood mill [in Lawrence], and worked [there] for Honeywell eleven years. I was mechanical inclined, so they put you on the table, and they give you some parts to put together. And by doing that, then you learn something else. The first thing you know, you're building computers. You were putting the parts in, but you wouldn't run them. You would send them, after it's all built, to another department, and they will adjust all the parts and see if the parts were good. If they were no good, they'd take them out and replace them. Then they'd run them for three or four days, and if they had no trouble in three or four days, then they'd send it to another department, and [if there was trouble] they'd pinpoint what was causing trouble. That machine will find it. So that's the way it went.

That's where I retired from [in 1975]. The Wood mill in Lawrence. I got a pension from there. You adjusted yourself to the closings and layoffs as it comes along. Well, they had to lay you off when it's slack-time. Last one in, first one out. They go by seniority. Mostly all the mills I worked in are all shut down today. But every place I worked, I got along very good. I learned fast and no trouble.

We had overalls with pockets where you can put your wrenches, your screwdriver, your hammer in your back pocket, and all your small wrenches in another pocket. You had to buy your own tools, your own clothes, yes, and your shoes. You had to buy everything. Nothing they give you. The mill never give you nothing. We never had vacation [time] in the mill, no. I had vacation when I was all done. In the Merrimack, we started having a week's vacation. One week a year, but it took awhile before we had that. When I left Honeywell, I had two weeks. I was going on three weeks the following year, but I retired before [that]. But I really enjoyed working in the mills. I loved it. I would go, if I could work today, I would go right back in the mill again to loom fixing.

Rigging, That's the Heavy Work

Henry Pestana
WARP RIGGER

Following family and friends to the Portuguese community in Lowell, Henry Pestana's parents found work immediately. When Pestana was old enough to work, he went to the Newmarket mills where his mother had once spooled and where other Portuguese, like John Falante, were employed.

As a filling hand, Pestana learned to pace himself to the requirements of his coworkers and to the pressures of his own piecework. He figured out shortcuts and as a battery hand watched the working looms and tipped off the overburdened weavers when to take off the cloth. Managers depended on this efficient cooperation among workers, but they took it for granted.

Working in the drawing-in room deepened Pestana's appreciation of the process of production. His job as a warp rigger was to place beams wound with warp threads into the backs of empty looms and draw the warp through the harnesses. His partner ran an automatic knot-tying machine, technology that largely eliminated the relatively well-paid work of drawing-in girls.

Mill operations at the Newmarket impressed Pestana. He was part of a huge, well-coordinated machine that possessed productive powers that seemed greater than the combined efforts of the individual employees. He also witnessed the reaction of those efficient managers to threats of unionization in the 1930s.

BOTH PARENTS and their families all originated in the Madeira Islands, in the capital city of Funchel, over in the old country, about five hundred miles from Lisbon, Portugal. My parents had just got married, and they came here in 1910 on their honeymoon. My mother was only sixteen. They came here with the idea of staying, because he had an older brother and his mother was here already. They lived near the Tremont and Suffolk mills. My father was an insurance agent for the Metropolitan Life Insurance Company for over ten years. But my mother was working across the street where the mills were.

I was born in 1912. My grandmother took care of me. And just as soon as I was old enough to get into the kindergarten at the Green School, about four years old, she took care of me after school. Then in 1918 we moved out to Tewksbury. At one point, probably in 1911, my mother worked for a short time in New Hampshire at the Newmarket mills. She used to tell me she would cross the street, set up her spooling machine, and get it all going. Then go home and do her washing, come back, and keep an eye on the spooling yarn. Once my father had a good job, she quit working in the mills.

My father never worked in the mills. He was the only one at that time that insured the Portuguese people in Lowell. And where he spoke four or five different languages, he even had the Italians and the French insured. When I was only about six or seven, I used to go with him especially towards Christmastime. I used to pass out the calendars from the insurance company to the people. He always bragged that I was going to be the next insurance agent.

My father picked up English while he was a cook on an English ship, and he had been all over, in Africa and all over. That's when he picked up all his different languages. There was a Chinese laundry in Lowell. Once I went with him. [That's where] he had his stiff collars cleaned. I got a kick out of him talking to the Chinese fellow there. I don't know how he spoke it, but he did make himself known to them. My mother spoke broken English. It was funny. We wound up with eight children in the family. My mother would speak to us in Portuguese, and we would answer in English. Until the youngest ones; they would speak English all the time.

Once my father got out of the insurance business, he took a fling at the restaurant business. He started a small lunch place, and they called it Bon Ami Lunch because it was in the French district. He stayed there for some time, then evidently he didn't make out too good. He moved and catered to the Portuguese and Irish; this time it was Pestana's Lunch. From there he broke away from Lowell and started to work in New York for a while, but the family stayed here. So then I wound up getting old enough to work, so I was working on a farm in Tewksbury picking rhubarb till [1928 when] I was sixteen years old. From there I went up to the Newmarket mills in Lowell.

I started right from the beginning, scrubbing floors on Saturdays and Sunday afternoons. Finally in 1935 I got in the weave room as a filling hand, that's delivering all the filling yarn for the top floor in the mill. That top floor had three hundred looms. I used to fill what they called pin boards that held the [silk] yarn for the weavers. I used to keep enough yarn there, so they wouldn't run out of yarn and keep the looms running. It was a system that eventually you got down to a fine point so you could control it and save time for yourself. If you didn't, you'd have problems.

You'd have to start with the first loom. These pin boards had twenty-four bobbins on them, and they'd run for eight hours for the whole pin board. So naturally, you don't give the weavers a pin board the first five minutes that you're in there. You wait and kind of stagger them around and help the weavers keep [the looms] going. Then you'd go down the line nice and slow, systematically, until you had gone through the whole three hundred [looms]. You'd take a half [full] pin board out of there and give them a full one and take the half pin board and piece it up and make a full pin board for the next weaver. This was all different kinds of yarn, so you had to watch what you were doing. The pin boards were marked with tickets and came down from the quilling room. I had two sisters working there in the quilling room where they fill those bobbins.

From there I got into being a battery hand, but I got out of that job after about a year and a half. It was too much for me. Then I got into the drawing-in department. I would bring up these big warps to put on the back of the looms when they ran out. These looms were running three shifts every day until Saturday. Practically every shift would be turning out eighty yards of cloth. These girls had to take these rolls of cloth off the looms, [first] stop the machine, take it off, and start another eighty yards. And the way they could determine when the eighty yards of cloth was done, there was brown chalk marks on the back of the warp, and they would watch for them. If they forgot and the marks went through the loom, they would have to stop the loom and pull all that cloth back to that mark before they cut the eighty yards of cloth. With forty-two looms, they had to keep watching them all. The battery hand would kind of tip them off when the end of the eighty yards was coming up.

The job I had was to take the warp off when the machine was stopped and the warp was entirely finished. I'd go up in there and strip off that empty warp spool [beam]. I would put a big clamp on there. These looms had seven, eight, nine thousand warp ends, and you had to put a clamp on there so the ends wouldn't be all over each other. The wooden clamp was about five feet long with felt on it. You would put it on the yarn ends, right in the groove all even and tie it up, before you dismantled the [empty] warp [spool]. Then you would strip off the back ends, cut them, throw them to one side, put the full warp spool in, take the paper off that big spool, take all the ends, and put on another clamp to correspond with the one that was running out.

Then the fella who was running the [automatic] knot-tying machine would come in with the machine and brush out [pull out] two thousand ends at a time and put them on the clamp in the knotting machine. It was something new at the time. The mill couldn't buy them; they used to rent them out of the Barber-Coleman outfit in Rhode Island. They had a meter on the machine. As much work as they got out of the machine, they paid accordingly for the use of the machine. Once the mill got really going good, they bought them.

You got in there, and we'd be punching the clock. And you'd go to the department, and I'd get my work. You would put one warp up in the weave room, and you'd go back down with the empty beam. They'd take it into the slasher room where they made up the warps, and you'd go for another job. You'd average probably four or five jobs in eight hours. This entails finding the warp that's laying on the floor on the stack pile, picking it up, getting it on the truck, taking it on the elevator, and going up to your destination in the weave room.

You go in there, and [maybe] it happened to be loom three hundred. You'd go to that loom, and you stripped it, and you'd put that one in. And then you'd go to the partner: you worked in partners. One ran the machine that tied in the warps, and the other was a rigger. That's how I started rigging. That's the heavy work, putting in the warps. You'd give him the ticket and say, There's your next job. So once he got that tied, he'd move to his next job, and I'd have to go where he finished and take all his work off the clamp, the whole row of nine thousand knots, and roll the warp back nice and slowly to take up the slack. There'd be slack there where you tied the ends up. Then I'd get in front, and I'd pull it easy and get all those knots coming through [the heddles and the harnesses in the loom]. And you'd have to take it easy, 'cause if you were too rough, sometimes some of those knots might let go [and come untied], then you'd have a lot of loose or broken ends.

Once you get it all done and if there was some ends broken, the second hand would call out the smash-piecer, and she'd check the warp before the weaver got a hold of it. The smash-piecer would check for any broken ends, and the loom fixer would check the shuttles to see if they were in operating condition, not worn out or anything. It wouldn't take much to throw them off 'cause the machine would run so fast. If the picker-stick [which propelled the shuttle] was a fraction out of the way, it would bounce the shuttle off. If there was any splinter [on the shuttle], it would tear hundreds or thousands of ends off. The machine would be stopped all day trying to repair it.

I'd seen where the picker-stick would slap those shuttles back and forth, especially on the outside row facing Market Street. It would shoot across the cloth and through the window and out into the street which was four floors down. So they had to put screens near the bottom of the glass to make sure that no one came after them. Those shuttle had steel points on them, and they're going and they're pretty heavy. They were made of a hard mahogany wood, so they could take an awful lot of punishment.

The warps would sometimes run four or five days for three shifts before they would run out. These warps were equipped with tickets, one ticket for every eighty yards on the spool. So when that [eighty yards] came off, the ticket would go with that cloth. And the next ticket would come up, and they knew accordingly how much more cloth they had left on [the spool]. By the time I got out of that department, they had taken the metal flanges off the side of the spool so that they would be two or three inches wider for two or three more days of weaving on there.

The warp beams averaged about three hundred pounds, and you were handling it by yourself. You'd have a little two-wheeled dolly that bounced. You would get that under the flange and catch it under on the dolly and grab the spindle on the other side and tip it up. After you got used to it, it was nothing. You'd push it to the elevator and go upstairs. This is all timed, because you're getting paid by what you put out. Eventually they kept changing the sides on the beams until they weighed four hundred pounds. You could feel the pressure in your ears when you picked one off of the floor. If you didn't feel just right, you didn't feel like picking one off of the floor, it was so heavy. Of course you're only picking one end, but there was still four hundred pounds, and it had to balance on a truck that had a little groove in it. The flange would catch on the groove, and you'd get on the other side and rush it up to the weave room. You'd get it set up for the knotter that would tie it in.

The looms would run continuously till they ran out of [warp] yarn, then they'd send the tickets down. They got pretty good at this. The office had a tube system running all the way down to our department, and they would take down the number of the loom, the type of cloth it was making, and instructions to replace with another warp corresponding to the same thing. It would shoot the message down the tube to the warp room just like a department store. The warp room boss would put it on a schedule. As we needed work, we would take the jobs off that schedule. Nobody got ahead of each other in the weave room. If your loom ran out first, you had first chance to get a warp in there. So everybody had an even break.

It got so efficient there, it was amazing. I don't know why the mill stopped. I never saw a mill that had such efficiency running. If you had a loom that was running and some of the ends broke, the weaver had no time to repair it. She had forty-two looms to watch. They had a little arm on each loom with little squares of colors on it, red, green, yellow, and black. If you wanted a smash-piecer to tie weaver's knots on the broken ends and run them through the heddles and the harnesses and put them right, you turned that signal up. The foreman or the second hand in the office had a glass window where he could see the signal and he would send a smash-piecer. If it was something else mechanical on the loom like a picker-stick knocking the shuttle back and forth, and it wasn't operating right, we would put up another color to call for a loom fixer. The second hand would send a loom fixer.

In the Newmarket, there were a lot of French. Then you had the Polish working there and the Portuguese and Greek people. There were some English, but they weren't regular employees; they were higher-ups. They worked in the office. The people out for production were the French. The French wound up as loom fixers; a lot were related: cousins, fathers, and sons working in there. The Greek people were up in the weave room, and the Portuguese were weavers. Sometimes the battery hands and the weavers would have difficulty talking [to each other]. Eventually they all got to talk good English to a certain extent. You had some Polish fixers too, and some Portuguese second hands.

The mill had a staggered set-up on shifts for our department. Everybody wanted to work the first shift, so they'd split it up so you alternated and worked all three shifts for a little more pay. They done that so that they wouldn't have to pay us for working nights. That's how they got around that. I would work one month on first shift, the second month on second shift, and the third month on third shift. It was amazing how the year would go by so fast, 'cause the next time you were come back to first shift, it was spring, and the last time you'd been working there on first shift, it was winter.

Each loom had a picker clock on it with three rows of numbers across it. The weaver, she would turn it to the first shift and it would take one thousand picks [strokes of the shuttle] to move it one number. They had a back-up system so that if any bad cloth went through to the cloth room [where it was inspected], they could trace it back to who did it. If there was too much of that going on, the boss would take that cloth up to the weave room under fluorescent lighting. They'd call the weaver over while someone was watching her machine, and they'd show the bad cloth. Lots of times, I'd see the woman come back crying. They'd not threatened them but give them a pep talk about the job that wasn't good, and if they kept doing that, they'd be out in the street. That's how they kept bad cloth under control. The weaver would be under pressure all the time. She couldn't turn out bad cloth, because it would reflect back on her.

If you wanted to be a loom fixer in the mill, you wound up oiling the machinery and cleaning the machines, taking the lint off the back of the loom, and you got familiar with the machinery. That way you could step up into another job if there was a vacancy for a fixer. The same with the battery hand. She would be a battery hand and got used to working with the machinery. If she was real interested in being a weaver, sometimes she'd help the weaver run the machines. Then if the weaver was out sick or something or quit the job, she could step in and take that job. It could happen in six months. Then the mill kept changing the gears on the loom. After the women had forty-two machines, they started changing the gears and speeding it up. It was so fast that some of the women were afraid to start it up unless they had been around and were acquainted with the machinery.

There was one funny thing about this company that was so efficient. Once they got wind of the union marching out in the streets and trying to pass out fliers to the weavers to have them join the union, they would always be one step ahead of the union. At the end of the week, you'd notice on the bulletin board, there would be a notice that the mill decided to give us a 5 percent raise, exactly what the union was peddling out in the streets. So the weavers had no need of joining the union unless the union promised more. So the mill kept going ahead of the union that way, and they kept the union out. The only way you could force a union in was over the help's grievances. The mill couldn't offset the grievances. If the work load was too heavy or the conditions weren't right, the union tried to step in and say, We will correct grievances. That's when the company said, If you put a union in here we will close up the shop. That's exactly what they done.

By the time the union was ready to step in, the weave room was [temporarily] shut down. That was about 1940. I was in the service then, and my job was promised when I came back out. [But when he got out] they had eliminated my job [as a warp rigger], and they had tied it into a loom fixer's job. So the loom fixer was doing two jobs under the patriotic system, they called it, during the war when they were short of help. You're going to help the country win the war; do that job too. We can't get the help. What happened when we come back, the servicemen did not have their jobs! They offered you a job that was not paying as much, and that's when I decided to leave that place, and I didn't go back.

Working in the weave room did teach me a lot about efficiency, how to work among machines and things, 'cause I wound up working places where you had to have efficiency. Where production was tops, you had to produce. Today, people have jobs but they don't really produce. They know things, but when it comes to producing production, I don't see how they do it. Electronics and all that has a different way of producing what you don't see; it isn't visible like it is when you're producing cloth. One of my last jobs I wound up doing was where we worked on presses and made hockey pucks, gaskets for cars and things. That was all production. I dropped out of that work, and I got into the Tewksbury school system. I swept out and straightened out the classrooms after the children left the school. Then the summertime you straightened out the school, painted classrooms, and changed furniture. It was a very easy job compared to working in production.

We Never Thought the Mills Would Close

Arthur Morrissette

LOOM FIXER

The American-born son of Quebec immigrants, Arthur Morrissette grew up immersed in the French community of Lowell, its neighborhoods, schools, churches, vacations in Canada with relatives, and jobs in the mills. His fast rise through the ranks of battery-boy, weaver, change-over man to loom fixer could not happen quickly enough for him. But his work as a fixer never paid him enough to escape the need to work two jobs.

When labor troubles disrupted work at the Boott mill in the late 1930s, Morrissette decided to go on the road in search of work to support his growing family. As all mill workers knew, woolen companies paid better than cotton, and when World War II created demand for khaki cloth, Morrissette went to work in Lawrence. After the war, he refused to return to the cotton mills. Instead, he worked in an elastic mill and quickly learned that the harder the weaving process was on the looms—and elastic was the hardest—the tougher the fixer's work. Promoted to assistant foreman, he was warned to keep his distance from the other mill workers, but he remembered clearly the death of a common laborer.

MY FATHER came to the States at about four years old, and my mother was about fourteen years old when she came to Lowell to earn a living. She stayed with her two sisters. I graduated from the St. Louis grammar school in 1927 when I was fourteen. I went to high school for a year, and I finished my school at the Lowell Textile Institute for three years. I was working at the shoe shop at the same time, but I was going to [the textile] school at night.

They were all French on my street. I don't think we had an Irish family. We used to fight the Irish with rocks, throwing rocks at one another. In the summers my family used to go up [to Quebec] to the farmland where my mother came from. My mother's name was Paquette, and that's all there was in St. Elfeche. All Paquettes mostly. Let me tell you we had parties. We used to stay there a whole week and go around from one to the other. Boy, parties every night! That was their week's vacation, my mother, my father. They always talked about it; all their lives they talked about the times when they used to go to Canada. And after I got married, we went with the kids.

There was a man, an overseer by the name of Mr. Deprey, who was living on my street, and I used to go out with his son. So one day he says, Why don't you come and work in the [Boott] mill? Gee, I said, what kind of money can I earn? Well, he says, I'll push you up. Don't worry about it. You have mechanical experience. So I started as battery-boy for three or four months. From there, I went to a weaver for another four or five months. And then a change-over man. I used to be pretty husky, pretty strong. [You had to be] in order to be a change-over man because the [warp beams] used to come down with the harnesses on them and you had to lift it up alone [and put it into the loom] and didn't have no help. All the work was done alone by one man, and that's how I learned how to be a loom fixer.

I think I had about forty-eight batteries to keep going [when he was a battery boy]. I didn't mind that; I was fast anyway. I had time off more or less to go sit on the window sill and look outside from the third floor. As long as you kept your batteries full, the boss never mentioned it, never gave you heck or anything. You had so many bobbins to put in there, and the bobbin-boy he used to bring the bobbins to you in a cart. Mostly it was all [girls], battery girls, but there was a few young fellows. Girls were much faster than men for filling the batteries. Then I went on to weaving which there was a lot of women weaving in those day. A lot of Polish, Greek, a lot of French that was working in the Boott mills in those days. There weren't too many Irish. I don't think they liked to work in the weave room.

Mr. Deprey was the overseer in my area and naturally every time he'd come by, he'd stop to talk to me, How you doing? and so forth. And I used to say, When the heck am I going to get on fixing? So I used to get on to him all the time every time I met him. I used to say, Hey, I'm due, ain't I? Not yet, he says, you've got to learn a little more. You've got to learn a little more. Finally I went on change-over. I used to love that because [that's how] I learned to fix looms, and I was mechanically inclined.

Any machine that runs for twenty-four hours a day is bound to give up. There was always [wooden] picker-sticks that was breaking up. They wear out the picker-sticks, things wear down, the gears wear down, and they get out of line. The operators used to come down, used to hail you, Well, I've got a job. And naturally you had to go. Well, I'm sorry there's two ahead of you. So we had to let the job go and done the small job which was four or five minutes maybe. Most of the girls, the weavers, were paid on piecework. The fixers weren't paid on piecework, but they had to keep those machines running. So naturally if they had two or three of them stopped for three or four hours a day, they were losing money and that was a big thing. So they used to hail you, Come on, come on; it's my turn, it's my turn.

Then I met a young man by the name of Wilfred Fortier, and he showed me. He taught me everything he knew, and he was one of the best fixers in the Boott mills in those days. And Arthur Paquin. Those were the two best fixers in the Boott mills. I was a little younger than they were, probably ten years younger, and they used to take me under their wings. So I was about the youngest loom fixer in Lowell at that time. We had a union, and I remember I got a prize for being the youngest loom fixer. I got a bottle of gin. Imagine a bottle of gin at the age of twenty-two! I came home, and I gave it to my father. My father said, Eck! It didn't taste good at all. I think he threw it away. It was cheap gin.

My father was a knitter at the Hub Hosiery. I have beautiful memories of my father working in the Hub Hosiery. We didn't need no pass to get into the mill. I used to bring his dinner, a hot dinner, mind you, in a special pail that had three compartments in it. I was about eleven years old at the time. That was during school lunch hour. We had an hour off from school; it kept you going. The parents in those days, you could not say no to your parents. So I used to bring him his dinner, not all the time, two or three days a week anyway.

My father used to pay me. I was the only boy [in the family] so we used to go to the B. F. Keith's [movie theater] on Saturdays. Saturday afternoon, stop at the five and dime for ten cents' worth of candy and ten cents to go in the "niggers' heaven" up there and ten cents [extra] for me. So for thirty cents, we had a big afternoon. Niggers' heaven was the third floor, the third balcony in the B. F. Keith, and it was very, very steep, and they used to call it niggers' heaven. I don't know why. I don't think it's a very nice word to say.

I was the only boy because I have five sisters. The youngest one worked in the shoe shop. My sister Theresa used to be a spinner [at the Boott]. They always kept the spinning room on the third and fourth floors. You try to keep the weave room on the first and second floor on account of the vibration, the vibration of the mill [from the working looms]. If they had the weave room too high, the mill would suffer by it. We accepted the conditions in the mill as part of our life. The humidity in there, the oily floors, and your hands always full of oil. We got a lot of boils on our necks from that oil.

In 1936, the entire first floor of the Boott mill was flooded. The work stopped for a whole week. They had the fixers carry warps which weighed four or five hundred pounds, no elevators. A warp is a big beam with warp threads all around it. There's probably thousands of thread, and they probably weigh three or four hundred pounds a piece. You put the warp which is all threaded on the looms. They wanted to save these warps, but they were all soaked in that muck [from the flood]. I remember Mr. Deprey asking me to come and work. I said, Oh no, I'm not feeling good. I really didn't want to work in that muck. It was dangerous, typhoid and diptheria. You had to be injected for it. I was working on the second floor, and the flood did not reach the second floor. That's why I did not want to go down there on the first floor and lift those heavy beams. All the muck from the water goes into the loom and makes the loom very, very rusty, and they all had to be cleaned. This was very heavy work. They had to hire people to clean them all up, and that was quite an ordeal.

I had beautiful relations with the people in the mill. I used to treat them right for one thing, and I wasn't afraid to work. I got so I knew Mr. Flather, who's the owner of the [Boott] mill, pretty well. Some sections were much, much harder to work with than other sections. If the man, your partner, on the other shift in the same section as you was a decent man, a decent loom fixer, he would take care of his looms as well as the other guy. I was always pretty lucky. I always had a good loom fixer on the opposite shift. I think it was a Mr. Martin who was on the opposite shift from myself, and he was a quick fixer. I considered myself a pretty good fixer. So between the two of us, we had a section that was very, very well taken care of. We used to strip one loom and overhaul it, one after the other, and the first thing you know we had them all overhauled. We used to take our time and keep the looms in good condition, so that the weavers were all very happy working in our section.

Then I got married in 1936. We used to go to the Lakeview Ballroom on Saturday nights. I never had a steady girlfriend until I was almost twenty years of age. Never cared for girls too much. I used to love to go to the YMCA, and I used to love playing ball and sports. And as far as spending money, we didn't hardly have any money to spend. We all had a lot of good friends, and we were playing cards at nights, and had a lot of sports going, and we didn't hardly spend any money at all.

Then I bought a car in 1935, an Essex, an oil burner more or less, and naturally I was the beau around that area. Nobody had a car. I was saving my money, and I finally got a car. Of course I had to ask Mr. Arsenault everytime I took his daughter out. In those days, you had to ask; it was difficult to get a girl to go riding with you. Finally I got married. I was working in the mill steady. I had a day job up there, but money was hard to get. I sold the car because the babies were coming in. So I asked them to go on the second shift for a while, so I could get a job in the morning. Around 1938 I worked at Brockleman's on the meat counter getting one dollar an hour dishing out hamburger two pounds for twenty-five cents. I never cared to be an officer in the loom fixer's union, because I was too busy. I always had two jobs, and in the early sixties, a friend of mine and I, we bought an old building and made eight apartments out of it. I was working nights and Saturdays. The only day that no one worked was Sunday. All my life I never worked on Sunday. It was for the family.

I worked at Brockleman's, and then I went on my own. I made myself a wallpaper table. A table to wallpaper. So I used to wallpaper in the morning, go home, take a nap, half an hour to an hour, and go to work [at one-thirty], come home at eleven o'clock at night. That was the life. I didn't have a chance to see my family for a couple of years. That was rough. Then there was a big strike in the Boott mill. I couldn't afford to stay out of work; my wife was pregnant. So a fellow by the name of Martin, I forgot his first name, a good-looking man, a little older than I was, but not much, he says, Arthur, would you like to come with me? I'll get you a job someplace. I know somebody in Rhode Island, in Connecticut. He didn't have a car. I still had my Essex, and we took off and finally landed in Paterson, New Jersey.

There we met a Mr. Brown, and he says, I only need one fixer. Martin says, Well, if you can't hire two fixers, you can't get one either. Oh well, he says, I'll take care of that. So he called up another mill, and he says, Okay, I'll toss up a half of a dollar here; whoever wins comes with me, whoever loses goes with this other company. So I lost. I lost the toss, and I went with this other company. It was all silk [in Paterson]. I had never worked with silk. And the fixer in those places was in charge of the [whole] room on the second shift. We were in charge of the weavers, and the battery hand workers, bobbin-boys, whatever. And I had a hard time because these people didn't want to listen to me at all. I had to fix their looms and try to take care of them, and I know they used to sneak out. I said to myself, it's only temporary anyway, so I didn't give a darn. So as soon I learned that the Boott settled the strike, I came right back to Lowell. I used to come back almost every weekend in that Essex forty-five miles per hour, right down to the floor.

We were on strike three or four times in the Boott mill in the space of four or five years I guess. They were hard people to bargain with, the Boott mills. Instead of getting $23 a week, when we won the strike we went up to $27. Finally in 1942 I went to work, and there was another strike, and I left them. I went to work in Lawrence in the woolen mills. They were all different looms, but I learned very fast. I was making $59 a week in the old Pacific Mills in Lawrence. I had to travel back and forth, but still the money was like two to one. We were weaving the big heavy khaki wool for the overcoats, and those looms were taking a licking.

After three years, when the war was over, the khaki was over too. So they had to lay off somebody. I was one of the fellows that was laid off. So I came back to Lowell to work, and I went to work in the United Elastic which was altogether different again. So from cotton to silk, silk to woolen, and woolen to elastic, and I think the elastic was the worst of them all. There was always a big, big strain on the loom. The fixer had to work twice, three, and four times harder than he did in the cotton. It was the same kind of loom that they were using in the Boott, dobbies. I worked on dobbies most of my life, so they were nothing to me. I knew them all by heart.

When I worked at United Elastic, I became an assistant foreman; I worked there for about ten years beginning in the late 1950s. There was this laborer in the United Elastic, a sweeper or something, and he was eating his lunch one evening. I was on the second shift. The assistant foreman had to work two weeks in the morning and then two weeks in the afternoon. They didn't want you to be too friendly with the help. This gentleman was eating his lunch, and he died right there eating his lunch with a mouth full of food. I had one of the loom fixers give him first aid [for a heart attack] while I went down and called an ambulance. I had to call the superintendent of the mill, and the medical examiner came over, and he made me shut the section down. Naturally the superintendent was not too happy about that when he came in. Two weave rooms shut down on account of this man dying. I'll never forget the way these undertakers—they just put him in a burlap bag and carried him out. They figured he's dead, that's it.

United Elastic was one of the last mills to operate in Lowell. By that time the Boott mill had stopped; the Merrimack was stopped; the silk mill was stopped then too. Then I got another job down at Raytheon which I did not like at all. I left that place after two years or so of working. Oh it was awful. I didn't care for that at all, working on the assembly line. Then I worked for AVCO [Corporation] for ten years as general maintenance, and that was about the nicest job that I ever had in my life. I really loved to get up in the morning and go to work. That's where I retired from in 1974. We never thought the mills would close. I thought I was going to have a job in the mills for the rest of my life.

Just Walking Up and Down, Trying to Keep Those Looms Going All Day Long Is a Job

Joseph Golas

WEAVER, SMASH-PIECER, FIXER

Joseph Golas knew little of the Poland where his parents were born except for powerful stories about Russian oppression. His father and mother became part of the small Polish community of cotton mill workers in a rural western Massachusetts town. The Polish people cooked much as their peasant families had done, making barrels of sauerkraut in the old communal way and storing away bushels of potatoes. Like their language, religion, and ethnic festivals from rural Poland, food rituals helped sustain the community's Polish identity.

In 1928 the mill closed its doors. The Golas family went along when the Newmarket mills in New Hampshire moved to Lowell to consolidate its operations in 1930. The depression years of the early 1930s brought lagging orders for goods, periodic layoffs, and low wages. Golas's main worry was a job. The mills required all those seeking work to report every morning whether or not there was work. It was clear that you had to know someone inside to get noticed, but Golas detested the only Polish boss in the mill.

In 1936 Golas began to weave rayon at the Wannalancit. He had respect for the mill owner. He appreciated a boss who knew all the operations and could perform them as well. He liked the generosity of a genuine paternalist who seemed to care about the welfare of the mill workers. But ask him for a raise? That was a different matter.

MY PARENTS both came from Poland looking for something better. My father landed in Galveston, Texas. Then he went to St. Louis, Missouri. He worked those places at whatever was available. In Galveston he worked at some farm there. After St. Louis, he went to Pittsburgh, and he worked in the steel mill I think. When he came to Clinton, Massachusetts, he worked in the cotton textile mill.

My father left Poland when he was just about eighteen, maybe in

1905. I forget what part of Poland my parents were from. They often said; I never paid much attention. They used to write to Poland every so often to the family there. Poland was terrible. The Russians took everything. If you were raising anything, the Russians took it. They wouldn't let them go to school to learn to read or write. They did it undercover if they could. If they raised any livestock or anything in the fields, the Russians took most of it. I don't know whether they let him go or they— his two brothers came too—just managed to escape, but they did manage to get here. They all came together, but they all went different ways. His brother in Clinton said to come because you could get a job, and it was pretty good. So that's why he went. Then his brother bought a farm, and the other one went to Rhode Island. My father stayed in the mill.

My mother came a little later, 1910, something like that. She had no skill; they lived on a farm. They were peasants, but they were fortunate that they had a piece of land that they could work in Poland. My parents met in Clinton through families in the Polish community. They talk to one another, and then they got together and that was it. They married.

My father and mother worked in the Lancaster mill. I was born in Clinton and went to public school there. First year of high [school], I completed. Then you had to go to work to help the family. There was six children, five others in the family besides me. The kids took care of the kids. My parents went to work in the morning at seven, and the kids that were old enough, like myself and my sister, they took care of the younger ones. Went to school, came back, start the wood fire so they could get the dinner ready. They used to come [from the mill] for dinner at noon. And then supper was the same way [as dinner], come from school and start getting your supper ready. You'd have to peel potatoes, start the fire.

We lived in company houses, and the Lancaster mill was just up the street, a couple of minutes walk. Everybody on the street, I'd say 90 percent of them were Polish. There was a few other nationalities there too, but most of it was Polish right from the top of the street to the end. The houses were all together in blocks. People were more or less like a family; they helped one another. They'd come in and see if you needed any help, and they'd give you a hand. The company took the rent out of the pay every week, like a dollar and a half out of ten dollars a week. It was good and clean; you had free electric and steam heat tied into the company's boiler room.

My favorite dish was cabbage and potatoes. For the winter they used to have a big wooden barrel. They used to buy the cabbage from the farmers that came down the street with a big wagon, and it was loaded with cabbage. So if they wanna make cabbage leaves stuffed with hamburg and rice, they'd have it. They'd buy maybe five, six, seven bushels of cabbage, and they used to take turns going from one house to the other and shred it. Then take this heavy wooden poker and poke that down [in the barrel], and make sauerkraut. They'd throw some cabbage, salt and vinegar in, and pound it. They'd want sauerkraut, they'd take it out of the barrel, squeeze it, and cook it. They used to get maybe ten bushels of potatoes and leave them in the cellar. For meat, ham, smoked shoulder, or fresh shoulder. You didn't buy for two or three days, you bought every day. The fellow from the Polish store used to come around and take your order, and he'd deliver it for noontime.

My father was a weaver; he learned in the mill in Clinton. My mother was also a weaver. Between the two of them, they brought maybe twenty, twenty-five dollars a week. My father claimed most of the time he had good bosses. They had to do what they're told or else they'd be out on the street looking for a job. They wouldn't be working. The mill went bankrupt back in 1928. They auctioned off all the houses, and the place closed down. Before that, they used to have their slack periods. My father used to take off to Rhode Island or Connecticut and look for a job, and we'd be home in Clinton. If he got a job, he'd send ten or fifteen dollars depending on what he made.

Then in 1929 or 1930 we moved to Newmarket, New Hampshire. The mill there moved us because they were anxious to get the people. They were having labor trouble, and they would move anybody that wanted to work there. That trouble was brewing from a few years back, but when we moved there it had more or less quieted down. I remember when we moved in, there was no picketing or anything. Everybody just went to work and that was it. We lived in company housing, but they had no steam heat. You had to have your own heat: wood and coal. One week my father got a notice in his pay that he owed the company money for rent. That week, he got a check for five cents! I'm sorry they ever cashed it.

When I lived in Clinton, I used to work on the farm in the summer, weeding and haying. I was twelve years old. You just go up to the farmer and ask if they need any help for weeding by hand, and then in haying season, you did the same thing. And you'd walk three or four miles in the morning and back again at night. My parents didn't say, you have to, but they'd kind of reminded you it would be nice if you had a job. You never kept the money yourself. You turned it all in. So you had to go to work to help the family, and that was it. [When] you went to work in the mill, you didn't make any money in those days. You were lucky to get $10 a week, sometimes five for fifty-four hours, sixty hours a week.

My first job, I was cleaning bobbins in a silk mill in Newmarket. Then they closed down the mill in New Hampshire and moved it to Lowell. They would be better off financially than by running mills in different locations, so they closed down. They paid the moving expenses, and the people that were up there came to Lowell. They bought the Lowell Silk Mills and converted it into the Newmarket mills.

My father and mother, sister and brother, were working there. I was stripping bobbins, and then went to twisting. From there I went to weave, and I was weaving on one or two looms, making two or three dollars a week. When the NRA came into effect, that was a godsend; they had to give you thirty cents an hour. So for the forty hours you worked in the mill, you got at least $12 a week. At that time you only had six looms, then they started going into automatic looms, and you were getting more and more looms. But the weavers weren't making much, between $10 and $15 a week. When the NRA came in, they had to give them [at least] $12 a week. So then they were making between $12 and $20 a week, depending on the type of cloth you made. Different types of cloth had different prices [piece rates]. The only ones that made good money in the silk mill were the ones that worked on Jacquards. They made fancy cloth and paid better than on the regular rayon looms.

There were slack periods when you probably wouldn't be working for a month, two months, three months. You didn't look for other work, because there was no jobs around. You'd go back to the silk mill. Some of it was running; some of it was shut down. You'd wait there maybe an hour or two until the employment manager came around and says, Nothing doing today. Or if he wanted somebody, he already knew beforehand who he was gonna take. You, you, you step over here! Nothing doing; that's all for today. Somebody that was working in the mill probably had that job spoken for [someone they knew]. If you didn't know anybody, it would be so much harder [to get them] to hire you; they usually hired the people who had been spoken for. You'd say, Well, I got a son. If you got a chance, can you see if you can get him a job?

The bosses had their faults, but who didn't? The worst fella [at the silk mill], who was really lousy, he was Polish. He thought he was just it! He thought he owned the mill himself. He thought he was God! He was a loom fixer, then he became a second hand. Nobody liked him. I don't think anybody had a good word for him. He got along with the boss. The bosses more or less try to get along with one another. That's how they got there.

If everyone in the family was out of work, they had a few dollars they'd put aside for a rainy day, and that's what they'd use. It used to be at that time if there was a certain style of cloth that didn't sell, they'd close that section down. You were out of a job. The people would still be working there, but you wouldn't be working because there wasn't a need or a call for that particular kind of material. You took whatever was available because there was nothing else.

If you were working, you were fortunate to be working. So you didn't have much choice. It wasn't a pleasant job. It was awful hot in the summer. Even with the windows open, it didn't do them people any good, because they were working in like 120 degrees [F]. It was noisy, and you couldn't make any money. Fifty-four hours a week, and Saturday morning we had to work. There was no such thing as vacation pay or bonus in the silk mill.

Saturday night was the big night. If you had thirty-five cents, you went up to the Commodore Ballroom, one of the best in the area. The girls would pay their way. You had a suit on, and the girls used to dress their best. The Commodore had big name bands on Wednesday nights. It used to be packed, and the prices went up for the big name bands. We went out after the dance, downtown there were used to be places where you could get a hot dog for a nickel, a hamburg for a dime, coffee for a nickel, and that's why you went down there.

Some Saturdays, you'd just go and make a tour of the barrooms of the city or hang around a café. Even if you didn't buy anything, you could go in there and chew the fat. It was a mixed crowd, and there was a poolroom right across the street. You'd stay there, and if you wanted a beer, Hey, let's go and have a beer. They used to have free pretzels, free cheese every Saturday night. Buy the beer for a nickel, and there'd be all the pretzels and cheese you could eat. There was a dance hall at the Lakeview Amusement Park. You'd take the trolley or else somebody might have a car. They used to have tickets to dance. Sometimes they were a nickel, sometimes they were three for a quarter, depends on the band. The girls didn't buy tickets. The guy that wanted to dance, he had to give them a ticket. But the Commodore was the place.

In 1936 I went to work for the Wannalancit Textile. I had no job, so I was looking around. So that's where I got the job from Alan Larter at the Wannalancit. They made rayon cloth. I started as a weaver there, then I went to smash-piecing. If there was a large breakout [in the cloth being woven] the weaver marked it on the board, and the smash-piecers tied up all the ends and started the machines up again. You tied [weaver's knots on] all the ends, and then you had to draw them through the heddles, through the needle eye that held them, and through the drop wires. Depending on the size of the warp, the type, the style, there were maybe three, five, eight thousand ends.

Your main concern [as a weaver] was production and first-quality cloth. An end might break and the drop wire might not drop right, and the loom would be going, so you'd have a hole in the cloth which was no good and get docked for it. We had eight and [then] ten straight looms [with no automatic bobbin changers] at the Wannalancit, but then they changed it. They wound up with twenty-four, then before they closed they were running sixty or seventy looms for one weaver. Just walking up and down trying to keep those looms going all day long is a job. Then I started fixing forty looms.

When I worked at Wannalancit, you're talking about cleanliness. That man, Larter, he wanted everything spick and span. He saw oil on the floor, he wanted you to wipe it off. That was Mr. Larter. He was a hard worker. He could do everything in the mill. The only thing I ever actually saw him do is fix looms, but he could slash, he could warp, he could twist. He was funny. [On payday] he used to come with a bag of money and ask, How much I owe you? Every week, but there was people that were really down, and he helped. He knew they were hard up, and if they asked for help, he helped them. He helped a lot of them, but if you tried to get a raise from him, it was hard.

When I first started I made two or three, then five, then $13 a week. Then as a weaver fifteen till I was making big money as a loom fixer, $24 a week. Then when I came back from the service in 1946, I was making $32 a week. The third week [I was back] I went to see the boss for a raise. How much do you want? I says, Well, at least $40. He gave it to me. So I hit up for a raise awhile later, and he says, If you want more money, you'll have to come in at three in the morning on Sundays and Mondays and start up the humidifiers. I says, No, if you want the humidifiers on, you come in. I'm not coming in at that time to get overtime.

I quit the mill in 1953 to make more money working for the corrections department of the state. It was a better opportunity there than in the mill.

They Used to Call Them Efficiency Men, And That Was a Bad Name

James Simpson

TIME-STUDY AND COST MAN

James Simpson had special status among second-generation immigrant children as the son of a Scottish father, but his father died during the postwar flu epidemic that claimed many lives among the Lowell mill workers. His mother worked hard in a woolen mill to support her young son and occasionally had to board him for months at a time with a local family. When, unlike most children of mill families, he graduated from high school, she got him a job. At the Lowell Textile Institute and in the laboratory of the Abbot Worsted Mill, he learned to check yarn for quality control and worked as a time-study man. Armed with clipboard and stopwatch, he figured the elements, cycles, and constants that determined the piece rate.

Efficiency men who studied and timed the moves made by workers faced resentment and resistance. Mill workers believed that these experts carried out company orders to increase speeds and cut piece rates. Getting their cooperation was not easy, but his day-to-day contact and the fact that worsted yarns could be speeded up only so much—the higher the twist, the slower the machine speed—helped Simpson win tolerance. Still, he realized that workers kept their shortcuts secret from time-study men.

James Simpson learned many lessons about mill work that seemed almost self-evident, especially the importance of cooperation with other woolen mills in the region to avoid wage competition and control the labor supply. Yet as markets slipped away, Abbot Worsted began to decline, and in 1956 the mill closed its doors. Simpson then worked as a time-study man for several companies, but when the last one folded in 1978, he found himself a little short of retirement age and in need of a job. He was then in the same position as many textile workers whom he had learned to respect, and he experienced firsthand the grim reality of being assessed for what a firm could get out of a worker for a few years.

I WAS BORN in Lowell [in 1917]. My parents worked in the local mills. My father came from Harwich, Scotland, and met my mother here, and they were married. He worked in the Hamilton mills and the Appleton mills; my mother [Elizabeth Barrie Simpson] worked in the Abbot Worsted Company and in the Uxbridge mills as a creeler. I can remember my mother working in the Uxbridge for $10 a week, and we were glad we had it. If you got a two or three cents an hour increase, that was great. If you ever got a nickel, that was big. When I went looking for my first job, I went to the Abbot and started as a checker.

I was the only child. My father died when I was three years old, and my mother worked most of her life until she died at an early age, fifty-seven. She loaded the creels for high-speed warpers. [Back] then the Entwistle Company used to manufacture machinery, and when they would send this machinery out to different parts of the country, she'd go with it and train the people how to operate those machines. I remember when I was a kid, she was in Rhode Island or Philadelphia, places like that, sometimes for as long as six months. I used to be boarded out for the week and come home on the weekends. I went to various schools depending on [where] the people I was boarding with [lived].

I graduated from Lowell High School in 1934, and then I started going to the Lowell Textile Institute. I went up there [to night school] for about twelve years for a diploma in worsted manufacturing. That included quality control, designing, and all kinds of math pertaining to the textile industry. I taught there two nights a week for five years on [worsted] spinning and how to [calculate] changes on the gears of the machinery. I got my experience in the mill when I started at the Abbot as a checker, and then they brought me into what they called the time-study and the laboratory. The overseers I was working for knew my mother.

They were on the incentive system. So as a checker I would make out the time cards and weigh material such as the imperfections that they cut out of the yarn called fluffing imperfections. That would all have to be weighed, and I had to record it on the card, add up the production sheets, and send them into the office. It was like being the bookkeeper for the department, but it wasn't that complicated. I got paid thirty-five cents an hour for a forty-hour week, no vacation, no paid holidays, no differential [wage] for working the second shift.

Then I went into the laboratory, and I learned to be a time-study man and how to do laboratory work. That means checking the yarn for count and twist. Count is the diameter of your yarn, and it has to be right. I became in charge of that department. Then when I was twenty-nine [in 1946], I was transferred to a large mill in Forge Village. Abbot Worsted practically owned the town of Forge Village at one time. Then they gave us aptitude tests and selected me to learn the business of the yarn mill and its operations. I had to go out into the mill, change gears [on the machinery], and work with the people. Then they started a mill down South, and they sent me down there to train the people how to run the operations. They offered me a job, but I wasn't interested in moving to the South.

My work [at Forge Village] took me out into the mill. Many people thought if you worked in the mill, you were the lowest, but you weren't. After I got out and found out how other people worked and did things, the mill people seemed very clean people in comparison. Very! When you used to see them outside the mill, all dressed up, they really had class, I'll tell you. They were nice people; good hard workers.

Many people resented the time-study. You set up these standards. The standards would tell you how much work the people could do. And you would take these studies and then you would rate them. You would do it with a watch and a clip board, and you would time them. Time everything the worker would do for a cycle that's liable to be an hour to five hours. I have taken studies of eight-hour cycles. Then you have to add up all the figures called elements. Like, if they had to cut yarn from bobbins, that's an element. When they doffed or took the bobbins off, that's an element. You have all these elements that you record and then you add the figures all up. Then you rate them on whether you thought they were going fast or slow which you judge by experience, and then you come out with a constant.

You take all these constants and figure on a master sheet, using all these constants, the total number of minutes. Then you end up by telling them how many points a pound they would be paid and how many spindles they could run. Sometimes they weren't running enough; sometimes they were running too many. Many people resented you because they thought you were a company man which really you are. They used to call them efficiency men, and that was a bad name.

After a while when they got to know you, they didn't resent you as much. They would tell you all their problems and get it off their chests. But you had to listen to them, and some of them sometimes got real mad. They would be swearing and everything else, but you couldn't swear back at them. You just had to listen, and by the time you got through the study and you left, they were generally more friendly. I remember one case of this woman on twisting. When I went in there, she started to cry, and Oh, we had quite a session! By the time I got through and left, she was saying, Well goodbye, Jim; we'll see you. But they got so they knew you after a while because the same men stayed there [working] and the same men would be studying [the work], so that they'd get to know you, and they'd call you by your first name.

You had to learn both the lab work and the time-study. If there was work that wasn't running too well on spooling, they would inspect the yarn. We didn't weave [at Forge Village]; we were just a yarn mill. We would have to go out and sit with a girl [the spooler] for an hour or so, and then we'd come back in and analyze the imperfections and where each came from. We'd pull it apart and say, Well, that came from a bad piecing where the girl pieced the yarn when it broke. Or something else. Then we'd have to make out a report and figure out how many knots [defects] per pound and submit that to the superintendent.

There was a fellow that worked in the rovers in the drawing room. That's where they take the tops [big balls of sliver from the card room], and they start reducing them to a smaller sliver. This is the last step in the drawing room before it goes to the spinning. Now this man, you would look at him, and he never seemed to be going too fast or too slow. He wasn't killing himself, but nobody could make as much money as he could. Everything he did, he did well, and it counted.

The supervisors didn't like anyone to tell their help what to do. The way you should do it was to report to the overseer or the supervisor and say, I think Mary could get out a lot more if she did such and such. Otherwise, it's a good out for any operator that's so inclined. You know, the supervisor goes over and says to the operator, What are you doing? Well, the [time-study man] came over and told me to do that. Then, look out! It's best for you to go to their immediate supervisor and tell them. And they in turn will take care of the matter. Then the woman knows who she's working for, and you're not caught in the middle.

Later on, I became a spare supervisor. I was still a time-study and cost man, but if a supervisor was out sick or on vacation, then I'd have to take his department and run it for that week. If it was the third shift, I'd have to take the third shift and in Forge Village, that was a big mill. I can remember having to be there at six o'clock in the morning when the first shift started, but it was a good education. That's where I got a lot of my experience, working in the mill, doing the actual thing. The night superintendent, George Pihl, he used to help me a lot. And [together] we'd go over drivers and drivens [gear ratios and proportions], where you have to know if you change a certain pulley or gear whether it's going to give you more or less of what you're after.

The company wouldn't speed up the operation unless we [in the laboratory] told them to. There were rules of thumb that they could go by. If we were running knitting yarns, you couldn't run a knitting yarn on a spinning frame too fast because there wouldn't be enough twist in it. If we felt that it could go faster or not, they would raise it or they would lower it. If the work wasn't running good, they'd have to lower the speed. Either that or put a little more twist in it if the ends kept breaking. We used to run mohair at times, and that had to be a hard twist. All your automobiles and your upholstery had mohair, but hardly anything has mohair now. When we were making khaki uniforms for the army, it was a fine yarn with a little crimp in it. A good suit will still have some wool in it. They need the wool to carry the coats and pants. Worsted has a harder finish than regular woolen, wears better, and your pants don't get baggy at the knees.

The woolen mills have converted now, and the mule spinning machines that used to spin the yarn are out. I can remember that we changed from what they called cap spinning. We used to get the little two-ounce packages [of yarn] off spinning, and then finally end up with a bigger package. We wanted to get eight or nine ounces off spinning. Of course, the longer you can spin without doffing, the more continuous the run, that's where the profit is.

We could express ideas on the operation, because while you're taking time-studies, you're supposed to be observing to see if they're wasting any motion or time. Sometimes the operators used to try to kid you. They would dog it. If they thought that they could pull a fast one so that they could get more time, they would. You could make a suggestion like why don't you put that barrel here instead of walking way down there? Why don't you do this instead of doing that? Your operators are your best time-motion people because they're living with that all the time, and they know every shortcut in the book.

Here's a for instance. When you're twisting, you take two ends of spinning yarn, and they go around a dolly cup, down through a guide, and then onto a bobbin. When those bobbins get down until they're almost run out, there's several ways of stripping the bobbin off clean down to the wood. If you want to get more time—fool the time-study man—you start pulling them off by hand [one at a time]. But when the time-study man isn't there, they don't do that. They take perhaps half a dozen of the yarn ends left on the empty bobbins and wrap them around the abrasive sleeve on the dolly cup. That dolly cup would run and take all the yarn off [all] the bobbins, and then they'd cut it off the dolly cup and throw it away. They're the smartest.

You didn't always take time-studies, only for new products or something going bad. Time-study had been in the Abbot for some time. The story goes that this Frenchman Bideaux [the man who invented the point system to calculate wage incentives] originally was a sand-hog: they dig tunnels under the earth. He came up with this point system to make it more efficient. As a sand-hog, he apparently figured in his mind that, Look, I'm working harder than this guy next to me. I should be getting more money, and it's unfair. You know how people are competitive when they're working. That may have been the seed for it. He must have been a pretty smart cookie. They claimed that during the war he more or less collaborated with the Nazis, and he lost favor in this country. Something tragic happened to him, but I forget.

[The company tried to keep up with the competition by rebuilding machinery, changing to new-style bobbins, buying new equipment to get fewer operations and bigger packages of yarn]. At the end of it, we even had some company from Connecticut come in and work with the time-studies, and they checked out all our customers to find out what yarn we were making for them and whether we were making any money. And if we weren't making money, they told us to drop them. Either go up on the price or get rid of them. So they really tried. Our company was a family-owned business for a hundred years: the Abbots, the Camerons, and the Sergeants. There were no stockholders from outside; this was their bread and butter.

Sandy Cameron was one of the owners. He was a perfect gentleman. He would come through the plant in the morning, every morning, and he'd say, Good morning, Jim, and how's things going? Are you running such and such? And well, have a good day. Everybody loved him. You didn't see Ed Abbot as much. I never really knew Ed Abbot. I knew Mr. Abbot's sons—they had to learn the business—and Bill Sergeant, another owner. He was the one that sent me down South and wanted me to stay and take a job. When I came back, I went to his home in Concord to tell him I didn't want it.

Abbot Worsted used to have a mill in Lowell and in the villages of Brookside, Graniteville, and Forge Village. Forge Village was the biggest one. It was a little village with a lot of Russian, English-Irish, and French people. Many of the supervisors were English-Irish that were brought over by Abbot to play on his soccer team. Forge Village had one of the best soccer teams around. They had a uniformed band and a baseball team. That's [in the twenties] before things really got competitive in the industry, and they had to start cutting down. At one time they owned all the houses in the village, and you paid them according to how much you worked. If you didn't work a full week, you didn't pay a full rent. But they got rid of their houses and sold them to the people for two or three thousand. Some of those people had cash to pay for those nice houses.

I never remember a strike in the Abbot or anyone trying to put us on [one]. American Woolen in Andover was the bellwether mill. If they gave a raise, then everybody else would give a raise, so that there wouldn't be that much unhappiness [among the operators]. Then after [World War II] it wasn't long before [we got] our first one week's vacation and getting paid [for it]. That was wonderful. The mills didn't give too much.

I worked in the Abbot during the war. We were considered a company that was working for the government because we were making government products. We were making khaki. You had to be fingerprinted, and you had to have a badge. There was a slack period after the war. Some of those people only worked one day a week, but everyone would get their six hours. They split it up so everybody got something. You didn't work a full week in the lab, except for the man in charge.

The company had been in business for a hundred years, and then it went out of business in 1956 after World War II. The government was giving everything away free after the war: Lend Lease and the Marshall Plan and all that. They were giving away better equipment than what we had here, and it wasn't long before we were put out of business. I liked the textile business. I thought I had a good future there, and it was interesting work. Our company was very progressive. They put in new systems and new types of machinery, but the move South wasn't a good move.

[Then] I worked over twenty-two years doing time-studies and supervisory work for three different companies including General Electric that made plastic laminates like Formica. It was entirely different, but as far as time-study goes, the principles are always the same. They're always the same. I retired when my [last] plant closed down in 1978. I stayed there until the last gun was fired. I was more or less in charge of closing it. I wasn't old enough to really retire, so I had to collect [unemployment compensation] for six months until I became sixty-two.

Don't let anyone kid you. Once you become sixty or fifty-five to sixty—I went into a company, and the guy looked at my resumé and said, Boy, you've had a lot of experience and you've made good money. I'm going to show this to Jack, the owner. So, I'm still waiting to hear from Jack. I know what the answer was. If I had been ten years younger, I'd have got a job. But they knew they could only get a couple of years out of me, not enough mileage and they couldn't be bothered. They tell you you're protected against this and that, but that's a lot of baloney. And it's not right because some of these older people can outproduce and outwork some of these kids. That's what they're bringing in now.

Those mill workers in Lowell, Boy, they would give you a day's work now, I'm telling you! In the hot weather, they would be in there, and those [spinning] frames generate heat, oh! And the humidity would get high, and they had overhead sprinklers shooting out water. And those people—the ends would be breaking down, and they would be trying to keep [them pieced] and would have to stop the machinery, it was so bad. It wasn't like today; they say, I'm going home. You couldn't afford to go home because you couldn't get a job that easy. Not everybody owned a car. You depended on the bus and the street car. You had to stay there, work, and take the good with the bad.

We All Worked in the Mill, and All in the Same Place

Raymond Gaillardetz

LOOM FIXER

The French Canadian parents of Raymond Gaillardetz immigrated southward to Lowell by stages, working in various mill towns and finally ending up in the Newmarket mill. There the family all worked together, utilizing the family labor system that depended on hard work and personal loyalty to the mill. Loyal family members expected a reward for their faithfulness. Gaillardetz pestered his overseer for a chance to learn loom fixing.

Once trained, Gaillardetz shared a section of looms in rotation with his father and a brother, each working alternate shifts on the same machinery, helping each other to keep it all in repair. The regional decline in the textile industry slowly eroded the basis of this family system of work. Unions made Raymond Gaillardetz nervous. Loyalty to the mill and the family seemed safer. Although he joined the union with much hesitation because of pressure from his coworkers, he believed that unionization killed the Newmarket.

When the mill closed, Gaillardetz made an easy shift to the Wannalancit, but things had changed. There were no family members to teach him or to help him. Only occasionally did new looms replace the old ones, and the old ones needed a lot of mechanical talent to keep them going. By the late 1960s, the Wannalancit was hiring no more loom fixers; this forced Gaillardetz to perform any extra work by himself. At first being a janitor for an electronic firm seemed degrading, but an increasingly heavy work load and the promise of better money finally convinced him to leave the mills.

MY FATHER comes from St. Lenore, Canada; my mother comes from St. Gregoire, Canada. At an early age they moved to Harrisville, New Hampshire, then from Harrisville to Dracut to Lowell. They both got a job in the same mill in Harrisville. And from there, well, they got married and raised a family of eight children. [He was born in 1910.]

We all worked in the mill, and all in the same place. The Newmarket mill.

My father was there first. I suppose when my brother was old enough, he wanted a job. So my father spoke to the boss about it, and they got him a job. After that my other brother got in there for the same reason. We asked for a job, and we got it because my father was there, and he was well known and well liked. I did the same thing during the shoe strike [in 1933] when I wasn't working. So I went over there, and I got a job. From there on, all our lives were in the Newmarket. I worked there twenty-three years. My father worked there until he retired.

I started to work right after grammar school as an errand boy for three different [grocery] stores. We'd fill up a little four-wheeled wagon and deliver the orders to different places. We used to deliver a hundred-pound bag of potatoes up to the fourth floor. It was only a small job. Then I started in working at the Wood Heel Company. But at supper-time, at meal times when we were eating, my father would be talking to my mother and to us about the jobs, and he would name the different parts of the loom while he was talking. He wasn't instructing us; he was just talking about it. I knew the names of the parts of the looms even before starting to weave. I had that advantage. When somebody mentioned a shuttle or a picker-stick, I knew what he was talking about. So I had that little advantage.

They gave me one loom to start. It was a woman that was teaching me. After a couple of weeks, they come over and they ask the weaver if I was ready to go on myself, and I suppose she said Yes, because they assigned me to one loom for a week or two. You get the hang of it, of how to run it. Then they assigned me to a job downstairs and gave me six looms with two shuttles [each]. We were weaving [silk] crepe.

Crepe takes two shuttles, one bobbin spun right and the other one is spun left. That kind of twist makes a crepe cloth. It had two colors, and there's two shuttles in the loom and an empty box. The top shuttle comes over [across the loom] and [then goes] back [into the box], and the box moves up [out of the way]. Then the other one comes over and back. When a bobbin is empty, this loom would stop, and you had to take the bobbin out yourself, put it aside, put a new [full] one in, and start up your loom again.

I was very fortunate. You keep asking the boss, I want to go weaving; when can I go weaving? From weaving I did the same thing. I told the bosses I wanted to go on loom fixing. I got an opening. My father was working on the first shift; my brother was working on the second shift on the same section. When my father went home, my brother took over. And then when I got on [in 1937] I come in on the third shift. So the three of us were working the same job all the time. You don't see that very often.

My father he was getting old, and [when they began to rotate the night shift around to everyone] he couldn't sleep during the daytime. So what we did is, my father worked the first shift, my brother would come in on the second shift, and I come in on the third shift. The next week, my father was supposed to move [to the second shift], but he stayed there [on the first shift]. So my brother went on the third shift, and I went on the second. We rotated like that every other month from one shift to the other. I thought I was going to die! I couldn't sleep. I couldn't eat. Oh, that was awful! Changing every month from one shift to another, you could never get used to it. Four weeks you sleep nights; four weeks you sleep days. That was a killer! I used to fall asleep on the job. It's just a wonder they didn't fire me.

My sister was a battery hand. There were no women loom fixers; that's not a woman's job. Women's jobs were weaving; you've got battery hands, filling girls, the warping room that was girls, and the spinning room that was girls. The winding room, there were girls. The harness [drawing-in] room, those were girls. Those were the women's jobs.

A loom fixer starts by putting in warps and getting them ready for the smash-piecer [to check]. If you have a big breakdown that the loom fixer can't do [alone], they use a spare fixer. That's how you learn to fix. They give you those jobs with somebody that knows how to do it, and you learn that. If you can follow the loom fixer around, he can show you when things are happening, why they're happening, and what you can do to fix it. That's the way you get it. Then you've got to wait for an opening. I worked there from 1933 to 1954.

A weaver's job is piecework, but a loom fixer's job is day pay. They pay you so much an hour. So it doesn't matter what you know and what you don't know, if they give you that job it's going to be a certain price per hour. If you worked in a cotton mill, they paid less than a silk mill, and a silk mill paid less than a woolen mill for the same job.

When an end breaks [on the loom], the [silk] weaver had to have a bag of chalk powder to put on your hands to tie the knots so that you wouldn't leave the grease and the oil from your hands on the white thread. It wouldn't show; you'd just make your knot and cut the end and let it go. When you go over and inspect the cloth where you had handled that thread, maybe there's a long streak depending on how dirty you were. If they decided that you should have done much better than that—carelessness in there—then they'd fine you for it. Oh, we were fined. I don't think there's a weaver that never was fined. I was; I know that!

The loom fixer couldn't be fined. The loom fixer could be fired. I've seen where a loom fixer got fired because he got mad and was fighting with somebody, then they fired him. I'll never forget when I was learning, a weaver went and got a loom fixer. I guess he had to come over once or twice before to fix it, and she had to call him two or three times. And the last time he came, he had a little tool box that you drag at the end of a rope. And he gets over there, and he was so mad, he kicked the loom. That stayed in my mind. How crazy can you be? What's the loom got to do with it? He's the one that wasn't fixing it right, but he kicked *it*!

We bought our own tools to a certain extent. We never bought the files. That was their problem. If they don't give me a file, I don't file it, but if you'd have to file something, a piece of metal that didn't quite fit, you'd have to file it. They'd give you the file, and they furnished the hacksaw blades, sandpaper, and emery cloth. That was all furnished by the mill, but the rest of the stuff, if you needed a tool you bought your own stuff. As far as wrenches are concerned, they were all my tools.

There was no union at the Newmarket for a long time when I was there, but the people started to get dissatisfied because the union men started to come around the mill, talking union. Talking union and the first thing you know [the others] got after you to join the union. There was quite a hassle because a lot of people were against it, and some were for it. I guess most of them signed up to join, and I hadn't signed up yet. They got after me for quite a while there. I didn't want to sign; I didn't know what to do. I was kind of leery about that, and finally I joined just like everybody else.

I had just come from a shoe shop strike [in 1933] and that wasn't very encouraging. We more or less lost that thing because there was so much darn trouble during that shoe strike. They hired strikebreakers, and there was fighting all over the place. It wasn't very encouraging, and that's the thing that you look at when they come in. That's the fear that you have. So when they decided to come and talk to you about unions, they say the union is this and that. I guess I wasn't very much in favor of the union. It wasn't long after that that Textron came and started to buy different kinds of mills and move them down South. The Newmarket was sold to Textron, and he closed the mill [in 1954].

When the union come in, it didn't last very long. My father's one of the very few that got something. At retirement they were getting a thousand dollars, and he did collect the thousand dollars just before the mill closed down. It must have been a big kick to him because he wasn't rich. He had six children working, and we always handed our pays in. My wife did the same thing. She used to run home as fast as she could to give her pay to her mother. I didn't run, but I did the same thing. I was twenty-five years old when I started to go with my girl which is my wife. My mother in the last couple of months before I got married, she let me have my whole pay.

I was one of the last ones to work there. I got through on a Friday in October 1954. The last Friday that I worked, the owner of the Wannalancit Textile [Alan Larter] came around with the overseer of the Newmarket. I guess he was looking to buy some looms or something. When he came by my place, I was working by myself. I was alone, the only one there. He introduced himself, and he said, Where are you going after the mill closes? I says, I don't know; I'm out of work. He says, If you want a job with me at the Wannalancit loom fixing. . . . I says, I never worked on those kinds of looms. Well, he said, we'll show you if you want to come. I says, Sure. He said, Come in Monday. I never lost even a day from Friday to Monday.

I started working days [on the first shift]. I worked there about three months on days working with other people to give me an idea how it was, the altogether different kind of looms that I hadn't even heard of. I was a Crompton and Knowles loom man, and all they had was Drapers. They have a different head on the loom to make it run. When they started to buy foreign cars, you would go to a garage, and they'd say, Well, that's a foreign car; I won't fix that. They had to have somebody to show you. [Another] difference is that in the Newmarket I learned with my own father which is a hell of a lot different. There was a lot of differences, but I learned it, and as soon as I learned it, they shoved me on the third shift, and I stayed there fourteen years.

They shoved me on [the third shift]; I had no choice. They were paying a little more money on the third shift than on the first shift. Like you get five cents an hour more on the second shift and fifteen cents more an hour on third shift, and I was a family man. I was broke, and I had to work. I took it. Quite a few years after that I was asked a couple of times if I wanted to go on the first shift, and I didn't want that first shift. There's too many people and too many bosses. At the night shift, there was only one man ahead of you, and we got along okay. He was all right, and I took it.

That was the worst part of my life, the third shift. I didn't like it; there was a lot of things I didn't like, but I didn't stop and think about it too much. [Otherwise] you go crazy in a sense. I knew I had to stay there; that's all there was to it. I come home in the morning [after the third shift], my kids were going to school. I'd just be able to barely say a few words, and they were gone to school. And when I got up at night, they were going to bed. A lot of times they were in bed. That's been my life, and that's not a good life. It's not a good life for your wife, and it's not a good life for your kids, and it's not a good life for yourself. But, hey, that's the way it is.

The looms at the Newmarket were old. Only towards the end, they had brand new looms for me. In the Wannalancit, it was the same thing. They had bought a whole bunch of looms there, brand new ones. That is the ones they closed the mill with; those were beautiful. Like a car, the older your car is, the more you're going to have trouble with it, and that's the same with looms. The older it got, the more wear and tear to it.

The Wannalancit also bought some Unifill machines. They took off all the batteries [automatic bobbins changers] and put in a Unifill machine. We had to learn that. It was a new, completely new process, altogether different. A man from the company showed us how to take the machine apart and put it back together so that we know what it was all about. Instead of having a [battery hand] come over and fill the battery with bobbins from the winding room, someone invented a new machine. They take a big cone [of yarn], and they put it on a spindle. [The Unifill machine] used to make [fill] its own bobbins right there as the loom was running. When the empty bobbin [leaves the shuttle], the machine starts over again and makes another [full] bobbin. So the thing is always full. It took away a lot of work; they didn't have no battery hands anymore.

Towards the end at the Wannalancit, they were bringing in people from different countries like Cuba, Portugal, Puerto Rico, [and Colombia]. It was a little bit difficult because in a very short time you tried to tell them something, and they knew it all before they really knew it. They didn't know they didn't know it. They thought they did, but they didn't.

The reason I left Wannalancit is they couldn't have no more help, and it was increasing the work for me. You could see that they were not breaking in loom fixers anymore. They were not replacing the floor man anymore. That means that with nobody to take the load off you, if you have a big breakdown on a loom like a broken shaft, that's going to take you two or three hours to fix, [and you have to do it alone]. You had to take a lot of stuff apart. That's a big job; that's a floor man's job. Well, if they don't have no floor man who's going to do it? It's going to come to me sooner or later.

I could see all that gradually coming, because they were not hiring. The reason they weren't hiring is they couldn't get anybody. I started to look around. I couldn't stand that, and I wasn't the first one. I had the experience of seeing other loom fixers quit, and they went to Raytheon. They had good jobs. They'd come over, and they'd tell me they were making $90 a week. At that time I wasn't getting anywhere near that, and I wasn't getting any younger. [At the Wannalancit], they had no retirement plan, no insurance, no nothing.

The first break I got to apply for Raytheon, I went over and applied for it. Some people think that it's degrading in a sense. That from being a loom fixer, then you go to a janitor. Janitor doesn't sound very good to a lot of people. 'Course if you had an education, you would never take it, but that's the way it goes. I quit my job at $2.60 an hour, and in three months I was making more than I used to make in the mills. In a few years I was making a bundle more than I ever could or ever had done in the mills.

I don't miss the mills; I miss my job at Raytheon. They forced me to leave work. I was fifty-eight when I went there in 1968, and the retirement age was sixty-eight. If I put in ten years [I'd get a pension]. So I said, I'll just make my ten years and then retire. But about four years after I began at Raytheon, the union put in a clause in their contract that you had to retire at sixty-five. There was a group of maybe ten or fifteen of us that were hired at about the same time, and we said, Hey, what's this? If they cut us off, we're going to miss our pension by two or three years. So that made them think, and they started to work on a plan, and six months after I spoke to them about it, the [union] man came over and said that they invented a grandfather retirement plan. All those that started at that time would work until they made their ten years and then you could have your pension. It's not much, but it's there. It's a lifesaver for old age.

I praised Raytheon to high heavens for the [working] conditions and the chance to get ahead. Whereas you could never do that in the mill. It's only once in a great while you could take a loom fixer and put him on as a second hand. You could almost spend a lifetime before that would happen.

Maybe there are a lot of things that you could squawk about working in the mill, but there was one thing. I never loafed. I worked all the time. I always had some work to do. I had three kids. I couldn't afford to loaf. I worked. The only time I loafed was when they were taking the looms out and putting some new ones in. There was one thing I could depend on; I was going to work. I was never afraid that I was going to be laid off. It was something I could depend on. It wasn't much money. I could get by, but we were poor. I never had a car. If I wanted to go someplace I had to walk.

My children went to high school. And from there, they could have better jobs than when I was working in the mills. They could work as secretaries, and the boy joined the service. [The mill] was a steady job for anybody that didn't know any better. For anybody that never had a good education, it was a good steady job. There was a lot of people working in the mill. There was over two thousand people in the New-market at one time. For every six looms it took about four people, and there were thousands of looms. When I was in the mill, the conditions were not good. It was no big money, but it was a living to me.

How Would You Like to Make Five Cents an Hour More?

Sidney Muskovitz

DYE HOUSE WORKER, CARDER

For a young man in need of work in 1937, any job in the mills would do. Sidney Muskovitz quickly learned that once he had gotten into the dye house of the Merrimack mills, he faced constant danger.

Muskovitz learned to operate a jig in which heavy rolls of cloth were submerged in a hot dye bath heated by steam coils in the bottom of the machine. Pressures to get the work done forced mill workers to invent shortcuts to save time, which intensified the dangers. No one in management tipped him off; he had to depend on his coworkers and his own wits.

When Muskovitz married he needed to earn more money. The lure of a few cents more an hour and the prospect of steady work led Sidney Muskovitz into the equally hazardous world of the carding operation. Each new job in the carding room involved alternating periods of pressure and boredom. Being identified by the boss as a "good worker" was a mixed blessing; the opportunity for different work often carried with it unforeseen dangers. Only personal vigilance made the difference between a ripped sleeve and a bloodied arm.

Sidney Muskovitz had contempt for those bosses who demanded to be called "sir," cursed his Jewish religion, cheated him out of vacation pay, refused to let him eat lunch, and ignored his warnings that the carding machines were about to catch on fire. When the strenuous physical demands of the intensifying pace of mill work finally wore him down, he suffered a nearly fatal heart attack. But Sidney Muskovitz still had the last word.

I WAS BORN in Lowell in 1917 and grew up in the Highlands. I graduated from the ninth grade and went to high school, but I had to quit it because my parents were sick. My parents were sick when I was born. My father was a tinsmith, and he used to put a hot iron into acid, and the fumes used to go up into his lungs and he got lung diseases. He couldn't work. Of course, they didn't have the medical insurance like they have now. Them days, they put you in the hospital to die. One doctor says, you quit your tinsmith job and try to get a job in the open air. You'll probably live a little longer. So he became a fruit peddler.

I had to go to work. Jobs were hard to get in them days. I had four brothers and two sisters; I was the third oldest of the family. I was a little young to work in the mill, but I used to work for a tobacco company delivering tobacco and candy. Then after high school I worked at the Wood Heel shoe shop where I was only getting between $5 and $8 a week on piecework. When I was nineteen, I started to work in the Merrimack mill dye house getting $14 a week.

My mother worked in the Southwell Combing Company. She started to work when she was fourteen. She came from Russia and was about eight years old when she came over here. They were both from Russia. I don't know too much about my father. My mother spoke better English than he did. She came here younger than my father and went to school. I'm Jewish, and my mother and father talked Jewish when we were small. Then we used to go outside, and we talked to all different nationalities; and when I'd come home I'd start talking English. So I lost how to talk Jewish. I even went to the Jewish school, but still you hang around with other children, and school is school. You forget your nationality and the words.

The Highlands was a mixed neighborhood. Mostly it was a Jewish culture. Where I lived they had three synagogues. Of course, the other part of the city, you had to beware. Little Canada, if you don't belong in Little Canada, you're gone. Chapel Hill and Back Central Street used to be Portuguese people. And of course Market Street was the Greeks. Them days, you had to stay in your own district. You couldn't travel the city. Only in the Highlands, it was all different nationalities.

It was just like a supermarket in Lowell because you had stores in every corner of the street and every section of the street, side street, main street. But we never had the canned goods or the bread already made. My mother used to make it in a black stove, even in the summertime. No linoleum on the floor, the floors were warped wood, and no electric light. You had gas light and oil lamps. And there were no bathrooms. The toilets used to be out in the hall, and you had to light a candle to get to the toilets. We had to take our baths in a big round tub. My mother would lock my sisters in her room while she was taking a bath, and when both girls took a bath, we'd be locked in our room.

I tried looking for a job to help my parents, so I went to the Merrimack mills. There was no jobs open. I kept on trying, and this man liked the way I was talking and asked me did I think I could ever work in a dye house? And I said, It's all I can do is try. He says, I'll start you working in the dye house delivering dye to the kettles and the jigs. The jigs is a dangerous job; you had to put in caustic to dye the cloth. I asked my boss, I said, I'd like to get on the jigs because I didn't like to be just delivering in the dye house because the dye would fly around the whole room, and, of course, your face is black or blue or whatever dye you're working on. I was about to get married and working on jigs paid $16 a week.

You start with a roll of cloth that's brown because the loose threads have been singed off. So to get it white, you had to fill the jigs full of water and put the caustic [powder] in the cold water. Pure caustic can burn your hand off if you touch it.* You can't put caustic in hot water or it will blow up in your face. The caustic is to take the brown off and turn the cloth back to white. There was a big chain with a wooden stopper, and of course you've got to wear rubber gloves. You've got two jigs, and each has a handle that you shift to go backwards and forwards. Then you give it eight turns back and forth and stop the machine. You pull the chain with the wooden plug like a bathtub. You drop [empty] the caustic solution, and you put the plug back in with a rod because it still has caustic. You can't touch it. Then you fill the jig with cold water and some other chemical to neutralize the caustic. You can feel your hands burning through the gloves from the caustic. You do that eight times, then you're safe to put your hands on that cloth.

When you start the process of dyeing the cloth, it's close to a hundred feet on each roll, and the hundred feet takes an hour and fifteen minutes in hot water and steam, and you've got to turn it over with a long pole. You got to hurry up; you can't stop. Once you stop the machine the dye will drip. You don't want the dye to drip because there will be a streak on the cloth. You turn the steam on. What I would do was, I'd run the first set about seven minutes, and then I set the other jig so it gives me time to jump back and drop, or empty, the other one. And the dye has to be hot. After you do it eight times back and forth with the dye wash, you keep running it and drop the dye by emptying the jig with the chain and a wooden plug. But the cloth is still turning in the jig. Then you put the plug back in, and you put in a cold wash. And you run it eight times back and forth on that. Then they put some kind of

*Caustic soda is a chemical substance that burns or corrodes organic tissue.

chemical on it to neutralize the dye so it would stay in the cloth. Then you'd drop it.

You'd cut a patch out for a sample and you bring it to the office, and they match to see if it's the same color. If it doesn't match, you'd have to add a little different color to match the color of the sample. And you give that four times back and forth. You'd drop it, wash it. Of course we didn't like that because you've got to make another set within eight hours. You have to eat your dinner on the fly; it don't leave you much time. But 99 percent [of the time] the second dye wash would come out right. But if you don't have no problems sometimes you could get two sets out at two o'clock and that leaves you an hour to wash up or do what you want.

I first thought I was going to save some time—you have to make two sets a day in eight hours—I thought I was going to beat the time and have a little more time to myself, and I was just about to throw the caustic [for the second set] in the hot water of the jigs, and this guy says, Stop! stop! Don't ever do that, he said. You've got to put it in cold water. I said to him, No one told me about that. It would have blown up. Not only the water would burn you, but the caustic would burn you. And there's no way of stopping it, the burning. I'm fortunate, he just caught me in time. Then we got some new help, and if I ever seen the new help was going to do the same thing, throw caustic in the hot water, I stopped them. There were a few guys, their faces were burnt right off almost.

When it's wet, the cloth weighs close to five hundred pounds a roll soaked in water. The jigs is high so you got a high truck. You make sure that truck don't tip on you or go too far over. Then we push the jig to the dryer and that's the process. I was getting forty cents an hour. I started working in the Merrimack dye house in 1937 and I put two years in it, and the dye house was about 102 degrees when the steam is on. Of course I'm not the only jiggsie. When you have around fifty jigs going at the same time, there's a lot of heat coming out of boiling water.

After a while I got married; and sorry I had to leave my parents, but we all have to get married sometime. My wife never worked. When her mother died, she had to take care of her five sisters and brothers, and she never worked. I was only getting forty cents an hour at that time, and my wife was having a child, so I had a job offered to me at Southwell Combing [in North Chelmsford]. They were having a layoff at the Merrimack. You know, you produce so much cloth or shoes or whatever, there is a backlog, and they lay you off. So I said I have to try and get another job somewhere that's pretty steady. So I went to the Southwell Combing Company. They were offering five cents an hour more. And before I got hired, I was told, keep your eyes open, ears open, and your mouth shut. The superintendent says, Instead of you looking from the inside, outside, you'll be looking from the outside, inside. I said, Yes sir. And you got to put that sir in. So, he gave me a job in the card room. That is the most miserable, hottest, dangerous job I ever had.

I started as a feeder. That was not dangerous, taking the wool out of the bin [and feeding the carding machine]. The raw wool goes into a scour room. It's washed; they got to take the oil out of it. They get the lanolin out, and they blow it upstairs to the carding room with hot air. You've got to have the windows shut. The wool's got to be dry, and the temperature is close to 120 degrees. Like I said, hot. I had to wear a dark hat and a dark tee shirt because it's dirty and of course dungarees. As a feeder I'd take the wool out of the bin. That would last pretty close to thirty minutes before you had to feed again. You had to feed six or eight cards, all depends what room you are in.

The wool goes on to a feed apron that pulls it along with spikes. Then it drops through the feed apron and goes to a feed roll. Finally it gets to a cylinder which is going close to a hundred to a hundred and fifty miles an hour. On top of the cylinder were metal workers and strippers. These workers grab the wool from the cylinder and the strippers take the wool off the workers and put it back on the cylinder. And it keeps chewing it up until it becomes smooth, and [then] it goes to a doffer, then to a comb, then to a feed-coil to be turned into a sliver and from the coil it goes into a can spun into circles [of soft sliver, see fig. B]. Each shift the foreman weighs the slivers by the yard. If it doesn't have enough weight, they feed more wool. If it's too heavy, less wool. From being a feeder, the boss says, Would you like to be a doffer? You got to start at the bottom. So I said, I'll try that. I was a doffer for about six years on the third shift.

The doffer takes the roll out of the coil and pushes it through to the next room called the combing room. As years go by, the boss says to me, Jeese, you look like a pretty good worker, and you're pretty intelligent. He says, How would you like to get five cents an hour more? I said, Sure. Like me, the dummy, seeing the job I was going to have and this is where the danger comes in and the dirty part. He said, How would you like to be an oiler? Oilers have got six or eight cards to oil, actually I never counted the oil holes but it was in the hundreds, the oil holes from the feed, the whole card, the coils, and the rest. But he says, You're kinda short. I'm only five feet five. You'll have some big machines. I says, I'll buy a special oil can; it'll give me two or three inches more.

Besides oiling you had to wipe the machines. Of course the wool flies on the machines. You've got to put your hand between belts, between pulleys, and between gears. The sweat used to go down in your eyes and mouth, and it blinds you a little. Of course when you wipe the machines, do not put your waste wool from the workers and the strippers close to the cylinder. It will pull the wool right in and your hand also goes with it because it goes so fast. The machine is operated almost six hours before you stop it to give a general cleanup. I got ripped with a hook, from two belts hooked together with a lacing. Going continuous it wears down, and when it starts up, I have a broken hook. Fortunate[ly] enough it caught my shirt on top of my shoulder and ripped my shirt. But other people wasn't so lucky. They got their hand so close to it that they had a gash about an inch deep in their arm.

Besides the other operations, I've got to pull the wool underneath the card out with a long stick. You've got a grille hanging under the cylinder which is going between 100 and 150 miles an hour, and there's wool hanging down from the grille. You take a stick, but if you push it up too much, the stick's going to go in there and everything's going to start flying. It could mean your job. The other job for the oiler is if the doffer forgets to doff the can of slivers, it knocks the doffer belt apart, and the whole operation backs up. You have to straighten out the backed-up wool.

Some doffers let their machines back up on purpose. That means extra work for me, besides what I'm doing, to straighten up the wool. It will take me at least fifteen, twenty minutes to get it straightened up again. So they could do less doffing and take a break. The union [in 1945] got us the privilege of smoking in a special room. Then it was my job to watch the doffing operation. If the doffer wants to go to the bathroom, he has to ask me. 'Course you can't say no. That means I had to stop. Oiling is not that easy, and it's not worth the five cents an hour more.

A card is a giant machine, and there are different ones for fine wools, semifine, and coarse wool. Not trying to give myself a pat on the back, but I used to keep the machinery going, all except for a general breakdown. I do not touch that. Like broken gears or broken belts, you'd have to have a fixer do that. My foreman liked the work I was doing, keeping the machinery going. He said to me, he says, How would you like to be a fixer? I said, I don't think I would.

Many fixers couldn't get the card machine operation. I used to tell them how to do it. They used to come and say, Sidney, will you tell me what's wrong with it? They used to wear the gears down in the coil, and the fixers couldn't find what's the problem. So, one of the fixers says to me, he says, The foreman's getting on my back, Sidney, can you help me? I says, No, but anything that's wearing down has got to be put perfectly straight. There can't be a set of gears pressing hard on one side and loose on the other. The one that's pressing hard is going to wear down, and she's going to skip and jump and skip and jump.

Well, he asked me if I could set it for him, and he was kind of shaky because he's supposed to know his job. I said, Well, I'll do it one time but who's going to do my work? He says, Well, he says, I'll oil the machines, he says, while you set the gears and straighten the shaft. Well, we worked piece by piece, and finally it ran loose and no bind. He helped me oil my machines and, of course, if he got caught doing it, he'd probably get fired because he wasn't supposed to help the oiler. And of course, I'd get fired if I helped him.

The superintendent comes to my card room and he says, I heard a lot about you, he says. You're pretty good. And I said, Not that good. He said, I want to ask you a question. I said, Sir, I don't want to answer it. Because I knew if I answered, I'm in trouble with the foreman and everybody else down the line. But I got along pretty good with this superintendent, you know, and I can get away with a lot of things because he liked me. I said, I don't like to answer because I'll be in big trouble, and I have to work, you know. After you leave, I'm going to be in trouble with the foreman and the fixers and everybody else all the way down the line. He said, You will not be in trouble.

So I says, The only thing I can tell you, the metal workers and strippers are not gauged right; it's letting too much wool through, and so it comes out in balls into the doffer instead of being smooth. So that means the wool is going through an open gauge on the workers and strippers. Thank you, he says, I'll forget what you just said to me. The fixer comes over to me and says, What seems to be the problem? I said, I don't know, but the superintendent says a lot of balls are going through. The fixer says, It's got to be gauged right; I'll try to regauge them again. Then the foreman came in; the superintendent had told the foreman which he said he wouldn't. The foreman says, Listen you, you work here, you don't know how to fix machines. I'm the boss here! You are not the boss here! I said to the foreman, You open your mouth about it once more, and I'm going to see the superintendent and tell him you're picking on me! That shut his mouth.

That foreman and I used to be just like brothers. He liked me and everything else. But one day he came over to me and he says, What nationality are you? I said, I'm Jewish, and I'm proud of it. He just turned around and didn't say a word. Then he started adding work to me. Talking miserable to me. Just because I was Jewish changed my whole working condition. The working people didn't like Jewish people.

So at the end of the week, we had to give the machines a general cleanup. In other words clean every speck of oil and grease from the feeder, doffer, and the card. We used to pair up and clean one side each at a time. So he came over to me that night and says, Which side did you clean? I said, That side. Well he runs his finger right across the card and says, It's dirty; clean it up again. And I had to do the double job of cleaning up.

The next week as he came over to me, I said to myself, I'm going to use a little psychology. He asked, Which side did you clean? I pointed to the other side. I says, Which side is the cleanest? He said, Right over here, look at it, nice and clean. I said, Listen you, that's the side I cleaned, and I says, Don't ever pull that on me again because I'm Jewish. He says, Well, all you Jews are no God damned good. All no good. I said, That's what I wanted to hear from you. That's just the words I wanted to hear from you. Now we're going to the office and show you where it reads no discrimination on account of race, religion, or color [in the Fair Employment Practices Commission directives]. And if the office don't do anything, I'm going to the federal government. Well, he says, I didn't mean it. I says, If you didn't mean it, you wouldn't have said it. At quitting time, quarter past six, he says, I'm begging you. I didn't mean what I said. I says, Well, I'll tell you, I'm going to let it go because I'm a nice fellow. I'm not like you, but you do that again to me and you're going down to the office. You bet your life he was good to me since that time on. You'd be surprised what goes on in the mill.

The superintendent asked me to do a favor. He says, We've got this new machine for nylon. He says, I don't trust anyone but you, he says, would you operate the machine for me? I says, I don't want to get my foot in something and not like it. It's going to be a little too much work for me. Oh, he says, try it. Will you please try it, he says? So I says, Okay. The superintendent is pretty nice and he likes me, so I said, I'll try it.

The machine looks something like half a card but it's got coarser wire that's straight instead of bent. It stretches the nylon and separates it. You've got to feed it by hand onto the feed apron and cut up the lumps with a scissors. Then you've got to pull it out and throw it into a bin and run back to the feed apron and feed it some more. At noon I asked the foreman, I'd like to have my lunch. Tough, he says. So right after work I went to see the superintendent and says, I don't want this job. I don't want to work eight hours without having a lunch or something. I don't want the job; I've done enough for this company and that's it. I don't want to do it. So he says, Okay, I'm not going to push you; you go back to oiling your cards.

The market for wool was a little slow so the mill started working on a new material: mohair. And that's another miserable job. Mohair flies. And if it ever hits the oil, it gets sucked right into the bearings and no matter how much you oil them bearings, they're going to heat up. Once it starts heating up, it starts to smoke and if it smokes too long it's going to melt the mohair and form a flame because it's so hot. So I tell the foreman, I need to fix it, take the bearing out, and don't you tell me I didn't oil that bearing. I oiled that bearing! In fact, instead of twice a day, I oiled it four times. And if you want the cards to catch on fire, just let it go. You've got to take a hammer and knock the bearing out, but if it's red hot the hammer will flatten part of the edge. So you use a puller and pull it, but even with a puller you usually couldn't get it out. You'd still have to bang on it because it was jammed right in.

So another time I saw the foreman and said, Gee, I need the fixer again. He said, Let it go, let it go. We can't stop production. That's the name of the game: production. I said, Okay, it's up to you. Fire started coming out of the card, and he came in and started to holler at me. I said, Don't you start hollering at me. You wanted the machine to keep going; it's kept going. He says, Well, you don't oil it. I says, I do oil it. What do you want me to do, oil every bearing every few seconds and not do the rest of the work? Well, finally they put the fire out and cleaned the bearings out. Then new material came in: cashmere. It's so light and fluffy, and the superintendent comes over and he says, How would you like to work on it? I said, Never. Do me a favor and put me back on wool. I don't want to be a good worker anymore.

Besides the rest of the work, at the end of the week you had to blow the ceiling down. You've got a long pipe with compressed air and you blow down all the wool that's stuck on the walls and ceilings. It's like a sandstorm from that wool. Of course I'm not the only one stuck in that room; there's the feeders and the doffers, and they're hollering at me, don't blow it towards me! I can't help it. At the end of the week, after you blow your nose, excuse my language, it would come out black.

At least I could get out and eat because I had no machines to watch, but the doffers and the feeders had to eat where their operations are. One doffer used to put his sandwich on top of the coil and then would start eating the wool and his sandwich together. That doffer that was eating wool in his sandwich, he told the boss he wanted to be an oiler. I says, Don't take it. He says, No, I want to eat in peace. He took the job. And the poor guy, he had the job about six months. He had a loose shirt, got caught between the pulley, and it turned him upside down and banged his head against the other card—you've only got about four feet between each card—and split his head right open. Within a year, he was dead. Must have had a concussion of the brain or something. That's how dangerous a job this was.

One time I was working overtime. I was an oiler, but I couldn't take the oiler's job on overtime. There was already an oiler in the room. So I took the job as the doffer. You can take any [available] job on overtime, but on regular hours you do your own job. I was doffing a can, ready to push it out. I heard the belt squeaking; I heard screaming. I ran over, and I sees the oiler's hand inside the cylinder. I shut off the machine, and I ran over and shut off all the machines [in the room]. I tried to get the strippers off his hand, but I just couldn't do it. It was too heavy. I told the fella, you have to stay here till I get help; does it hurt too bad? He says, No. I says, It must be all numbed up. You'll feel it later.

I ran into different rooms to get the fixer, and we lifted the machine off his hand. His hand was stopping nothing. I couldn't bear to look at his hand. It was just like hamburger; you could see the bone. After he got the man's hand out, the fixer went to call the boss to get an ambulance. So the boss says to me, *Why did you shut your machines down?* I says, What did you want me to do? Leave the machines run? With no one there, and the guy's hand caught? And have all the machines jammed up? He says, Well, you should have called the next room and got help and keep the machines going. I says, Okay. 'Cause if you talk too much, you're fired.

Well, they started up all the machines, and I says to this boss, Wait a minute! I'm not alone in this room. You have to get another person here. 'Cause it's against the law to be alone in a room. Then he says to me, You're gonna run those machines. I says, *I'm not gonna run them!* You fire me, I'll go to Boston. Well, he says, you run three machines. I says, I

Sidney Muskovitz in 1946. *Courtesy of Sidney Muskovitz.*

won't be in this room by myself. I'll run three machines, and the fixer can sit here or you can sit here, long as there's someone in this room. So he says, You can go home. I can't find another man to be with ya. I says, That's fine with me. Well, I went to work the next day, and the boss says to me, I don't think I'll give you no overtime.

That poor guy got a few thousand dollars, lost his job; nothing coming in his house. Fortunately when I hurt my finger, they paid me workmen's compensation, but I had to go to court. I got caught in the burr roll. There's a burr roll that knocks the burrs off the wool. I got a little too close to the burr roll, and it cut my finger. When I went to the hospital they wanted to cut the whole finger off; it was just hanging. I said, Nope; sew it back on. If it doesn't take, then cut it off, at least I'll have a piece of a finger left. It's okay now, but it will never be the same.

During World War II, I was drafted. My wife and I had one child. When I left the mill, they owed me one week's vacation pay. In order to get it I had to work until May 1 but I had to be in the service on April 29. I used to write my wife, Did you get the vacation pay? She says, The company won't give it because you missed one day. Well, I went to see the lawyer on the base, and I explained to him about that one day and here I'm trying to help my country out. They've got an American flag flying from the top of that mill which they never had before until the war. I says, I'm proud to fight for my country, and he's listening to me and shaking his head: it can't be true. He says, I'll verify what you're saying and see what I can do for you. But the company [still] says No, you got to stay until May first, and the lawyer says [to the company], You have a government contract, and if you do not give this man the vacation pay, I will see your contract is cancelled. So my wife wrote to me, and she says, They gave you that week's pay.

When the war was over and I was discharged, I didn't have to report to work for thirty days, you know, just getting straightened out and settled down. But I couldn't live on twenty dollars a week discharge pay, so I went back to work the following week. The boss said, I should take you back, all the trouble you caused us? I said, Look, I'm going to tell you once, you can fire me and send me home, then I'm going to see the federal government about what you done. The law says you've got to take me back. I'm in the service. He says, What law? I says, Well you better read the law. If I go home right now, I'm gonna get paid for a full day, and the day after, and the day after that, till I go to work. Well, he says, I'm going to take you back out of the goodness of my heart. I said, Don't do me no favors. I'm easygoing but when you start pulling that stuff, I can talk. I fight for my country; you stay back and get a high salary. I get a lousy eight dollars a month, and you, a good American, threaten me because I ask for a measly week's pay and all. Well, he said, we'll forget the whole thing. I says, That's all right with me, as long as *you* forget it. So I swept floors that day and cleaned walls, and the next day I was back in my own job.

Well as the years go by, we got a union [United Textile Workers' Union, CIO] in there and we got a few raises. The more raises we got, the more the operation went faster. Say the doffing goes from twenty-five minutes to fifteen minutes. You get another raise, the operation goes faster. The union came in around 1945. I became a steward, and if I see anything wrong, I tell the feeder or the doffer or the scourer or whatever, I tell them is that so, is that true what the company has against you? And if they say no, I fight for them. And if they said that they made a mistake and didn't mean it, I'd still fight for them. But if they do it on purpose like the doffers [forgetting to remove the can of slivers], I will not fight for them, because they're hurting their own union members.

I became a union trustee. That means you have to check the books
and the checks. Well, there was one check paid out that didn't have a
bill or a receipt. And of course you go through the books, you got to sign
that you went through them. And the president of the union says to me,
How come you're not going to sign it? I says, I didn't get a receipt and
the check is out. I'd like to know where that money went to. He said,
Well, what's the difference? I said, My conscience is going to bother me.
I'm not going to sign for it. Well, he says, I'll see if I can dig it up. I'll see
if I can get a hold of the treasurer and dig it up. I said, You'd better dig it
up because I'm not signing for it, I'm telling you right now. So he
blackballed me from being a trustee.

I'm not a company man, but the unions asked too much. When I first
worked, we only had two holidays, Christmas and Thanksgiving. We
didn't get paid, either. Now the unions wants to have about ten holidays
with pay. You can't do that with any business. All your materials and
your food goes up, 'cause the manufacturers and the shops or anybody
else is not gonna lose money. They're gonna push it [on] to the consumers [in higher prices]. Then you have inflation. The buying power of
your dollar goes down. I don't believe that someone who doesn't work
should get paid for it. If you stay out of work, then you don't get paid.
Get an honest day's pay. I don't want to be overworked, but I don't think
the company should be paying someone if they don't work.

Once they got a union in the place, the machines start going faster.
Instead of a feed lasting forty-five minutes, it lasted a half an hour.
Instead of a doffer lasting eighteen minutes, it lasts fifteen minutes. We
got another raise, the feed lasted only twenty minutes, the doffer only
ten minutes. And of course they got a few more machines. I used to oil
six; I had to oil three more. You gotta be very careful. One mistake, you
won't have no arm. It was starting to be a lot of tension; it was starting to
bother me; I was starting to slow up. Then I just couldn't keep up.

The year after I got nine machines, I started to have pains in my chest.
When I had pains in my chest, I couldn't go as fast as I can. Especially
when I'd go under the card to pull the waste out. I was sweating more
than I really should be sweating. I don't wanna lose my job, had a family
to support, and that was the only job around.

I had worked twenty-nine years in Southwell when I started getting
pains in my chest. So I went to see a doctor and I said, Doctor, I've got
pains in my chest. He says, Indigestion. I went back to work, same thing
happens. So the superintendent says, I'm going to give you a good job,
more money, ten cents an hour more. Want to be a fixer? Well, I'll give it

a try. That was 1969, the day before Labor Day. He says to me, Fixers have got to lift the metal workers and strippers up off the card. I said, Yes, I know that. I'll try it, but I can't guarantee I'm going to take it. I tried to lift it. That's when it happened. I couldn't breathe, getting dizzy. Pains in the chest. I didn't say anything to the wife and children. We drove to Plimoth Plantation for Labor Day, and I got sick and we drove home to the hospital where they revived me.

All the rumors are flying in the mill that I am dying. A few guys came to see me in the hospital and said, Sidney's gone. He'll never make it. I was dying, but I am stubborn. I stayed over a month in the hospital. The doctor said I'll never work again. I believe it was the heat and the dust that irritated my heart.

I'm glad the mills are out of Lowell. All you get is tension; your body vibrates from being nervous, afraid to get hurt. I had left my working clothes in the mill, a navy-blue shirt, a jersey, my hat, my working shoes, and my dungarees. I heard some of the fellows in the locker room say, Gee, Sidney's clothes. Wonder what we should do with them? Give them to his wife or something? I walked in, and they all say, Hey, here's the ghost. Then I went to see the boss and he says to me, You're not going to work here no more. I said, I wouldn't want to work here if you gave me five thousand dollars a week. I says, you half-killed me. You're not going to finish me off!

I Was Young and Strong and Fast
and Earned Twenty-five Cents an Hour

Henry Paradis

LOOM FIXER

The parents of Henry Paradis were determined to keep their children out of the mills, but in 1937 a young man had few other opportunities in Lowell. When offered a job, he did not hesitate, but the Lowell textile mills in the 1930s offered little encouragement of his hard work and ambition. Increased skills did not necessarily mean pay raises or better shifts. While on the job and off, Paradis hustled to supplement his earnings at whatever his ingenious mind and fingers could devise.

As part of a group of young, single men with the boundless, carousing energy of youth who worked the late-night shift, Paradis exulted in the nonstop weekend recreation that left them exhausted but still able to handle the routine of work on Monday night. His marriage followed the pattern of his parents'. Ethnic families sought to contain their children's choices within the community and censored all serious contact with girls of other nationalities. Paradis regarded the routine sexual harassment of young and inexperienced women workers by male supervisors as part of a timeless if regrettable system of male privilege.

Henry Paradis remembered a childhood of special treats from an indulgent mother, the wild freedom of play, and the texture and closeness of tenement life in Little Canada. But he also remembered that his relative success as a mill worker was an exception to the rule.

MY FATHER came to Lowell as a young man. He was born in Quebec, and my mother was born in Suncook, New Hampshire. I was born in Lowell in 1918. When my father came here, he got a job in the Suffolk mills. He worked there forty-eight years. He said to me when he retired, I thought I had a steady job. Forty-eight years is a steady job in my book.

He had six children; four girls and two boys. I'm the youngest one of the family. Actually he started out working twelve hours a day, six days a week for $5.50 a week. That wasn't much money, but in those days it was. Cigarettes were five cents a pack. He worked so hard that he said to my mother, I'll make sure that our children do not go to work in the mills.

I grew up in Little Canada. It's all torn down [now]. We lived in what they call two large blocks. There was ninety-eight tenements in one and ninety-eight in the other one. The French people had a way of doing things day-to-day. Monday was washday; they washed by hand. So they had a clothesline from one building to the other. They got their baskets and hung their clothes on the line. Every Monday morning you thought it was raining, it was dripping so much. In the summertime the kids would get underneath there; it looked like a bath. We used to take a bath on Saturday in the tub. And then my mother used to make ice cream by hand. Now that was a treat. We all had our turn at the crank. We all played together between the two buildings. If there would have been a fire, that would have been it. So old and so close together, and all made out of wood. It would have been terrible.

When I was eight years old [in 1926], my mother decided that we're going to move to the neighborhood of Pawtucketville. By then my father's making more money. We were paying seventy-five cents a week rent, but where we were going was five dollars a week. But it was a cottage, and we'd be all by ourselves. We didn't have electricity in Little Canada; we had gas [light]. My mother used to put twenty-five cents in a meter for gas. In Pawtucketville we used to go around and push the electric switch, and my father would run after us and put it out. My father gets all of us together and said, If you need it, put it on, but if not, put it out! There were a lot of bootleggers in Pawtucketville, and they were selling half a pint of whiskey for twenty cents. So, what we used to do, go to the dump and pick up bottles, and go to these fellows, and sell the bottles for a penny a piece. Then I had a paper route. I used to go up Prince Street to get the French paper, *L'Etoile.* I had sixty customers.

My mother was very good at sewing and at cooking. She made your jackets and coats, hand-downs from one to another. I remember what we used to like on Friday. One of us was allowed to bring one friend; my sisters and brothers, we would take turns. My mother would bake bread, okay? And she'd take the inside of the bread out for bread pudding. What would she do to fill the bread? Full of salmon. And then she'd make fried rice. And she'd put this on the table. The beautiful bread full of this hot salmon with fried rice. Everybody liked it; everybody went, When is it my turn? Friday night, that was her treat to us. We had a lot of fun. Come the Fourth of July, fireworks; we didn't have that. What we used to do is get cans and tie them together one after another.

We'd make a line of sometimes fifty, sixty, a hundred cans, and we'd run around the block. Vroooo, I'll get you! All kinds of noise.

As the youngest son, I used to go and visit my father once in a while in the mill and became interested in the work. I came out of school, and I got a job in a bowling alley, setting up pins. Three cents a string. Now that was from ten in the morning to twelve o'clock at night, six days a week. So Tuesday was my day off. It was July 2, 1937, and I used to like to go to the beach a lot. This day was such a beautiful day, I got up early. I walked down to the mill area, and there was two hundred people waiting to see if they could get a job. So I was talking to one of my friends, and this gentleman, Paul Whittier, comes up to me, and he says to me, Let me see your hands. So I showed him my hands. He says, Come with me, and I walked with him to the office. He says, I got a job for you. Do you want to work? I said, Yes. How old are you? I told him, Eighteen. He said, Go to the city hall and get your working card. Then I went home and told my mother, and she didn't like the idea. She said, Your father's not going to like that.

At one o'clock that day I went to work at the Newmarket mills, and it was very hot, lots of noise, and we worked from one until nine-thirty at night, second shift. Between five to five-thirty was our lunch hour. I didn't live too far from work. And after supper, my mother's talking to me, and I can't hear a thing. But I liked my work. My work was to put full bobbins in the automatic batteries that fed the looms. I had a hundred looms to feed. So I really had to move fast. I was young and strong and fast, and I earned twenty-five cents an hour. In those days it was good money, and when you got home, your mother was going to like this, and you gave her your pay envelope unopened. In my spare time I learned to be a weaver. I told my boss, I said, I can weave. He said, You can weave? And I said, Yes. So he said, Okay. You come Monday at nine-thirty. You're going to work the late shift, the third shift.

So Monday night I went to work nine-thirty to six in the morning. The boss says, Okay, these are your looms. Sixty looms. Now I knew how to weave, but I didn't have the experience of running sixty looms! So I really worked hard all night. The night went by so fast that I didn't even see it. So I went home at six-thirty, and I fell asleep. My mother woke me up at seven o'clock that night and said, Are you working tonight? I said, Yes. So anyway, I became a good weaver in no time at all. Because I was working on the late-night shift, I went to the textile school to learn loom fixing. If you lived in Lowell, if you went at night, it was free. The Lowell Textile School was all about textile machinery. People came from all over the world to learn weaving, loom fixing, dyeing, and designing. Then after the Second World War, people didn't want to study anymore about textiles; that was going down.

I didn't tell anybody, but when I graduated I walked in the mill, and I said to my boss, Here's my diploma in loom fixing. Gee, he says, I'm going to give you a job on the floor repairing the looms. Now I was making $18 a week [as a weaver]. That was very good pay; the wages were low in those days. So he said to me, We're going to start you at $16. I said, Wait a minute. I had my diploma; I was independent now. I'll go somewhere else. There's other mills. I said, If you give me $16, I'm losing $2. Rather than that, I'll stay on weaving. He comes back and says, We're going to give you $19. I said, With the understanding that you'll give me $21 in one month. He said, Yes. My supervisor died of a heart attack in my arms six months after I was there. So they asked me if I'd take over as supervisor on the second shift. Naturally I said, Yes.

I was well paid then. I had my own office. I had sixty-eight people working for me, and they were all nice people. They were people who needed to work and knew that I was new at the job, and they figured that if they do good, I'm going to do good. If it's going to be good for them, it's going to be good for me.

I dated girls in the mill. It was funny; you know the French people. Well, not only the French, the Greek and other nationalities too. Your parents wanted you to go out with your own nationality. For instance, I met this Polish girl at the mill, and I told my mother I had a date, and she asked me what was the name of the girl. Her last name was Polish. She said, That's not French. I said, I know, she's Polish. Oh, she didn't want me to go out. So I came home at nine-thirty at night; I'm twenty years old now, and she's waiting for me. Gee, you're late. Where'd you go with that Polish girl? And another time, I met this girl. She was a student at St. Joseph's High School. And her mother was French, but her father was German. So it was a nice night, and I said, Let's stop at my house, and I'll introduce you to my mother. I did that on purpose. She was very nice to her, as nice as pie, and she was very nice to my mother. So when we left and I came back home, my mother said, What nationality is that girl? I said, Her father's German. She said, I don't want you to see her anymore. Oh yes, they didn't like you to go out.

I did things on the side. These guys would play cards, and Hey, Henry, get me a beer. For ten cents; I'd take the money first. Then I'd give my mother a buck for the electricity to use the refrigerator. Selling beer at ten cents, I could probably make three cents a bottle. But, you do that two, three times a week, it gets to be a lot of money at the end of the week. And I was well known; I was very popular with the city of Lowell.

I also made weavers' hooks. You see, a weaver had to have a hook to draw in the yarn through the heddles and the reed. It would be twelve inches long and the last two inches would curve a little bit, and then at the end, you would make a hole. That would be to hold your yarn. To draw the yarn through the reed and the harnesses. The hooks were made of harness rod, and it was very hard steel. It was very difficult to drill a hole through that. So what I did, I asked a dentist to save the very hard steel drills for me instead of throwing them away. It did the trick; it was wonderful.

But it took time to make them. First of all the rod was a little too wide. So you had to put it on the emery wheel and make it narrow, see? And to bend that, you had to heat it up, so it would get really hot. And then when the steel is hot, you can bend it much easier, see? And then, I'd burn the tip to drill the hole. Then you had to get emery cloth and keep polishing because it had to be as smooth as can be. Now, what would we do for a handle? Used to cut off the end of a tooth brush three or four inches long. Different sizes for different people. A woman would want a narrow handle; a man, a five-inch handle. Then I'd drill a hole, that was simple; and I'd put some glue in it and glue it. A lot of weavers would put it in their shirt pocket and when you bend down, get it in the eye, see? That was very dangerous. A lot of people lost their eye for that. So, the company said, no more pocket; any place else but your shirt pocket.

So I used to have probably twenty, twenty-five hooks all the time. I made them at the mill when I was head loom fixer, when the boss wasn't around. So, a weaver would say, Hey, I lost my hook. You got one to sell me? They had to have it. Sure. So, I'd go to my tool box. Now you have your choice. Well, I'll take this one. Give me a buck: you had to take your money before you'd give them the hook, see? A lot of times they didn't have the money. I'll give it to you payday. So, okay. Then you'd look around, and you'd find that [lost] hook, clean the handle, or put another one on. How many times did I do that? And not only me, many.

At the Newmarket mill, where I worked eighteen years, I went to see the nurse once. I happened to hit the edge of my tool bench, and I got sliver under my fingernail, and I couldn't get it out. It was in. You know, when you got something under your fingernail, it hurts. So I said to the boss, See what I did? I got a sliver, a wood sliver. The boss said, You go see the nurse. She was a Polish woman, a big Polish woman. I'd never talked to her, but I knew who she was. If I'd see her on the street, I'd say, that's the nurse from the Newmarket. So, I go down, and she said in a gruff voice, What can I do for you? I said, Well, I got a sliver under my finger. She said, What did you do that for? And you know what I did? I turned around, and I went back upstairs. The boss said, Okay, okay, but oh I was suffering! So finally after eight working hours, I went to the clinic at St. Joseph's Hospital, and they took it out for me. They were afraid of her; they were all afraid of her. I'm telling you, the women went when it was time for them to be sick, once a month, or they felt faint or whatever. They would go, but as far as the men is concerned, she was too rough. What did you do that for? If you get hurt, naturally, you don't do it on purpose. Oh yes, she was a tough one.

Very few got hurt. But I'll tell you about the worst thing of all that happened up there, and I thank God every day it never happened to me because I'm not that big and I was never that strong. We used to put these warp beams in the loom. You had that warp on a two-wheel truck. So you pushed it down and picked up one end, then you had to lift the other end to put it on the frame of the loom. Now all of these fellows, when they'd lift those beams, they got ruptured hernias. So, somebody wouldn't come in one day; where's so and so? Oh, he's in the hospital for a hernia. And I did a lot of lifting, never got hurt once.

You could not open the doors or the windows. The warmer it was, the better for the yarn. The less it would break, the better the room would be running. And the more the room is running, the more production you would make. The reason why they had three shifts in the mill is because there was big expense in the mill. All mill machinery on the first shift was taxed. From eight o'clock in the morning till five o'clock at night, they were taxed, each individual machine. The only department that made money was the weaving department that was weaving cloth to sell. The rest of the departments were all expense. So the first shift, no more taxes on the machinery, but the third shift was all profit. Beautiful for them, and they made sure they had a third shift. To work on the late shift, they'd give you seven cents more an hour which was big money at the time. I remember one time we got an increase in pay: two cents an hour. We worked forty hours; that was eighty cents. So that wasn't much of an increase, but you know, you got your pay, Hey, eighty cents more!

Working late-night shift is hard. The reason for this is because it might be very hot that day, and you're not going to sleep too well. So you're going to get up and go out, and then you've got to go to work all night. Now that's going to be a long night because come two o'clock in the morning, your eyes start to close. But, you know, the funny part of working on the late-night shift, you don't sleep that much; you go to work all night and two, three o'clock in the morning, oh, you could sleep on a picket fence! Come five o'clock, it's getting daylight. Oh, cripes, you're wide awake again; you're good for the beach for the day.

Like on Friday, I used to get up early, well, all my friends, a group of ten. We all worked the late-night shift at the Newmarket mill. Some were weavers, some were battery hands, some were fixing looms. Fridays—why we'd get up early, see, because it's our last night at work. Come five or six in the morning, you're wide awake. Now it's Saturday, see? We'd go and have a few beers in the back of the police station. We could have got arrested. Then, let's go to the beach for the day; we don't have to work tonight. So we go to the beach, and that night we'd go home and get dressed and go out. Then we'd play cards all night at my place. These guys who were dead tired Friday night, they're going to play cards. Sunday morning we go to six or seven o'clock Mass at St. Jean the Baptiste. Okay. So to the beach again for the day. Sunday night, play cards all night. Now Monday, you went to bed. You were dead. So we'd go to bed, then at six o'clock my mother would wake me up and then I'd have supper, I'd go to the textile school, then I'd go to work at nine-thirty.

Most of the fellows in the group were French, but after a while other nationalities started to join the crowd. Polish, Portuguese, more Polish, a few Irish guys, and then the Greeks, one by one, kinda scared. One Saturday morning we were having a few beers, and I said to the fellows, You know, McQuades is having a sale at nine o'clock this morning. You get a hat, you get a shirt, you get a tie, you get a suit, you get stockings, you get shoes, and a bag for eighteen dollars. So, one of the fellows says, You going? Oh, I'm going. I was kind of the leader then. Well, if Henry goes, so will I. At a quarter of nine we were in front of the store waiting. I knew the clerk; Maurice was his name. I said, Maurice, we all want to buy what you've got on sale. Cripes, he's as happy as can be; he's going to make money, ten of us. We paid twenty-five cents a week. So it's my turn this week to go pay McQuades. Everybody gives me twenty-five cents, and I go pay it. Then next week it's your name, so we all pay you. At four o'clock that Saturday afternoon, we're all going down to get our clothes. You had to have a cuff put on the pants. We all went down to the Commodore Ballroom that night to dance. We thought we were the cat's meow. Well, finally we paid them. My mother was against that; too much money, eighteen bucks.

The boss was very strict. They made sure that you kept busy. If you didn't have anything to do, they'd find something. They had to because if not, they would be replaced themselves. Some of them got caught smoking, and they got fired right away. If you got caught doing something you weren't supposed to, you got fired right away. I don't care who you were, a sweeper or head loom fixer.

Actually as far as trouble goes, the trouble was with the supervisors. Let's say this girl comes and gets a job. Well, hey, he likes her, you know? I'll get you a raise. It won't be much, but I'll get you a raise. But he's not saying when. A week goes by. Oh, I'll get you your raise. Oh, don't ask me, don't worry about it, I'll get you a raise. But you know what would be nice? To go out together. Oh cripes, she's going to get a raise, hey. The boss is asking her. That's an honor. So, they would go out. First thing you know, she can't work any more, if you know what I mean. But she never got that raise because she got into trouble. Oh yes. That happened many times in my father's time, in my time, and I'm sure it's still happening now. And naturally we knew that, see? A girl would come in neat and nice looking, and oh cripes, you're not going to stay here long. Because the supervisors, the Romeos, they think they can do anything they want to do or have anything they want.

As a loom fixer, I had ninety looms. The head loom fixer was different; I had the whole floor to take care of. But I had men to do that. My job was to assign these men to different looms to repair them and keep them in good condition so they would run good. If a weaver would put up the flag, really a piece of wood, I'd see the flag. Yellow was for the loom fixer, and green for the smash-piecer. I'd see the yellow stick, I'd go over, and then I would know. I could tell what's wrong with the loom by the feel of the cloth. A good loom fixer, he looks at the cloth, then he knows. If it's all curly on one side, there's something wrong on that side. If you get skipping, then it would be your harnesses. If there was an end out, then you knew it was the stop-motion. Your yarns broke, but the looms didn't stop, something else. If you knew your cloth, then you were in good shape. And to be a good weaver, you also had to have knowledge of your material.

There were many, many women in the mills. Some of them were grouchy, and some were nice. If they were ambitious, they were very nice to you. If they say, My loom is broken, [then] okay I'll be there in a minute. If you didn't like her or him, you didn't go right away. You made them wait. So, while they're waiting for you, their loom is stopped; they're losing money. You had to do it anyway, but if you liked the person, man or woman, oh, right away. Or if they didn't like you, they wouldn't tell you. They didn't care how much money they were losing. Your production would be lower, and you'd get hell. So it can work both ways.

My wife never worked in the mill. I wanted her to stay home. Her father worked for the Boston and Maine Railroad. When she graduated from high school, she was only sixteen years old. Graduation was Sunday afternoon, and on Monday morning she had a job at the Boston and Maine in Boston. In those days, if a woman worked in the office for the Boston and Maine, you had to be single. Once you got married, you lost your job. So when we got married, my wife was all done working, and twelve months after that, we had our first child. My mother did the same.

I got very interested in politics in 1952. I was working at the Newmarket mill, and Christian Herter's going to run for governor. The Herter Republicans in Lowell were James Gaffney and Brad Morse. So they were talking, we want to get labor's vote here in Lowell; who can we get? So Gaffney got me because I worked in the mill, but Brad Morse didn't know me to talk to. So one night I went to work, and my supervisor said to me, James Gaffney wants to see you in the office! That's how they talked, nothing nice. They talk as if they were mad at you all the time. And he wants you now! Cripes, I said, what does he want? So I went down. He said, Henry Paradis? I said, Yes. Then he started to tell me about Brad Morse, and Herter is going to run, and they'd like to get the Republican vote in Lowell, but they'd love to get the labor vote. Would I help? I says, What do you want me to do? Well, he says, you're going to come with us to the Republican meeting. So, I liked that; I was welcome as a king. They were very nice to me because I was going to get all the vote at the Newmarket. So I take Herter into the mill and introduced him to these people before working hours, after working hours. And don't forget, you've got to vote for this guy. Okay, don't worry.

We also made some radio talk, and they asked me questions about the mill, blah, blah, blah. So at the last Republican meeting, I'm voted to be an elector for the electoral college. The next day in the newspaper, my picture there: local loom fixer chosen as elector in the electoral college. Well, the phone was ringing then! When we went to the statehouse, it was a big deal, a big day. I was on t.v. I didn't realize how big it was. So that gave me the title of Honorable. My name is Honorable Henry L. Paradis. We got a kick out of that. A friend of mine, he's a traveling salesman. Send me a card no matter where he goes; Honorable Henry

L., all the time, never misses. The Republicans got the vote in the Newmarket. Herter got all the votes in Lowell. A lot of them were Democrats, but they voted for Herter on account of [me] and because they thought it was a big deal. They were proud of me. Local loom fixer.

I worked at the Newmarket mills for eighteen years. I had another job for seventeen years at United Elastic. They asked me if I'd go to Belgium when they closed down. I said, No thank you. They said, You should go, you speak French, and they're all French people there. I said, No, I'm too old. When the Newmarket closed in 1954, I was thirty-seven. I didn't care; I was still a young man.

But I knew the textile business was going down and down and down, so I went to school in Boston to learn to be a fireman in a boiler room. Then I took my state test, and I passed and I got a second-class fireman's license. Working on the second shift at the United Elastic from two-thirty to eleven, that gave me a chance to go to work at the House of Corrections in Billerica. If you get a job there in the boiler room on the late-night shift, you sleep four hours a night. So the chief at Billerica said to me, What shift do you want? I said, I'd like the late-night shift because I'm working second shift, and the place is going to close down, and when they do, then I'll stay here steady, see? So I'd leave United Elastic at eleven; I'd go to work at Billerica at eleven-thirty. The other guy on duty says, You going to sleep first? I'd say, Yes, I'll sleep first. So I used to sleep four hours, and he'd wake me up and he'd sleep four hours. So that was good. I was making good money. I got a pension from the county; in the mill you didn't get no pension.

If I was a young man, I would want to work in the hydroelectric plant on the Merrimack River. Today, all the textile mills in Lowell, they're all gone. Where are they? Who knows, now? Thailand or whatever. Now Wang computers is going to be bigger than the mills in Lowell. There's no end to computers. You buy something today, and you go next month, it's changed. It's better. Sometimes I sit home and I say to myself, did I do the right thing or do I regret working in the mill? Sometimes I say, No, I don't regret it because I had a steady job. I'd work hard; we all did. I made sure that my children would do well in school. I made sure they were clean and neat and well dressed, and as soon as they came home they would do their homework. Like when television came out with children's programs, Oh, Mama, I want to watch. Before you watch, you do your homework. They did their homework.

I see these fellows from the mill once in a while, and [told them] there is going to be a textile reunion in the fall [of 1985]. Everybody in Lowell that has worked in a textile mill. We're all going to get together. And I said, That's a wonderful idea because some of these people I haven't seen for a long time. Hey, hi Joe; how are you, you so and so. That'll be a great day, I think. So, I see different people on the street [and tell them about it,] and they say, Oh, no! Count me out. I don't want any part of it. Why? Hey, I worked hard in the mill for no money while those people were getting very rich. Which is true.

Never Screamed Before;
Never Have Since

Nicholas Georgoulis

DYE HOUSE AND BLEACHERY WORKER

Nicholas Georgoulis remembered the texture of his childhood and youth growing up in the oldest working-class neighborhood of Lowell, the Acre. At the turn of the twentieth century new emigrant groups from southern and eastern Europe, especially Greek and Polish people, began to crowd out the Irish who had lived there since the founding of the city in the 1820s. The Acre became a thoroughfare and a battle ground for conflicts ranging from rock fights among children to sadistic assaults by adults. Each child knew his neighborhood, face by face and house by house.

Play could sometimes be helpful to the depression-strapped family. After a snowstorm, the children—as though they remembered some ancient ritual—stretched their arms over a fallen tree in the nearby Common, claiming it for their family's stove. Railroad tracks were scoured for coal, the gas works for coke.

The Georgoulis family of eight children exchanged rough and tumble and taunts and blows. Home was mother's place. Men inhabited the public world of church and coffee houses where politics buzzed, while religious factions within the Greek Orthodox community debated the perennial question of old and new calendars. There, Nicholas Georgoulis watched satirical puppet shows about homeland politics that meant nothing but fun to his young eyes. None of this prepared him for the physical hardships and dangers of the dye house. Georgoulis worked various construction jobs in the late 1930s, but when he found himself unemployed in 1939, he very reluctantly tried for a mill job.

I WAS BORN in Lowell in 1917. My parents were born in Greece: my father on the island of Theos and my mother on the island of Sefoloina. They married in Greece sometime around 1912. After the birth of my oldest brother, my dad came here to this country in 1914 and left my mother there. Then he sent money over to my mother to come to this country, and he had eight more children. Nine altogether, eight who lived. My only sister was born in 1916. My mother landed on the island of Ellis in New York, then came to Lowell.

They often spoke about grandparents that none of us in the family had ever seen. We weren't that inquisitive about it. Being children, we always wanted to go out and play. Which we did. Then in the afternoon, we'd come back home from public school and take Greek lessons. Our first language was Greek, the one we learned first. My dad would teach all of us at home in the afternoon. Or in the evening when he had time. When the churches started having their school sessions, we'd study the Greek language, reading and writing at St. George's. We had started with the Holy Trinity, but when the factions in Lowell split into two different groups, we went with the groups that became St. George's.

My group was the old guard who believed in the old calendar, the Julian calendar. The officials at city hall set my birthday on April 11, but it's actually April 24 by the old calendar. There was a two-week difference. My folks adhered to the old calendar, and all of us were registered on the dates of the old calendar except for the later births. We are now on the Gregorian calendar, but the Greeks for quite a while followed the Julian.

Every Sunday we went to church, the whole family. My dad would hold us by the hand and take us down. My mother stayed at home and did the cooking. She would go to church when she didn't have any cooking to do or she would go to the Saturday night vesper service or some midweek service. But Sunday, the poor soul had to cook, and she had a family to cook for.

I was the third oldest. A boy ahead of my sister, my sister, then myself, and then the other boys followed. It was a seventeen-year span of children. My mother was illiterate in both English and Greek, but she did pick up some American words to speak. My dad was quite a scholar in the old country, but he left there and came here to pick up the gold in the streets.

My mother was a hard-working soul, and she stayed home. She didn't have to work for a living. Until he passed away, my dad supported her and the family pretty well, figuring it was the Depression. He passed away in 1943 while six of us were in the service. We had a brother who lost his life in the service, and several of us were wounded. During the war she went to work in the Boott mills. She was four foot eleven inches tall, a short woman and slender, and she was always happy and singing in a happy way. She worked on one of the spinning machines; she was fifty-two years old at the time. In 1946 she quit. She never worked at a job before. That was her first and only job, but she was with some women that she knew so she got along just fine. She didn't like the work, but she had nobody at home and she had to.

My mother, the poor soul, she'd be up at six o'clock in the morning trying to wake us all up, hustling us up, trying to get us fed and out. Those that went to school, to get to the school, while she passed out chores to others. We were chopping wood and gathering wood during snowstorms. We lived [in the Acre] across from the North Common, and whenever a tree fell down in a storm, we'd all go out and stretch our arms out [over the tree]. We owned that portion of the tree until somebody from the family came out with a saw. Then we started cutting and lugging the wood home. We had chores splitting wood; mine was doing kindling. I chopped my finger with the axe one day. Didn't swing hard enough to chop it off, but I still have the scar.

Chop the wood, gather the wood, bring it in the house. Go down with the wagon, down by the railroad tracks, pick up coal and coke. Bring it home and burn that. And sometimes the engineers in the train would see a group of kids coming by, and they'd throw the coal out to be picked up.

One time they parked a freight load of number one coal near the gas company. They just parked it there, the train men did, for some reason or other temporarily. I'll tell you they were missing a few tons before they picked up that freight again. We loaded up bags. The freight train was just chest high to you, so you'd hold a bag there and load it up. It was the Depression; money was scarce. Some of the healthier and stronger kids would climb the fence of the gas company and steal the coke or toss it over. But that freight car of number one coal, everybody did a job on it! There must have been two hundred kids filling up bags. It was like a swarm of bees. It was stealing, yes, but it was still Depression. There was nobody to stop you.

We also had to help with the wash. We used scrubboards. Sometimes I used to stay home from school when she wasn't feeling too well. I was out in the backyard doing the scrubbing, and the truant officer came along to see what was happening. I wasn't playing hookey. He thought I was, but [when the officer saw the boy] he just laughed and took off. [His sister] would help out with the cooking and the ironing, and the boys would do the washing or help with the washing. If my mother hadn't caught up with it, they'd finish it off for her. Myself mostly.

There was just one sister, and she wasn't the queen bee either. She had her battles with us. We had some royal battles between us, all of us.

She being one of the older ones, she thought she could lord it over the rest of us. And every chance we got to beat her up, she got her beatings. Nothing about inequality then; she was an equal. If one of the boys got mad at her and he wanted to punch her, he'd punch her. But she would strike back just as hard. Fortunately we lived across the street from the North Common, and we could just go to the park and play so you weren't a nuisance in the house.

I liked the Acre; it was a community. There wasn't a soul in the entire Acre that a child growing up didn't get to know. If you lived in the Acre, they knew them by name. If not by name, by sight. They could almost tell you exactly the house they lived in. And the people would walk down the street, and everyone was saying, Hello, and speaking nicely. We formed an athletic team, the Black Hawks football team. Some people called us a bunch of bums or delinquents, but we had the best teams in the city. And we were the wildest group. We didn't molest anybody or bother anybody, but if they bothered us they were in trouble.

We chased the Irish, and the Irish chased us. When the Irish were too many for us, we'd go and join in with the French and fight the Irish. If the French weren't handy, we'd jump in with the Polish and chase the Irish and fight them. They had to come through our Acre to go to St. Patrick's Boys' School. But they used to beat the heck out of us, and we in turn retaliated by beating them. Bigotry is a great thing in Lowell even today, and it was greater then. If you were of foreign parentage, you were considered a foreigner by most and the Irish in particular.

When I came back from the service, I had my eye on a particular [Irish] cop; I could have killed him. But when I came back, he was dead. I never forgot him because he beat me up when I was twelve years old, because I happened to be of foreign [parents] and was selling newspapers. He took my license [to sell newspapers] away from me quite often, but this time he thought he [really] had me. He said, Come here, kid, I won't bother you. Took me in the back alley behind a lunch place, asked me to put my newspapers down, then he started whacking me. I couldn't go home and tell my folks a cop had beat me up for nothing, 'cause I'd get another licking. They believed in respecting the law. So I didn't say anything.

When I came back from the service in 1946, I was going to look him up, but he was gone. Never forget it; I was only twelve years old. To be walking down the street and be called a G.D. foreigner by anybody in a uniform wasn't right. The French and the Greeks and the Polish got along very well. It seemed that they banded together for their own

Acre children on Adams Street, 1939. *Courtesy of Lowell Housing Authority and the Center for Lowell History.*

protection. This cop was called Bull Liston. I used to go down to the city hall and buy a twenty-five-cents license to sell newspapers that had a big safety pin. You needed that to sell newspapers. We bought the newspapers for a penny and a half and sold them for two cents. And the son-of-a-gun would take the badge away from me about once a month. Every time he caught me. Bull Liston preyed only on children. He sneaked up on us and got hold of us, and he'd use that stick; he did with me. Sometimes the other patrolman, a very nice man, would warn us. He'd say, Jesus, kids, here comes the Bull! Then we would scatter.

We lived in what had been a one-family home, but as the Greeks moved into the Acre, the Irish moved out. It had been a small cottage, and it had six rooms downstairs and the bath. The bath was just the toilet; we bathed in washtubs in those days. My father rented this place from a landlord by the name of Joe Fay, who later sold the house and the cottage next door as the Depression came on. My father and the next-door neighbor bought them. It was a beautiful little place, backyard for a garden, had a little tool shed in the back that I used as a playhouse. I played there with electrical wiring and batteries and got it lit with lights when we didn't have electricity in the house yet. We did all our studying by oil lamps until we finally put in electricity in 1932 or '33. The house was torn down, and the family was forced to move for the housing project in 1939.

We got our first radio in 1935. My father loved to dance, and he would pick up a broomstick or a chair, and he would dance. He was a happy man. He was very, very jolly. He was a flirtatious man. He was a ladies' man. He'd flirt with every female that came along. When I was going out with this girl that I married, she would come by, and he'd flirt with her mother. He was always singing, joking, dancing. He wanted to go on picnics. As little children we were loaded up on trucks, and everybody took their picnic baskets out to a field. Everybody spread out their lunches, and they enjoyed themselves. He would take my mother to a beach on Sundays when she wasn't feeling good. Don't go to church, do nothing. The whole family would pack in a car and go to the beach, usually in Lynn, to Nahant, but always a beach.

He got involved in Greek politics, never in [Lowell] city politics, but he always made it a point to vote at every election. He never failed to vote. My mother didn't vote because being unable to read or write, she didn't bother voting or trying to learn the language. She was too busy raising a family. I would hear him speaking about Greek politics in the coffee houses. I'd go visiting with him, but it was way above my head. But I knew it was Greek politics, and that's how the churches began to split. I started shining shoes in the coffee houses. The coffee was a nickel for a little demitasse cup. The churches got mad at the coffee houses for being open on Sunday mornings, and the churches weren't that full. So they tried to get the city fathers to close the coffee houses on Sundays to get the fellas to go to church, but it never worked out. They would play cards. It was just a place for the guys to hang out. It was a club house for them, a very inexpensive club house. It was all men; never saw a female in there.

Market Street used to have probably twelve coffee houses, and they would all be full. My father's generation, sometimes they used to have shows. They'd have a screen, and they'd have little forms or caricatures of people pinned on a clothes line. They'd be talking behind the screen and playing like a Punch and Judy show. It was a clown show, and we'd gather around and listen to that.

Growing up on the North Common as a youngster, the city used to have free movies. My father had a little push cart with three-holder ice cream cone stands, sell ice cream for a penny a cone. I was just a little shaver. My father would go twenty-four hours a day if he could. He'd put in a ten-, twelve-hour day at the mill, and then he'd go out and make ice cream or buy it for the little cones for a penny. Every night in the Acre at nine o'clock there was a strict ritual; all the kids would get off the street. You heard the words start: Nine o'clock! Everybody would run to their house. We'd just pass the word down: Nine o'clock! In the entire neighborhood, every kid disappeared from the street at nine o'clock.

I stole many a sewing machine belt from my dad. He was strict. He used to carry one in his pocket and whip us with it. When he fell asleep, I'd go take it. Unknown to me, he had a spare one somewhere! God! Ya know they couldn't reach ya, there was so many [of us], just like a pack of rats. They didn't get ya, but whoosssh, they used the belt, and you got hit. But it wasn't to hurt you; just to punish you. Let you know that you have to get in line, toe the line, that's all. They were strict.

I remember one time two of my brothers and myself were running around the house. We thought, Ha! Ma can't hurt us. She can't do anything to us. By gosh! If she didn't get all three of us! I was running by, she got me by the arm, twisted me over, flattened me down, put her foot on me, and grabbed the other one going by with the other hand, and she had both of us. She put her foot across both of us and caught the third one. She put us in our place. We were horsing around in the kitchen. We thought we could get by with something. We must have been eleven, twelve, thirteen. When she can just flip you over flat on your back, she was pretty good.

My father worked first in the Massachusetts mills in the dye room, and he eventually wound up at the Merrimack. The same owners had a hand in all of the plants. I have an old book of the history of Lowell. It explains how all these owners: Moody, Boott, and the others, were all part owners of the Merrimack and of the Appleton mills. They were all a combine of sorts, so it still had to be the same way.

My father worked mostly with velvets and light pinwale corduroy. The bleach house, they called it the bleachery, had huge tubs. You walked on a big ramp [around the vats], and the cloth would be cooking [in the bleach]. Then after they cook it, they would take it out and put it through this liquor. I don't know what it was. Some guy fell in [once]; they took out parts of him, that's all. You walked on a ramp. You looked down at the cloth that was being boiled in this liquor. To me, some kind of sweet-smelling liquid they used to put in.

The first experience I had in the mill was when I was applying for work in the dye house. I saw all these fellas with their feet [and legs] wrapped up in cloths. Later I found out that they wrapped their feet in cloths like they did and boots [underneath] so that the dyes and the acids wouldn't burn through to their skin. It was the harsh chemicals. They looked like a bunch of gypsies. They had different colored cloths from the dyes that fell upon them. Or if they were mixing up a dye, it would fall on their clothing. Even work clothes, you'd have to make something up from what they had there or take some old cloths and wrap rags around you and work that way. You worked usually stripped to the waist, so you just had a tee shirt on.

You had no other choice 'cause you were working in a hot area, in a steam area whether you were bleaching or you were dyeing. If you worked in the dryer, it was extremely hot in there. As you put the rolls through the dryer, they came out the other end. It was always hot; the dryer had big drums, thirty or forty drums that the wet cloth went in and out of, dry on the other end. They would extract the water, pass it into the dryer, and then fold it up.

When I went to work, they were using the new machines that looked like wheat harvesting machines. You had five bays of cloth going back and forth and around and around with separators so the cloth wouldn't tangle itself. One was hot, another was cool water. You would push the cloth over with a long lever and hold that lever till all the cloth was in that reel. You have to keep going and keep going. Builds up the muscle in your arm. The machine keeps moving around, you're wearing boots, and you're in water all the time. It's easy to slip, easy to get hurt. From there it goes to the air-suction machine that extracts the water or to a round drum to spin dry. You had to let it spin until most of the moisture was out. Then take it out and into a folding machine. And lay out the cloth layer by layer. It would go into a regular dryer and then would be taken upstairs and inspected, then rolled up and run through the cutting room where they cut the velvet or the pinwale corduroy.

The dye vats were all the same. The [rolls of cloth in the jigs] were all held with a rosin strap with weights on each pulley to keep the things from slipping. But then the rosin would get too hot, and eventually it would just slide. That's when the troubles came. The dye room was a long room, a huge place, with a bunch of vats [or jigs], and each man had two vats to work on. The cloth went in, down, around, and up over the steam pipe, then came up and rolled up on the other two pulleys. One would unravel, and the other would roll up. Then you'd reverse the process and go back and forth until you got the right color or the right bleach.

When you reverse the machine, you pull a lever towards you, and it would start to roll back the other way. If you weren't there to watch it, the end [of the cloth] might fall through and you'd have to weave it back through again and it was a hard job. It was hard trying to weave it back through because then you had to work through heat, acids, and hot water, sometimes 196 degrees. When you're dyeing cloth, you've got to have hot water anyway, but for bleaching your caustic was a little bit stronger. For some dyes, the vats had to reach 200 degrees for certain colors. You couldn't start the machine till it was 196, and you had a temperature thing you stuck in and read it.

The rosin strap is supposed to hold the pulley from rolling [the cloth] too fast. In my case [in late 1941], the rosin strap let go as I was feeding this [jig.] Now I'm waiting for this machine [with caustic in it] to come back up to temperature and waiting to push the lever that would put it into gear. As I pushed the lever forward, the [rosin slipped] and the cloth [which had filled up with steam from the pipe] exploded, like blowing up a paper bag. It filled up with hot steam and caustic, 196 degrees. All that liquid went up in the air, and it caught me. I screamed for the first time in my life. Never screamed before; never have since. I got it from the neck to the waist. I jumped in a [nearby] barrel of [acidic] water. [Nicholas Georgoulis's burns were severe even with the emergency barrel of acidulated water to counteract the lye. The caustic burned his flesh to the bone; his injury required sixteen skin grafts. When his arm had finally healed, he was drafted into the army in the fall of 1942, and he never returned to the mills.]

I Can Take It; I Can Stand the Grind

Del Chouinard

SLASHER

The son of French Canadian immigrants, Del Chouinard combined two essential elements of their culture in New England: religion and mill work. The family survived because of its fierce belief in the moral good of earning your own way.

Del Chouinard spent a few years as a seminarian, but in comparison to the stifling obedience expected of him, even mill work promised self-reliance and mobility. As choir director of the biggest French Catholic church in the city, he cherished and preserved the French language and traditional sacred music, while church and society around him abandoned them.

Del Chouinard took pride in being a slasher, which involved complicated work that prepared warp yarns to stand up to the pounding of the looms, but the market for synthetic fabrics soured in the mid-1950s, undermining his trade and forcing him, if he wished to work full time, to accept any mill job that needed doing. In spite of his own narrow escape when a roof caved in, he blamed accidents and injuries on the foolishness and ignorance of mill workers. He clung to the traditions that assured a man's authority and dictated the separation of men's work from women's work, despite his own involvement in jobs that violated those boundaries for both sexes.

I WAS BORN in Lowell in 1930—to celebrate the Depression. My father and mother both emigrated from the coast of Quebec along with my two older brothers. They were having quite a time to make a living up there. My father had a farm, and it wasn't paying off too much. So finally like a lot of others, he had to immigrate to this country. Of all of my relatives, we are the only ones here. The rest of them are all in Canada. Some of them, I don't even know; I lost track over the years. Or I've never seen [them]; some of my father's brothers I've never even seen.

He immigrated around 1927. They were poverty stricken like a lot of the other emigrants from other countries. My father came here [to

Lowell], and he got a job at the Merrimack mills. He stayed here a few weeks, and then he went back to get my mother and my two brothers. When he came back, somebody else had gotten his job. So he was an entire year without work. Fortunately they came across some good people that had a boardinghouse, and my mother was quite a cook. She worked for this boardinghouse as a cook, and my father was more or less a caretaker of the property. That's how they got by for a whole year. It was a private boardinghouse close to the Merrimack mills.

After that, my father started picking up work in different mills as a weaver. From there he went to Lawrence to work in the Pacific woolen mills, and he worked for them until the place closed down. By that time, he was ready to retire at sixty-five, which he did. Then he got a small part-time job as a house painter, and he passed away at sixty-nine. When he was at work in Lawrence, he worked on the second shift. He used to leave the house around one-thirty because he started at two or three. He'd come home around eleven o'clock at night. By the time he'd come home, I was fast asleep with my five brothers and one sister. My father was the sole provider up until my brothers got old enough to go to work themselves. Then, like I did, you go to work, you come home, you give your pay at home, and then you get a small allowance and you get along on that.

My mother, she'd get up in the morning and make breakfast for the entire family. My father was a meat-and-potatoes man, three times a day. There was no such thing as just a bowl of corn flakes; that wasn't his bag. He'd need meat and potatoes, three times a day. And my mother was a fantastic cook, and she never wasted an ounce of food. She always managed to take any leftovers we had and turn them into something else which was just as good as the first time. Her day's work was just being a housewife: taking care of the family, doing the cooking, taking care of the apartment, doing the washing, and doing the ironing. She never worked except maybe in the later years when she worked part time in a hospital. She never was in any factory.

My mother was very friendly with everyone and was always willing to help anybody that needed help. She was a strong, hefty woman. Always managed to do hard work: wash floors, wash windows, wash walls. It never bothered her much. She always looked after us very, very well. We never went to bed on an empty stomach, never went without shoes on our feet. My father was a good worker, never a big provider, but my mother manipulated the paycheck to make both ends meet. When times would get hard, they had these insurance policies, five and ten

cents [a week] insurance policies on the children. If times would get
hard and my father would be out of work, they'd cash in one of the small
insurance policies and start us another one once they got back on their
feet. And that's the way they managed to get through. They always
found a way out.

My mother taught us how to be morally good. She taught us never to
steal from anybody. Or to try to hurt anybody by saying things against
them whether they were true or not. Never knock down another person,
and if a person gets down, don't kick him. Try to pick him up. That's
how we were brought up. They taught us to be happy with what we have,
providing that you have earned it. There is no such thing as a Santa
Claus. You're not going to get anything for nothing. If you want something, you go out and work to get it. Nobody's going to give it to you for
nothing.

That's the way we were raised. My brothers were all the same. Nothing was given to us. We didn't try to hurt another person or play favorites
with somebody else to get something out of it. You don't go out to help
somebody with the intention of receiving something back. If you do get
something back, all well and good, but the primary thought in doing it
was not to receive or get in return. You gave without expecting something in return.

My father was very, very strict, and God bless him for being that.
Because we were brought up morally, and we never shamed either of
our parents. We never back talked to them either. Whether my father
was right or wrong, he was still my father, therefore he was always right.
In turn, I've brought up my three daughters the same way. I am the head
man; I am the man of the house. Whether I am right or wrong, I am still
the father and the man of the house. I reserve the right to be right,
although I am wrong.

I never stood up to my father, never, never, no way! My brothers, yes;
let's face it, brothers will do that. And the stronger of the two will come
out the victor. If I had stood up to my mother and tried to scare her and
my father had known about it, then I would have been in big trouble.
We were taught to respect a parent, respect older people, our neighbors,
and all those that we had to deal with.

The church was definitely important in my childhood. I was born and
brought up in the Acre section, and I attended the St. Jean Baptiste
Church. When I was a child growing up in the Acre, the Greeks stayed
on one side of the street, the French stayed on the other side, and the
Polacks would stay on their side, and there was more or less of a battle

between the nationalities. That all changed during World War II. Then everybody moved in together. There was no such thing as the Greeks on Market Street and the French on Salem Street. You had French, Greek, Portuguese, all living in the same section.

I sang in the church for forty years. The last twelve years, I was choir director up there. It started out as a hobby and turned into a full-time job. Between the hours that I was putting in then at the mill, approximately fifty-five to sixty a week, and teaching the choir—whatever I had to teach them, I had to learn all the parts myself first—it became too much. I was also in charge whenever they had funerals and weddings. I had to make sure that I furnished the church with a singer and an organist. The entire music in my church was my charge. Anybody that wanted anything had to go through me.

Over the years as all the new changes took place in our religion and they demanded more and more congregational singing instead of choirs, the choir dropped out. I was leading the congregation in singing during the Masses. Then I started a small choir, and it grew and grew to a point where I could no longer handle it.

I sang in every church in the city of Lowell. When I was working at the Wannalancit mill on the second shift or the third shift, that's what I used to do every morning, go from one church to another. It gave me an extra income. I was raising a family then, so you always need an extra income somehow. I used to do that every morning.

I started singing at the age of eight with Rudolph Pepin, the organist at St. Jean the Baptiste church. I joined the boys' choir. From then on I never stopped. I kept right on going. In 1944, I entered the Oblate Seminary in Bucksport, Maine. At the time, I thought I had the aspiration of becoming a priest. I worked for the church from a very early age. After three years, I finally found out that it wasn't my calling. I couldn't take orders. I couldn't see myself having to report every time I went up and down the stairs. Or if I wanted to do something, I'd have to ask permission first. If I didn't, I'd get reprimanded. I was very stubborn, so that wasn't the place for me. So I came out, and I went to work. I figured I had cost my parents enough money by putting me in the seminary, so then I went to work. I also went back to singing in the church.

I was born in the Acre, and I was still living there when I got married. We lived in a three-tenement block which was always, always immaculately clean. My mother was very ticklish on cleanliness. I was born at 217 Salem Street, the tenement block in the front on the first floor. And shortly thereafter, we moved to the rear on the third floor. It was a very comfortable apartment; the only thing that I didn't like was that we lived on the third floor. Each of my brothers and myself, we had the everyday chore of going downstairs in the cellar and bringing up wood and a bag of coal for the wood and coal stove. Then on Saturdays you had to bring up more than one bag because the next day was Sunday, and you didn't do that on Sunday. So you had to double up on Saturday. That was the only chore I hated.

The coal used to be delivered right into the cellar. My father used to buy in the summertime the wood we needed in the wintertime. He'd buy a truck load of wood for three dollars. They'd dump that next to the tenement block, and you'd have the chore of passing it through the window to get it in your cellar. Then every Saturday, my father'd go down there and spend the day cutting it up. And I'd go down and help him chop it up. Finally my father decided to convert to oil, and that wasn't too bad. You only had two jugs of oil to bring up every two or three days. That kept you going.

Many a dish I dried because my mother couldn't do it all alone by herself with a fairly large family. My sister was the youngest one. You couldn't depend on your sister to do a lot of the housework. She was only a baby. So we helped out; we helped in the house.

When I was young, mostly every weekend somebody had a party. One week it would be at someone's house, and another week it would be at somebody else's house. There was always somebody that could either play the violin or the guitar or the accordion. We always managed to have a good time for ourselves. The biggest holiday for the French people is New Year's Day. This goes back to Canada.

I went to a French-speaking elementary school on Merrimack Street. We started learning English in the very early years of school because you learned American history and that was in English. Then we learned geography and that was in English. And you learned arithmetic and that was in English. Certain subjects were in English, and others were definitely in French.

At home we always spoke French. I have three daughters, and the oldest one can speak and understand. My second one can understand, and my third one, forget it. As long as the children were small and in the house, it was French. But the moment they started going out, they learned English with their little friends. When television came out and everything on it was in English, they picked that up. Even in the French schools. They gradually got away from French. You'd meet a nun or a brother on the street, and you'd say, Bonjour, and they'd say, Good morning. As soon as the children started going to school, it turned into mostly English. Even us, if we spoke to them in French, they would answer back in English. So automatically, we fell into the same.

For twelve years, I fought heart and soul to keep the French in my church when I was choir director. I was teaching twenty-two young girls, three-quarters of them that never could even understand French. I used to make them sing in French. It wasn't any harder for me to teach them to sing in French than it was for me to sing in Latin. When I was a child, I didn't know what I was singing. I was just repeating what the choir director was teaching me.

My first job was [in 1946] during my first vacation as a seminarian. I was sixteen then. I worked at the Boott mills in the spinning room on cleanup. Later after I came out [of the seminary], I went back to the Boott mills, and I was working in the card room. Then about 1948, I left that and went to work at the American Plastics in Fitchburg [Massachusetts] for eighty-five cents an hours. American Plastics went on strike, so I finally got a job at the Merrimack mills as a spinner and doffer. I was making $1.12 an hour, but I left that to work at the Wannalancit for a dollar an hour to learn my slashing trade. I've been there ever since.

The slashing trade eventually would pay me more than what I was asking there [at the Merrimack], although I would have to take a cut for leaving one place for another. After a six-weeks' training period, I'd be making much more than I was making at the Merrimack. My brother was a supervisor [at the Wannalancit] at the time. It was a very flourishing company [in the early 1950s]. They had three floors of looms, running three shifts. We had an entire warping department running three shifts. The mill at that time was really booming, making nylon and Dacron.

They were supposed to give me a six-weeks' training period, but they put me on with another man for three days. Then they put me on the machine by myself. The training program meant that they gave you six weeks to learn the job with somebody looking over your shoulder. But this guy stopped looking over my shoulder after three days. My six weeks were very, very short, but I managed to master my job.

Over the years, I've managed to learn six different operations on the floor that I was working. In the mid-1950s, business began to go very, very sour, and two-thirds of the mill [workers] were laid off. I was working seven days a week. There wasn't enough work on any particular operation to keep full-time men going, but there was always a little

Slasher. *Courtesy of MATH.*

bit could be done on this particular job over here. And then a little bit to be done on the other one. I knew every one of them, so I'd jump from one job to another, and that's how I managed to keep working seven days a week while two-thirds of the people were out. This is what I liked about the Wannalancit because I gambled leaving the job that paid more to take one that paid less but eventually paid off more in the long run.

One of the operations was spooling. You buy [synthetic] yarn from the DuPont Company, and they sell you packages which weigh five or six pounds a piece. Now there's no way that [the Wannalancit's] twisting machine can handle that [package]. You have to transfer a six-pound [package] onto a one-pound spool that will fit the [twisting] machine that we had. That's called spooling. From spooling it goes to the twisting department to add a certain amount of twist per inch to the yarn to give it more strength for the fabric you want. From twisting it goes to the warping.

The warping department prepares [the yarn] for the slashing department. Slashing is the process of running the yarn through size or starch or gelatin, depending on the yarn. This is in order to give the yarn more body and durability [during the weaving process]. If you did not size the yarn before you put it in the loom, you'd have just rags. You'd never be able to weave a decent piece of fabric. After the cloth is woven, it is sent to a finishing process, and the sizing is washed out of it. But it had to be sized before it's woven into a fabric.

My machine doesn't make much noise. The sounds that you heard when you were working were coming from the top floor where they have the weave room. But the heat—you have three machines running at 275 degrees Fahrenheit. You have nine cylinders in the machine which produce 240 degrees [to dry the sized yarn]. So during the summer, it really gets hot. In the wintertime, you kind of enjoy it if it's cold outside, because the boiler [in the mill] can't always keep up and give you adequate heat. The heat doesn't bother me. It never did. I can take it; I can stand the grind.

If you want to, you can wear shoes with steel caps, just in case you drop one of these big heavy beams. There's no law that says that you have to do it. I've had no really serious accidents outside of cutting my finger with my scissors. The most serious accident that I had was the time I was trying to wash off the yarn with live steam. I dropped the hose, and it fell on my foot. It kind of burned a little bit. I've never seen anybody else that's had a serious accident on the slasher. The weave room would be the place that you would have most accidents. Those shuttles, they go back and forth. If one comes out and strikes you, it is traveling quite fast. If the operator sticks his hands or his fingers in there, then there could be a serious accident.

Other accidents have happened on elevators because of not taking enough precaution. We had one young fellow one time that was coming up in the elevator, and he had his foot stuck out and got his toes caught in there. Common sense will tell you that you should keep your feet inside or never get on or off the elevator while it's in motion. We had this old fellow that used to work at the Wannalancit only part time. One day, I'm coming down with the elevator, and he's hanging over the gate sweeping inside. If I hadn't been fast enough to pull on the cable to make the elevator go up again, I'd have chopped his head off. These are foolish things that some people do. You have to have common sense.

A man would have to be foolish—if he wants to test the size [in the slasher] to see how hot it is—to stick his fingers in between the squeeze rollers and the steel roller. You'd have to be pretty stupid to do a thing like that because there are no guards over those rollers. It's just a matter of using your judgment and paying attention to what you're doing.

One time the roof on the sixth floor caved in. If I had gone up there

ten minutes after the time that I did, I would have been laying underneath that roof. Our size kettles were gravity fed. The slasher was on the
fifth floor, but your kettle was on the sixth floor. At night, if there was no
third shift, you'd have to empty out your size bucket, transfer the size
back into the kettle, and shut the valves off so nothing would leak. That
particular night my usual procedure was to do that at twenty minutes of
ten, 'cause I was finishing at ten. I did that, and at ten minutes of ten, the
roof caved in. Right over the size kettles where I had just been. It broke
the sprinkler line, and the water was coming out of the sprinklers, all
over the machines, all over the yarn. Something just gave out. Nobody
was hurt. The place was a mess, but nobody was hurt. After that, I
thought twice about going up there.

I've always been in textiles. I've never worked at Raytheon or any of
these electronic shops. I don't know what they do. [In textiles], each
process is a different one from the other. Slashing is more difficult than
warping, and warping is more difficult than twisting, and twisting is
more difficult than spooling. You adapt to the job that you have. I'm sure
that a spooler could not slash, because all your spoolers are women.
During the war [World War II] they did have women slashers because
there were no men around, but you don't see them anymore. It is a
difficult job, and it can be a strenuous job at times. Women weren't
allowed to work at night on the third shift unless you had government
contracts.

We had no union at the Wannalancit. We never had because we never
felt the need of having one. We've always been treated decently by the
Larter family, so there was no reason to go out and make trouble for
ourselves. I remember quite a few times [beginning in the mid-1950s]
the union did try to come in, but the help never voted them in. The
Merrimack started their own union, what they called the Independent.
The Boott mills had the AFL-CIO. So did the Newmarket and a few
other mills on Market Street, but we never did. We had all the major
holidays throughout the year; we had master medical, Blue Cross and
Blue Shield insurance which we paid little of; there's always been a
Christmas bonus and your vacation pay. We never saw the need of [a
union].

Textiles was the backbone of our city; years ago everyone worked in
the mill. That's all you had. It was all textile mills. Working in the textile
mill was the bread and butter of the people of the city. Then one mill left
after the other, and new shops started coming in. The cloth was being
produced down South at a much cheaper price than we could sell it, and

that's what hurts the textile business. I remember when I first started working at the Wannalancit, we used to slash DuPont crepe and American viscose taffeta. That was a good seller for us until it was being imported from Japan at a much cheaper price than we could even make it. It was being sold on the market exported from Japan at a cheaper price. So Mr. Larter just dropped it. Hey, if you're going to lose money on something, there's no sense of going with it any longer. That's what killed textiles, and that's what's killing textiles now.

I Won the Respect of All My Mill People

Fred Burtt

PAYMASTER, PRODUCTION AND
PERSONNEL MANAGER

A native New Englander, Fred Burtt decided to study textile engineering at the Lowell Textile Institute, graduating in the inauspicious year of 1931. His teachers were men who had worked in the mills and took pride in their scars. After a lot of practical training, he took his "smattering" of time- and cost-study to the Newmarket mills.

Although he was surrounded by the hazards and crashing noise of the weave rooms, Burtt feared those dangers less than the looks on the faces of the mill workers when he handed them their meager pay envelopes. The Newmarket was a "tight outfit." He knew that the bosses could pay higher wages, and he welcomed a better job in a worsted mill.

Burtt became production manager at Abbot Worsted when war orders for khaki yarns poured in but mill workers were scarce. Strapped for fixers, he worked on the machines himself at night, then supervised the first shift. As personnel manager after the war, Burtt closely observed the lives of mill workers.

Industrial decline and the shrinking of the textile program at Lowell Technological Institute turned Burtt into a consultant who supervised the sale and transport of millions of dollars of machinery from New England to the developing textile industry in Latin America. Once there, the worsted machinery in these new mills produced cloth that undersold anything made in New England.

I WAS BORN in Lowell in 1908. My father worked for the New Haven Railroad for forty years, and my mother, Edith Flint, graduated from Lowell Teachers' College in 1900. In the fall of 1927, after I graduated from a private academy in Maine, I went into the textile engineering program at Lowell Textile Institute and got my degree in 1931. These men [at Lowell Textile] knew their business. A lot of them came right straight out of the mills. Just like Jim Kennedy [who] was only a wool scourer down at the Arlington mills [in Lawrence]. They brought him up, and they made him an instructor. He finally became a professor and head of the wool department.

We had over fifty woolen mills all around in New England: places up in Winooski, Vermont, they had five or six mills. William Wood when he was president of the American Woolen, he built Shawsheen Village in Massachusetts. We had mills up in Skowhegan, Maine, and out here in Maynard, Massachusetts. We had mills all over the place. The biggest woolen mill was the Wood Mill down here in Lawrence and the biggest worsted mill was across the street.

In the system that descended from English mill practices, we took wool and made roving and then made yarn from that. It was all done between rollers and the drafting [occurred] between rollers. The other system was the French; they had these little pin rollers called porcupine rolls and the wool was fed through there. It was straightened out, but with very little twist. The English or Bradford yarns were very coarse with quite a bit of twist in them and not too soft. French yarn was very, very soft with no twist.

We used all kinds of wool: mohair, angora, cashmere from China, alpaca and vicuna from South America, South American wool, domestic wool from New England to the Middle West, territorial wool from the Far West, Australian wool, and wool from Africa. Even musk-ox from the Arctic. Mink hair, dog hair, cat hair, rabbit hair. When I was a student we were doing work on the side for people like DuPont and Eastman Kodak and all kinds of chemical companies when they first were perfecting their [synthetic] fibers, rayon and nylon. That's where we got a good working knowledge on all these new fibers that helped [us] later when we went out into industry.

During the four years that we were students, we got a very good all-round education. A lot of it was practical because when you go out into the mill, and you talk to some of these people who have come from England and they knew all about it, they would have to listen to you once in a while because you knew what you were talking about. They would respect you after a while, but it took a long time sometimes to break down that wall. They figured we knew nothing, but we did. We were well trained. In our fourth year, we got cost accounting, business administration, and mill engineering, and just a smattering of time-and cost-study.

After I graduated I went to Eaton Rapids, Michigan, as a wool trainee. If I had stayed—I only stayed for six months—and married the boss's daughter, I'd have been head of that company, but after looking at the young lady. . . . So I came home, and I worked for the Newmarket mills in Lowell. A fellow who was a year ahead of me in class, he was down there as production manager, and I took over later on. After the New-market, I was production manager at the Abbot Worsted Mills until 1950.

It was rather rough in 1931, but most of our boys [in his graduating class] survived. When I went to work at the Newmarket, they were weaving a rayon casket cloth. Silk warps and rayon filling. Everybody was being buried with those in the caskets. We also made [silk] taffetas, rayon taffetas, and rayon print cloth. They had come down from New Hampshire because they had a strike there, and they bought in the mills down here. They stayed in business quite awhile.

When I went to work for them, I used to do cost work and motion- and time-study. I went around and read the picks [numbers on the pick-counters] on looms twice a day. The noises were deafening [in the weave room]. The minute you open up the door. . . . I mean the decibels were way up about two or three hundred. No wonder most of the people ended up deaf. One day I felt a little [thump] in my back. I turned around, and there was a shuttle on the floor. It hit me in the shoulder blade. It flew out of the way of the loom, and it hit me.

We would [record] the number of picks that they did per day, and they would be paid according to the number of picks and the style that they were weaving on. Some of the girls were only making four or five dollars a week down there, and they'd come up to me [as paymaster] and say, Can you give me [a little more]? I'll do anything if you give me a few dollars to buy a piece of bread. It was terrible the wages in the early 1930s during the depression years. The Newmarket could but wouldn't pay them more. They were one of these tight outfits that were playing on human misery.

It made you feel pretty bad sometimes to see some of the pays [marked on the pay envelopes]. When I used to be paymaster and go out and pay the people in the mill, I'd turn the envelopes over. I was ashamed to hand it to them because it was three, four, five dollars for forty hours to forty-eight hours [a week]. I used to turn it over and hand it to them. We began to have strikes all over [in the early 1930s], and they began to pay a little more. In 1933 we had the NRA. We were marching through Lowell celebrating the National Recovery Act. Everybody came out of the mills carrying flags, and after that things got a little better.

We made unfinished cloth, "greige" cloth, and it was sent out to places around Rhode Island and New York for finishing. They would buy it by the yard from us, and then either put it through print machines or dye it. We had a lot of Jacquard weaving too, the [mechanism of which was the] forerunner of the computer. You could make all kinds of different beautiful designs on Jacquard looms.

I was not getting very much money with the Newmarket Company and went over to Abbot Worsted Company in 1933. I was also taking credits at MIT [Massachusetts Institute of Technology], and I got a Bachelor's of Business Administration degree from Boston University night school in time- and motion-studies. Just before World War II, I was a civilian textile inspector for the Quartermasters Corps in Phila-delphia. I was too young for the First World War and too old for the Second. Then Abbot Worsted called me [back] in early 1941. They were making khaki yarns for uniforms, shirts, leggings, underwear, and caps. I had to come back to run the mills because they couldn't get executive help.

We were operating at 65 percent during World War II where a lot of mills around here were down to 35 percent. We hired busses and sent them around to people's back doors and through the side streets of Lowell. The only thing we didn't do was serve breakfast on the busses taking them up to work. We gave them a lot better money too. I ran a spinning room from six o'clock in the morning to eleven o'clock at night. Trying to keep a spinning room going when we couldn't even get a second hand or a fixer. I was a fixer and a second hand besides my executive work during the day. I still carry the scars of [those days in] the mills on my hands.

I was one of those patriotic fellows. I felt I was doing my duty to try and do what I could. I won the respect of all my mill people. When I became personnel manager at Abbot with eight thousand people, three mills in the North and one in the South, I could go around, and I could speak to everyone in the mills and call them by their first names, pass the time of day with them. If I needed a little extra production effort, I'd say to him, Jim, can you get me a couple of extra boxes of yarn? Sure, we'd be glad to do it, and they'd pitch in and they would do it because there were good relations between myself and the help. Give them a smile, ask them how their family was. How's the little child? Is it sick or something like that? People used to call it human engineering. I call it good rapport.

When I was personnel manager, I was in divorce cases, in abortion cases, in despair cases, and everything else. I was like a father confessor who people came to with their troubles. Some people were a little bit unreasonable, but if a woman had a grievance with an overseer or a second hand or anybody else in the department, she came in and sat down, and started talking to you. It's surprising; you become a good listener. And all of a sudden, she'll start to smile and say, Am I saying this? I haven't any troubles. Just to talk to you, I've solved my problem, and I have no more grievance.

Sometimes I'd have to go into homes and straighten out people because they were abusing their wives. I tried to keep out of the homes. But every Monday morning, we used to stand at the mill gates and watch our help come in. If we saw any of the men glassy-eyed or staggering around, we wouldn't let them come to work because it was dangerous. The accident frequency rate in our mill would be high, and our insurance rates would go sky high. So we turned them back, tell them to go home and sober up, and come back when they were ready.

When I went into the Abbot Worsted [operation] in Lowell after I left the Newmarket Company, we had spoolers there complaining about pains in their backs. I looked up and saw the sprinkler heads that they were using to condition the [atmosphere in the] mills, and they were coming right down on the women's backs. We found out they were taking raw water out of the canal, putting it into the system, and spraying it on those poor people. Polluted water; anything went into the canals in those days. We finally had to make them go to city water, and that cleared [up] a hell of a lot of troubles with back pains and so forth.

I was on the Lowell Industrial Accident Safety Committee; all the mills had representatives. That's again where I met a lot of the mill people. Many of them are grown old, and a lot of them are gone, but they were all good workers, they were good friends, and I had good public relations with them. This is what helped me.

The work force at the Abbot was a mixed group. The first people that worked there came over from England. From Benchley, Bingley, and Bradford. A lot of them were of Irish descent. When they came over here, they bunched together. Abbot Worsted had invited them and brought them over and set up houses for them. They had these big soccer teams there in North Chelmsford. They imported these Scotch and English soccer players who were [woolen] experts and had them in the mills. Many of them didn't do a damn thing in the mill but walk around, but they got well paid.

Then the French Canadian people came in, and they weren't too, too bad. Then we had Russians and Polish people working out at the mill. So we had a very cosmopolitan group. I'm a mongrel with English,

Irish, French, and American Indian blood in me all mixed up, but I would love to have had a mill full of Polish and Russian people. They would give you a fair day's work for a fair day's pay. You would see them get up at four o'clock in the morning, they'd get their kids ready for school, they'd get their lunches ready, and they'd come into the mills at six o'clock in the morning. The women and the men. They'd work through to two or three o'clock with just probably a half hour lunch break. And [during the shift] they would never leave the mill; they would work all the time.

Then they'd have to go home and start getting dinner ready for the night and take care of the kids. Those Polish and Russian women practically worked around the clock. They were conscientious. If you started to give them heck for bad work once in a while, they said, Me no understand, so you'd get a Russian or a Polish interpreter. They knew what you were talking about: that some of it was bad work, and that they had to quit it. We don't want to lose our business. There's still a Russian cemetery out there full of good old workers for Abbot Worsted. They're right next to the Catholic cemetery. They had to go over to Maynard and bring a Russian Orthodox priest to bury them or officiate at weddings and baptisms.

The women I always admired. The men would work, and I had no problems with them because they knew what they were supposed to do and they would do it. And they'd put themselves out to help you. But to see the women doing double duty. Double duty. You [had to] admire them. I thought the world of them. They'd have their pigs and chickens running around through the house, and they had gardens and raised great big cabbages. They came from Poland and off the steppes of Russia. They were better off here.

In 1926, practically every Ford in the country was running around with Abbot Worsted yarn in it. Mohair fabrics in all the Ford cars. We would make the yarn and send it down to big finishing plants in Rhode Island and Connecticut [to be woven] and finished in whatever colors and type of finish they wanted. [Abbot] didn't want the finishing to do. They had enough headaches making yarns. Let somebody else have the headaches on the finishing or the cloth end. We had plenty of headaches. We'd get back imperfections that got through. We'd have to go around and pay for pieces of cloth that were spoiled and sometimes didn't show until you finished it. And it might go on for yards and yards and yards.

The textile program at [Lowell Tech] had to end; it was inevitable.

The mills were closing or going into bankruptcy. Some mills went South and took the help with them, then closed down. In the South they could take the cotton right from the fields and put it into the mills. Woolen mills wanted to move South for lower wages. We had strong unions up here that were fighting the mill owners and putting them out of business. Their demands were at times unreasonable. This was in Lawrence, Lowell, Manchester, all over New England and in New York, Rhode Island, and Connecticut.

I tried to get a job down South for a fixer once. We sent him down to Arkansas. He was fixing card machinery down there. He said they didn't pay much attention to him. One of them happened to walk by his coat and saw his Masonic pin. He came over and asked him, Are you a Mason? He said, Yes! Well, Jeese, why the hell didn't you say so? Welcome! My God, from then on he got along very nicely with people. They thought he was Catholic.

Abbot Worsted tried to start in Seneca, South Carolina, but we got there ten years too late. The day they opened the mill in Seneca in 1952 after I left, the people came down from up in the mountains, and they wore these great big broad butternut-dyed skirts. Great big skirts and these kerchiefs and bandannas around their heads. We had to stop them and put them into dresses or they would get wrapped around in the pulleys in the machinery. Homespun material and home dyed. The day the circus came to town, you might as well shut the mill doors. Nobody would show up for work. The circus was the thing going through town, and everybody would go to the circus.

The biggest mistake that Abbot Worsted made in Seneca, they took all our old machinery and shipped it down there into a brand new mill and put in new machinery up here. By the time that the old machinery started to wear out, the Jantzen Bathing Suit Company came in across the street. All the people left one side of the street and went across the street because they got more money working for Jantzen than for Abbot Worsted. We were using junk machinery down there.

The Uxbridge Worsted Company also went down South. They took some of their key help. One day one of the overseers swore at one of the workers. He either told him: get the hell to work or get the hell out or something like that. The southerner sat right straight down in front of him and said, If you-all don't apologize to me for swearing at me, I won't do another stitch of work for you. And [as] the overseer said [later to him], I had to apologize. Up here if I told somebody to go to hell or do this and that, they'd take it. But not down there. They were a very, very beautiful people.

I shipped a million and three-quarters [dollars worth of] textile machinery out of New England. I bought the stuff from up in Manchester [New Hampshire], around Lawrence, and shipped it to Uruguay. As a member of a textile faculty, I was a consultant and was certified by the United States government to clear shipments. I'd go up to Manchester and [oversee] the packing. I knew some of the things that went into the boxes, but a lot of it was undeclared parts with no duty on them. I used to get two hundred dollars a day for going up to Manchester plus my expenses. I would take the manifests on all the boxes, and we'd ship the machinery down to the docks in Boston. I'd go to a ship's broker, and we'd get clearance.

We'd go out and buy hundreds of yards of colored ribbon, and we'd stamp these ribbons on each document. Then the secretary of state of the Commonwealth would put the state seal on there. When we'd get through, and we'd go down to the Uruguayan consulate and get them to okay the shipment. More ribbons, the most beautiful documents that you ever saw; they were masterpieces. Then we'd go down to the docks, and here's an old tramp steamer, rusty as hell. We put the machinery in boxes on that ship, and they'd go down to Montevideo.

I went down to Montevideo [too], and saw the stuff coming in off the dock. We had to get a manifest from the legislature of Uruguay to ship the machinery onto the docks. We [had to] pay payola or baksheesh. In the Middle East, [it's] baksheesh. Then we'd have to pay the trucker to take it to the gates of the mill, and then we had to pay to unload it and get it inside the mill. Then we set it up, and we were making cloth that could sell in the New York market for three, four, five dollars cheaper a yard than it could be made in the United States. Beautiful worsted machinery.

There were just two classes of people in South America: the rich who wore English oxfords and tweeds and the peons who had a little blanket over their shoulders. The state wage was [the equivalent of] $13 a year. You'd find Juan, one of the men on the looms, making bad work. You'd say, Juan, bad work. He don't care. He'd take out a bottle of sweetened water, that's what kept him going. I don't know what the hell it had in it. We'd say, Juan, bad work; you're fired. Go ahead, and fire me; you've got to pay me state wage under the law. Thirteen dollars, so you might as well keep him working; so we did. They're still in business down there, but now's there's a middle class. Between the elite and the peons, there is now a middle class.

Even when I was teaching [at Lowell Tech] in the fifties, I was consultant for twenty different woolen mills in New England. If they had a mechanical problem or a processing problem or they weren't getting the right finish or weren't producing enough, [they'd asked me]. And when I went to Egypt [on a Fulbright Fellowship from 1965 to 1967], students over there in the Alexandria University where I taught, the oldest university in the world in mechanical engineering, the students would say to me, How do you know so much about the mill, the machines, and the business? I said, I actually worked there. I carry the scars of the mill.

Unions Were Few and Far Between

James Ellis

DYE HOUSE WORKER, LABOR ORGANIZER

When he was just nineteen, James Ellis had an unforgettable experience in the Merrimack dye house that set him on his course as a labor organizer. Born in the Greek section of the Acre, he grew up with an ailing father and a mother who worked double shifts to support the family. Like many older boys in the depression years, he assumed responsibility for himself and left home. He returned to Lowell when his father died, and he began working in the dye house.

The daily attempt to get work was similar to the shape-up system that longshoremen faced: job seekers showed up every morning but only a few were hired that day. If a worker was willing to kick-back part of his wages, there was a better chance for a job. When Ellis began to organize, the Merrimack management fired him and threw him out of the main office.

Ellis turned for help to an experienced union shoeworker, also a Lowell Greek-American. Increasing orders for cloth from European countries, which were at war by 1939, helped the new independent union win recognition, but Ellis became the target of a local vilification campaign that tarred him as a Communist. He continued to put pressure on the Merrimack, but the attack on Pearl Harbor changed everything.

The government's call for uninterrupted war production made strikes seem unpatriotic. The establishment in Lowell wanted Ellis and the other union leaders at the Merrimack safely in the U.S. Army. The local draft board altered his draft status, and Ellis was denied admission to Officers' Candidate School because he supported the CIO.

When he returned to Lowell after the war, Ellis set up a small labor newspaper that criticized Lowell's overdependence on textiles. The remaining mill owners feared that the development of new industry would disturb local wage levels and substandard working conditions. Ellis gave up and left to organize mill workers in the South.

There he confronted racism, violence, and the naked combination of industrial wealth and police power arrayed against labor organizers. When he returned to Massachusetts, his organizing days were over. By *then, the new industries that he had called for in 1946 had begun to diversify the industrial base of the region, while the remaining textile mills closed their doors.* *

IN 1938, at the age of nineteen, I was working in the dye house at the Merrimack Manufacturing Company. The dye house is what is commonly known as the color room where the cloth is dyed after it is woven and finished upstairs. I had a partner working next to me, and we used to start work at seven in the morning. From seven till nine in the morning, you couldn't see one or two feet beyond you because of the steam that was generated as you started to work. That steam would sort of fade away round nine or ten o'clock.

One morning as the steam evaporated, I looked for my partner, and he was lying on the floor from a heart attack. The man had seven children and was sixty-five years old. At that time we were earning [around] $13.40 for a forty-hour week. I went to his assistance, and my boss immediately came forward and instructed me to get back to my machine. He would not let me administer aid to a man who was at that moment dying. It was at least half an hour before the nurse came down with the doctor who then declared the man dead. From that moment on, I'd made up my mind that the only way that we workers could elevate our standard of living was to organize collectively into a union.

I was born in Lowell [in 1919] and lived there in the Acre until about 1935 when I went to New York City, then came back off and on until the war, and stayed until 1942. In 1951 I changed my name from Boutselis to Ellis. My father died in 1940, that's what really brought me back; he was sick. He drove a laundry truck, but there was sickness. My mother worked as a spinner in the Boott mills all through the 1930s. She worked two shifts, from six in the morning till late in the evening, to bring up the family.

There was no such thing as a [family] bank book; it was a struggle. But during World War II there was a scarcity of goods, and they were making better money. My mother bought war bonds, and she cashed them in after the war and bought the first house we ever owned. A five-thousand-dollar, three-tenement house, one thousand down and fifty-five dollars a month.

When I worked in the Merrimack mill in 1939 it was really a slave

*James Ellis's narrative is reprinted courtesy of the Lowell Museum. It appeared in a slightly shorter version in Mary H. Blewett, ed., *Surviving Hard Times: The Working People of Lowell* (Lowell: Lowell Museum, 1982), pp. 141–48.

Bleaching and washing in dye house. *Courtesy of MATH.*

shop, like the shape-up system on the docks of New York City. We used to report in the morning to the dye house, maybe forty or fifty of us. The boss would say, You're working today, and, ah, you're working today. It was a daily routine. There was the bosses who had their own little clips and rackets. One boss might be in the shoe business, and if you didn't buy shoes from him, you didn't work. One fellow, he was connected with a grocery in the neighborhood. If you didn't buy your groceries from him on payday, then you just didn't work. It really depended on what you did for them, whether you worked or not.

I got together with a friend of mine, Jimmy Angelopolis, to organize the Merrimack. He worked in the weaving end of the mill, and I worked in the finishing end. He spoke no English, didn't know how to read or write. He was a socialist in a way, like a little boy looking for the justice he couldn't find anywhere. He took it out on organizing. I became the business agent when I was twenty: the youngest paid business agent in America.

Unions were few and far between. The plant that we worked for employed about three thousand people. I immediately set out to organize, not knowing anything about unions. I had several thousand so-called membership cards printed. The entire operation cost approximately $12 for three thousand cards. We didn't have the money. We had to pass the hat around to collect it, and once we did that we circulated the cards throughout the mill.

At the time I was organizing the Merrimack, Louis Vergados, who was also born in the Acre, was working in a shoe factory. I took him out of there to help us. He was shop steward. He had been involved in the unions over the years, and he knew more about the unions than we did. He was involved in some vicious strikes before the war. We brought him in; he was also a business agent. He became involved in the day-to-day grievances with the people and with the shop stewards. He was drafted into the service before me.

We divided the plant into two divisions: weaving and finishing. Within two or three days after we started circulating the cards, the company's personnel department discovered that I was one of the ringleaders, and they immediately discharged me. I continued to work around the entrance gate, getting cards signed. And after a month or so, we had enough signed cards to petition [the National Labor Relations Board] for an election.

When the cards were signed, I took them into the superintendent's office, and I said, My name is Jimmy Boutselis, and I represent the employees that you by law must bargain with collectively. They threw me out of the office, bodily. They called the guards, and they threw me out. I went to the state agencies [of the NLRB], and they had to recognize us. I presented them with the cards. A meeting was called between the company and the union that we had formed. In the meantime we had meetings with the mill workers. We had to have a seven-week strike before we really gained recognition.

The members selected me as business agent, and an election was held by the state board. I was making $20 a week as business agent, and the dues were one dollar initiation fee and ten cents a week. Just enough to make expenses such as $25 a month rent for an office. The main union demand was a 10 percent wage increase. At the time workers averaged about $20 a week. The wage increase meant workers getting [about] $2 more a week. We also asked that they grant us a one-week's vacation with pay. Prior to that, nobody received a vacation with pay, no matter how long they had worked for the company. Some had been there for fifty years. And there were no paid holidays, and we asked if they'd give us Christmas and Easter as two paid holidays. The company refused all those demands, forcing us to go out on strike.

We called mass meetings first. The people voted to enter into the strike, and for seven weeks we were picketing the company for our demands. For seven weeks nobody was receiving any pay. There were hardly any welfare benefits at the time, and the business community was against the strike. We were vilified and called Communists and radicals and everything else because we were trying to elevate the standard of living of the people.

The loss of a day's pay for any reason was a major burden on these people. They had large families they were trying to put through school, grammar school and high school. They needed the money. One lost day was a catastrophe. Absenteeism at that time was at a minimum. You had to be really sick to lose a day. There were no [textile] unions to my knowledge in Lowell. This was a new thing in the city. In order to support the union [on strike] we used to hold tag days to raise money. We were able to get a permit without a great deal of hassling with the city of Lowell. They gave us a permit to solicit money from people in the streets and give them a tag. They'd give us some coins in a box, and the tags would say: "We are supporting the strike at the Merrimack Manufacturing Company."

During the first seven weeks of the strike at the Merrimack, they brought in trailer loads of so-called scabs, people who meant well but didn't know the meaning of trade unionism. They were unemployed [textile workers] and had been unemployed all those years. The company would go to New Hampshire and Vermont and bring these people in, load them in these trailer trucks, and try to bring them through the picket lines. In some cases they were successful; in other cases they were not successful. The violence was kept to a minimum because we were able to talk these people into not working and hurting those who were out picketing for a decent living.

Finally, after seven weeks, the company acceded to our demands, not because they wanted to, but because at that time Europe was [at war], and the company had orders from the War Department to produce cloth and other orders from France. And the United States Army and Navy were also contracting, and cloth was at a premium. So the government—the governments of these countries as well as the United States—was pressuring the Merrimack Manufacturing Company for production. Out of necessity they capitulated. They granted the wage increase, and we went back to work. That was my first experience with the union. The following year, we struck again and again. We had three straight strikes.

We were out on strike in December 1941, at the time of Pearl Harbor, and we were doing navy work. Navy officials would come to me and say, Now look, there's a war on, and the war's being fought by their sons and daughters, and they had certain rights. The army and the navy made an effort to bring the parties together, and we solved things. We knew there was a war, and we could have been a lot tougher, but we relented because of the war. Not too much, however. We got two paid holidays and a one-week's paid vacation. We felt that we had some economic strength for the first time, and we were trying to use it.

I went to the [union] office in the morning, and I left late in the afternoon about six o'clock. The major portion of the day was spent in the company office with the personnel director running through grievances. I had a stack of grievances every day. In the beginning I had to go around and collect ten cents dues from the workers. I'd give them a little book, and they'd give me a dime, and I'd put a stamp in the book showing that they were paid up for the week. After a great deal of fighting with the company we were able to get a check off [deduction of dues from the pay envelope]. I didn't have the check off when I went away in 1942. They wouldn't give it to us because it would stabilize the union's finances and make it stronger.

The cloth room at the Merrimack was mostly Irish and French. All the loom fixers were French. The dye house and the spinning room was mostly Greek. The velvet and the corduroy cutters, the high-priced jobs at the time—twenty-five dollars a week—that was mostly Irish. It wasn't just in the Merrimack. It was [like this] in all the other mills as well. If you had any sort of education and you spoke fluent English, you would try to keep away from textile mill work. You would go into a shoe shop or another kind of job that paid better wages and required a little better skill. With your shortage of labor during and after the war years, the Irish found better things than the cloth room and the cutting room and this forced management to take others in these positions, the Poles and the Greeks.

In those years, the people were afraid [of unions] because the employers had created the impression in the minds of the workers that by joining the union there would be an automatic strike and you'd be out of work for months and months without pay. Unions weren't welcome in Lowell. They were anti-American. Unionism was something bad, something vicious, something completely un-American. They had been successful for years making people believe this. But there were people who believed in unions. A lot of immigrants, people who had come from European countries, had some knowledge of unions because many of them had dealings with organizations long before they got here to America. The Polish-speaking people pretty much accepted the philosophy of the labor union.

I'd spend my leisure hours with people who had the same type of philosophy I had. We talked about a better world; what's going to happen after the war. We talked about a stronger labor movement, about what direction to take. We believed in social justice and were people with socialist interests. We weren't very organized. We had contact with but shied away from Communist cells in Lowell. We discussed moves with them, but we saw them change from being anti-Hitler [Popular Front] to pro-German [after the Nazi–Soviet Nonaggression Pact in 1939], back to anti-German when the Germans attacked Russia in 1941. They were amateurs, drifters, but they were searching like all of us to find something better.

All the companies in Lowell were against me personally. [They thought that] I was a Communist and this and that. I never hid the fact that my philosophy was Socialist. [They believed] I was a radical, and [that] this was no time for concessions. They gave me the business. My dad had died in December 1940, and under the Selective Service Act, I was entitled to a 3A classification. I had three younger brothers and my mother. At that time, I was trying to organize the Boott mills which was controlled by the family of Congresswoman Edith Nourse Rogers. They made sure that I was drafted even though I was entitled to a 3A classification. I was in Washington, D.C., at the time, and I called my mother. She said, We got a draft notice for you on Monday morning. There wasn't even a fourteen-day grace period before reporting. I didn't appeal. I knew the people on the draft board: a judge, a banker, an industrialist. I didn't have a chance. So I was drafted in 1942, and that ended my organization days. One troublemaker was away.

So this left the union to Jimmy Angelopolis who spoke no English. All the young union leaders were drafted. So he got a hold of an old-timer, an English fellow Neil Clark, who kept the union going through the war years. The war was on, and the company had plenty of orders. They were afraid of strikes, and they wanted to maintain order. They didn't try as hard as they might have in normal times to destroy the union. Maybe the government had something to do with this.

I remember during the war at basic training in Oregon, I was interrogated by the intelligence officers. I had applied for Officers' Candidate School. They asked me questions like: what do you think of John L. Lewis [president of the CIO], what do you think of the labor movement, what did I think of the coal strike that was in progress? Never asked questions about what I was supposed to do as an officer or where I was supposed to be trained. I was rejected from OCS simply because I had been a business agent, the union guy. That was made clear to me. They had a dossier [on him] from the 1930s. They knew that in the 1930s, when I was living in New York City, I was involved in talk about the Spanish Civil War and all that stuff. I wanted to go to Spain; I was young. I wanted to join the Lincoln Brigade.

Living in New York City, you couldn't get a job or a bowl of soup. Like many of the artists and writers at the time, you would follow all the political movements simply to get a loaf of bread or a sandwich. The Christian Front would have a meeting on 29th Street. You would go there because they'd advertise a buffet. You'd go there, and they'd pass around petitions and nobody cared. They all signed them: the Christians signed them, the Communists, the Social Democrats. We were there waiting for the meeting to end so that we could get a bowl of soup and maybe a sandwich. I think that's what happened to John Garfield [the actor]. After the war came the McCarthy years. They looked back into the 1930s, and they found files and petitions that had been signed by people like me to get a sandwich.

Right after the war, the Boott mill was organized, the Newmarket was organized, and many of the smaller shops were organized by the textile workers' union of the CIO. The Merrimack union was an independent. [At first, in 1939] nobody would finance us. We did this all on our own. We scraped up some dollars, printed a couple of thousand membership cards, and distributed them. We knocked on doors, and that's how we organized the Lowell Textile Independent Union. When Louis Vergados wanted to come back after the war, they wouldn't let him. Angelopolis and Clark had control of the union. They had built a little empire for themselves. They fought him, so he went to work for the CIO.

After the war when I came back, I realized that the only salvation for the independent union was to affiliate with the CIO which had organized the Boott and the Newmarket. I tried to use my influence on them to bring the CIO in [and] let the independent become part of the national organization. They fought me on that.

Finally I succeeded in getting Jimmy Angelo to go along with that, but the company fought affiliation. They used all kinds of gimmicks to stop affiliation, and they were very successful. They were able to put their own people in the leadership of the independent—company people, and it became a company union. We were never successful in bringing it into the CIO. It remained an independent union until the day that the Merrimack liquidated and closed its doors.

In 1946 I gave up being a business agent and started to publish a newspaper, the *Industrial Journal.* I was very active in the labor movement for the CIO. I fought the Lowell city council and the mayor to set up an industrial commission to bring in other types of industries and diversify the city. One industry was bad for Lowell. When business was bad, there was a lot of unemployment. Diversification would cushion recession. But the textile manufacturers controlled the city, controlled everybody. They weren't anxious to bring in higher-paying industries. They wanted to maintain the low wages and the same conditions. They failed to diversify when they had the opportunity to do it. When the last mills migrated to the South, the whole Merrimack Valley found itself in a very depressed situation with high unemployment. Lowell missed the boat because of the newspaper [the *Lowell Sun*], the bankers, and the investors.

In 1948 my newspaper folded; it didn't get any advertising. I was too radical for the system at the time. I left [Lowell] and joined the Textile Workers' Union of America as a business agent. Louis Vergados and I worked together [after the war] in the textile workers' union in the CIO. We worked together as organizers and business agents for a number of years until I was transferred out of state. He left the textile workers' union and went into the state, county, and municipal workers' union.

In 1948 I was called upon to go down and organize the southern textile workers who were very difficult to organize because of the great economic pressure that was exerted by the companies in the South. The very wealthy textile owners controlled the towns, controlled the hospital, the police force, the fire department, and the local stores that were in the town. And that made it extremely difficult for employees to organize.

Organizing in the South was a lot different from organizing in Lowell because in the South, the state police would fight you and the local police would fight if you tried to hold meetings. The companies had spies who would come to the union hall and record the names of all those who attended the meetings of the tentative organization. So it was a very, very tough thing. In many cases when we called a strike, the other half [of the mill workers] would be working. They would not permit us to picket peacefully. The Wagner Act [in 1935] gave us the right, but picketing was denied us. We were clubbed, the cottages we lived in were set on fire, many of us were beaten and put into jail. Organization was extremely slow for many, many years there.

The Ku Klux Klan played a major role together with the state police and the town fathers in trying to keep the unions out of the South. As a union organizer, I can remember the Klan burning a cross for me and trying to beat me out of town. They tried at one time to burn the hotel that I lived in. The Klan slashed the tires on my car and stoned me. They did everything. They threatened to tar and feather me as they did to other labor leaders down there. In many cases the Klanners were the policemen and the firemen in the town and the foremen in the mill and workers who were scabbing.

In the South there were professional scabs. They were [paid] rabble-rousers. They would go to work in a struck plant and taunt those who were out on strike, trying to get them to go back to work. They were trying to create the impression that the strike was being broken and the cause was lost, [that] if they wanted to preserve their jobs, they should cross the picket lines.

What was also different in the South was the discrimination against black people. A black man in the South made less wages than a white man, even though they did a similar job. In many cases the union discriminated against the blacks down there because if you didn't do that, you were considered problack and that would kind of slam the organization. In order to be successful in the South, the unions in many cases practiced race prejudice in the forties and the fifties when the unions were fairly strong. They had the economic ability to support a strike by paying strike benefits to people and giving them food. I recall in many cases the black man would not be permitted to be in the line to collect these so-called commissary goods. He would have to wait and get the dregs. In all cases, he was last, and in many cases there wasn't anything left for him.

Finally I came back North and worked in Worcester, Massachusetts, in an administrative capacity [for the CIO]. I was negotiating contracts in mills that had been organized for years. I was no longer organizing. My organization days were over. I stayed with the CIO until 1955; then I resigned and became a professional labor arbitrator and a consultant in labor relations.

The Children

Introduction

THE CHILDREN of the last generation of mill workers were angry over what their parents had endured. They admired the fortitude of their fathers and mothers, regretted their parents' lack of choices, and rejoiced over their own escape from the mills. They could name what it was that they feared. For Hubert LaFleur, it was the physical danger of unsafe working conditions; for Cornelia Chiklis, the long, exhausting hours; for Mary Karafelis, the difficulties of taxing, dirty work and unfair bosses; and for Ronald Bacon, the ensnaring trap of "those wretched mills." The textile industry was in the last phase of its regional decline while they were growing up.

Some of these children were lucky enough to be able to leave the mills shortly after they began to work, because they learned another trade or a skill that got them out. Others had the luxury of finishing high school and getting some further training. Some were the youngest in the family; other family members got out of the mills while younger ones remained. The boys, the "mainstays" of the family, usually had the first chance to go to college, while their sisters continued to turn over their pay envelopes each week.

As children they saw the lint in their mothers' hair and the exhaustion on their faces; they worried about their fathers' safety. When they delivered dinner pails at noon to the mills, they watched the machines whirl and pound and were both fascinated and repelled by what they saw. They breathed the hot, humid air and smelled the sweat and the grease. They became as determined as many of their parents were not to let the mills get them.

These clever, resourceful, hard-working parents left deep impressions on their children: some because of their adaptability and talent for speaking many languages; others because of their toughness on the job; and still others because of their ability to provide a decent life for their families from whatever they earned. Almost all had known want or despair. To their children, the strongest of them seemed monumental. But because their lives were hard, they could be hard on their sons and daughters. Discipline was swift and sharp. No one could fool them. Children did what they were told without question. They handed over their paychecks and swallowed their complaints. Like their parents before them, the children lit fires after school, hauled coal and wood up tenement stairs, and helped with the never-ending wash.

Yet those who escaped retained vivid memories that evoked life in a twentieth-century New England textile city: memories of mill people flooding the streets with each change of shift; of steam rising from the mills and turning to snowflakes; and of stories about their parents as young mill workers, meeting, courting, and beginning the family. They recalled their fathers teaching them how to do things and the physical strength of their mothers. They remembered their parents and their childhoods with the gratitude of those who had been given a better chance in life.

There Wasn't an Inch of His Body
That Wasn't Black and Blue

Hubert LaFleur
AUTO MECHANIC

As a boy, Hubert LaFleur, like thousands of other children of mill workers, took his father's dinner to him in the mill and watched him work. This was the initial experience that led them into the mills. Like so many of them, he too left school at fourteen and started at the bottom of the job ladder in the mill. Then his father suffered a terrible accident, and the boy, who knew about his father's dangerous work, feared the worst. When the tough father survived and later stoically returned to the mill, his son drew his own conclusions and got out.

MY FATHER AND MOTHER came from Canada. My father wasn't a citizen. He worked in the mill most of his life. He never became a citizen. We tried and tried, you know what I mean, to have him [become naturalized]. He would never go along with it. Neither would my mother. They used to go back to Canada every summer for a visit in a Reo touring car.

[My father] worked in the Shaw Hosiery where he was a mule spinner. They used to make men's stockings there. I always remember this about my father. In the place that he worked, they had these mules [mule spinning machines] that came back and forth, and you had to do your work before the mules would come together. That was a very dangerous job. Because I remember I used to watch him work. I used to bring his dinners, and then I used to watch him. When the mule started to go out [back up], he had to do the work, whatever was broke like a thread, you had to repair [piece] it. The mule runs on tracks, and I should say it's about twenty-five feet long on both sides, and [the sides of the mule] they come together. My father had to do his work and pull out before they came together. There was no safety. All you had to do was watch it, do your work fast, and pull out.

And when I was about eighteen [around 1921], my father got caught in one of those mules. He got caught in between. He was a long time in the hospital. And there wasn't an inch of his body that wasn't black and blue. He was very bad; we never thought that my father would live because he stopped both sides of the machine with his body. But my father pulled out of it.

He was a big man, 210 or 220 pounds. He was lucky he was a big man because it never killed him. He was very lucky that nothing punctured his body. All it did was it pinched his body just like you pinch yourself or hit yourself with a hammer. He was black and blue. He suffered blue murder; I'll always remember that. And he went back to the mills. Well that's all he ever done, you know. He was a mule spinner all his life, for a long time.

My uncle used to do that, too. He never got hurt. I don't know how my father got that job. I think he was taught; he went into the mill, and they taught him how to do that kind of work. It was really very dangerous work in those days. After he got hurt, they gave him a different kind of job. But he came out of it very good. He got workmen's compensation [from the state]; nothing from the mill.

My mother never worked. We were a big family. There was four girls and three boys. When I was fourteen years old, I didn't want to go to school, so my father says, you're going to work. So I went to work at a bobbin shop, Parker's Bobbin Shop. And from Parker's Bobbin Shop, I went to the Hamilton mills for probably a year or so. Then from there I went to the Plush mill where my sisters worked.

I was a bobbin-boy and yarn boy. I worked setting in bobbins and taking them off when they're filled. You'd carry a basket. The bobbins used to come in by trucks from the Parker Bobbin Shop where these bobbins come from. They'd bring them upstairs in the elevator in big trucks. And we used to take them out of the trucks to put them on the [spinning] frames. The doffers—five girls called doffers—when the bobbins were full, they'd come along and they'd take the full bobbin, put in the empty one and then tie a thread on to it so it would join, so it would spin by itself when the frames were going. In our spare time the bobbin-boys picked yarn: cleaned the threads out of the waste cotton that the spinners left. There was two bobbin-boys for a whole floor. They were the errand boys.

After that, I worked in the Depot Cash Market. And then from there—my uncle, Jack Pomerleau, was a mechanic—I worked in the automobile business all my life after that. I didn't work very long in the mill. I worked probably about three years until I was [about] seventeen. There was no future; I didn't care for it. I didn't like the smell and the

Hubert LaFleur (at far right) and his family, c. 1915. *Courtesy of Hubert LaFleur.*

heat. It was awful warm. I worked outdoors almost all my life, and I hated to be locked in. I was pretty lucky. My uncle taught me what to do. He was a crackerjack mechanic, a great guy for building automobile racers. He was a very clever man.

As a mechanic, I never lost a day's work in my life. I worked thirty years for Packard, and seven years for Middlesex [Auto] Supply, and then eighteen years for Bournival Chrysler. My uncle used to be the repair man for the Depot Taxi in Lowell. In them days, it was Fords. The old mayor, Tom Braden, used to be the man that owned it at that time. The Fords in them days, Boy, anybody could fix them. At first with my uncle I worked for Alcott Motors. I used to pick up cars at Cambridge where they assembled them. I used to take a wooden box and put it over the gas tank and come home just sitting on the gas tank with a box. I drove them back to Lowell, from Boston to Lowell, from Cambridge to Lowell [about thirty miles], winter and summer, only hand-wipers, no electric wipers. If the car broke down on the way, I'd have to walk. I did that for a long time.

I worked in a garage; some fellows can't stand the fumes. The fumes never bothered me. Never bothered me at all. But I remember one time, my Uncle Jack was underneath a car, trying to find out something, and the motor was running. And I hollered at him, Jack! I didn't hear him, and he wasn't moving. And I says, Jack! He didn't say anything. He didn't talk to me. I pulled him out and sure enough he was ready to pass out. I brought him outside and brought him to. If I had left him in there another two or three minutes, he would have been a goner. From the fumes and the doors were closed. I had a lot of narrow escapes. My boy, he's working out to Raytheon. He's a lead man at Raytheon. He never went into the mills; he's been in electronics all his life.

They Never Saw the Sun

Cornelia Chiklis

TOP STITCHER

To Cornelia Chiklis, long hours spent in a cotton mill were the penalty of poverty and a fate to be avoided. Her mother tried to conceal her experiences of hardship from the children, but at night they saw the lint in her hair and the exhaustion on her face. Chiklis's sympathy extended to the entire first generation of her community who sickened in the mills far from the sun and pure air of the Greek homeland.

To Cornelia Chiklis, being Greek meant having a strong, capable, and shrewd mother who knew the value of things and how to manage people. Being Greek meant having an honorable, toiling father who refused charity and took on debt so that no child in his large family went hungry. It meant learning the ancient craft of embroidery around a kerosene lamp and living so that the children would be educated in the old faith. It meant the coffee house and political talk for her father and special treatment and college for her brother. It meant her parents' satisfaction at witnessing their nine daughters married, and their son trained as a professional man. All safe from the mills.

I WAS BORN in Lowell in 1909, but I went back to Greece [with her family] when I was three years old. Came back in 1912 [the same year]. My parents were both born in Greece. My mother came to an uncle in Lowell, and he married her off. Her sisters came later. My father came to this country when he was sixteen. He went out West; he had a brother there. He had twenty-five cents in his pocket, and he worked building the railroad. Well, he stayed there for some time, and he didn't like it very much. He went to New Orleans, then he came here because in Lowell there were many Greek people and, they said, plenty of young, marriageable ladies.

My mother was a spinner in the Merrimack mill. He didn't know her, so he went and he stood in a corner and was watching her. She got aggravated. Why was he looking at her? So she took one of the cones which they spun the thread on, and she threw it at him. Almost split his head open. She was so mad at him for watching her; she didn't know why. Well, he ended up marrying her, and they had nine girls and one boy. She worked in the mills when she could. She had a big family. When she could, she helped. My father worked in the tannery.

My mother was a spinner. It was hard work. My sister Anna went to see her one day, and she was shocked. She says, I didn't know our mother worked so hard. The cotton was all over. They were breathing this cotton. No masks; noisy. Terrible, terrible! The cotton was so thick that the nostrils would fill up with cotton. They'd be throwing up cotton; they'd come home throwing up cotton. From their noses, from their mouths. Their hair was full of cotton. Some of them would wear little caps to cover their hair. It was terrible. They worked from six to six. They never saw the sun.

Most of them in the early years, most of them turned tuberculos [tubercular], because they didn't eat well. They came here, a lot of the women and men. They would bring a piece of bread and a piece of cheese and expect to work hard in the mills, not having the right food. They could eat bread, cheese, and olives in Greece, but they were out in the fields, out in the air. They could get milk from the goats. But here they were indoors, and a lot of them got tuberculos. When they worked, they got $6 a week, and they'd live eight or ten people in one apartment to save money and go back to Greece. When they got sick and had no money, they'd pass the hat around in the coffee houses. Make collections to send them back to Greece. Men and women went back. Their lungs were full of cotton. It was terrible.

Before my mother stopped working, they had speeded up the frames. They were speeding them up so they could get more work out of the people. It was terrible. I remember as a little girl standing at the city hall, and they were coming from the mills along the railroad tracks on Dutton Street. Hundreds and hundreds of people. All the cotton mills were busy. Then they moved out. Then the next generation started with shoe shops, dress shops, and the hosiery.

My mother never complained. She'd be so tired—being up with the children at night—that the boss would ask her to sit, try and take a nap, and he'd have somebody watch her work. He felt so bad because she had a big family, and, if one was sick, she was up all night. And then work from six to six. We'd bring the children to the baby-sitter, the little ones, the milk, the diapers, and the food. Then come home from school. Light the black stove with wood and coal. Put the big tub on top of it, so the water would be hot. Then we'd have two tubs to wash. And she'd rinse them out, and that was going on all the time. Between washing and rinsing.

We had a big round table with a kerosene lamp, no gas light. And the little ones would do their book work, and we would embroider, the white cut-out work. My mother would crochet. She would crochet lace to pay for our embroidery lessons. If we had homework, we'd do our homework. We were all around that table. There weren't lights in the other rooms. And we ironed with the irons on the stove. That's how we heated them. One stove. Six rooms, one stove. No steam heat. We had six rooms, but still we'd sleep two in a bed, and the little ones would sleep three in a bed sideways.

My mother did the cooking, and she was a smart woman. She knew how to manage. If she knew how to read and write, she'd have been a businesswoman. You couldn't cheat her a penny. She knew how to handle nine girls. None of us went wrong. She knew how to handle us. My father worked in the tannery, wearing big high boots in water. He'd come home, have his supper. He'd wash up, have his supper, and to the coffee house. Greek men all went to the coffee house after supper. Sit and talk politics, Greek politics, but they always came home early. And the women knew if they wanted their husbands they knew where to find them. That was one thing.

My father couldn't put a nail on the wall. My mother did it all. He did bring up the coal for the stove, the wood and the coal. My brother, Peter, was too young. My father could read Greek and taught himself to read English by reading the paper. He spoke good. My mother didn't speak English too well, but you couldn't fool her; she knew everything.

My father had steady work in the tannery until they closed. And then the Depression come on. We have the grocers to thank, because in those years, you bought your groceries, and they put it all in a book. Then you paid them at the end of the week if you had the money. A lot of them didn't get paid for a long, long time. If anyone had to go to the hospital, you'd go to your grocer. He had a horse and buggy, and they'd bring you.

In 1928, we moved to Keene, New Hampshire. There was no work. My father had no work. So they told him that we could get work in Keene. My sister Julia and I worked seven weeks without a penny to learn a trade in shoe work: top stitching. I think my father was in the stock room. But once we learned, they paid us. It was a good paying job, but we had to sacrifice, both of us. We gave our pay at home because we were a big family.

I eloped; it was Depression. My father couldn't afford a wedding, and he asked my George to wait a couple of years, and if things went good then we could get married. George was twenty-nine. I was twenty-three, and we had been going out for quite a few years. So he told my father, I'm not going to give you my word. If I give you my word, I'll have to keep it. So we just took off, and we got married at ten minutes past midnight by the justice of the peace in Nashua [New Hampshire]. And two weeks later we got married by the church, and we moved back to Lowell in 1932. My father called Roosevelt the second Christ. He brought the WPA which gave people work. They were getting $13 a week, digging. We were ten, twelve of us, yet we managed. Some of the women sewed at the WPA, nightgowns and pillowcases and sheets.

All of us went to the Greek school at the Holy Trinity [Greek Orthodox Church] and paid tuition. My father paid. He always said that he'd never walk up those stairs for welfare at city hall. He was very proud. He went in debt, and he paid his debt. Pile up some more debts, and his life was that way till we all grew up and helped. We never went without. My father always said, Maybe I can't dress you well, but you'll never go to bed hungry. And none of us ever went to bed hungry. We all went through high school; some went through secretarial school. Peter went to college and is an optometrist.

The parents worked in the mill, and they set their minds that their children were gonna get an education. They worked very hard. They went without to send these boys to school. And it was a sad thing because these boys got an education and met girls that were educated, but they were non-Greek. And they married non-Greek girls. Their parents couldn't see that, and a lot of them just broke off from their families. The families didn't want to mix. My brother married a non-Greek girl, and my uncle says when he comes to Lowell, Don't leave him in the house. And I said, He's my brother, and he's coming into my house. These boys got an education, and they wanted an educated woman too.

All of us got married. All nine girls, and my mother lived to see them. My father didn't, but my mother lived to see all her daughters married to good men.

I'd Think of My Mother in
Those Wretched Mills

Ronald Bacon
SALESMAN

In 1985 Ronald Bacon helped his mother, Leona Bacon Pray, give an interview about her life as a mill worker. Her hearing had been damaged by the years she spent in weave rooms as a drawing-in girl. That interview also preserved his own vivid memories as a child supported by his hard-working mother. It captured his feelings of intense pride in her abilities and of grief over her lost chances. These feelings were shared by many other children of the last generation about their own parents.

MY MOTHER was seventeen when she graduated from the McIntosh Commercial College in Lawrence in 1923. She and her older sister who was nineteen, each had offers to be federal government secretaries in Washington, D.C. They both already had some work experience.

In those days things were a little bit different. Everyone in the family contributed to the general welfare. Society was much more conservative sixty years ago. And a seventeen-year-old person in those days was still considered a kid. My mother's father thought that she was too young to be leaving home and going hundreds of miles away to pursue a career of her own. And in fact, he wouldn't let her go. So instead she wound up entering a dying industry. It was already dying [in the 1920s]. She was young and had a chance to go to Washington, D.C., and she instead entered a dying industry.

She was one of the hardest working people I've ever known in my whole life. She was so good they always wanted her to work. Wherever they needed a hole plugged, they'd call her. Dedication. She was four-teen when she was working forty hours [in Lawrence]. The kids then brought their pay home unopened. There was no allowances. They gave it to Mom, and Mom gave to the kids as she felt fit. This was the normal thing in those days that the kids working at fourteen, fifteen years old, bringing the whole pay home to the parents. And the parents using a good part of the pay for household expenses with a few treats for the kids for earning a full-time pay. Of course, they'd provide for your needs.

Her first husband, my father, was half Greek. My mother's fluent in French, and if you know one Romance language, you can pretty well figure out close to every European language that is spoken. She picked up languages. My mother's father-in-law, my grandfather, came from Salonica, Greece. The old man went to the University of Athens. His first name was Aristides. The last name was originally Battous. When coming to this country, they wanted to Americanize it, and they decided on Bacon. My father's name was Ulysses and his brothers were Homer, Socrates, and Euclid. He had all the old, old Greek names for his children.

When my father left us in 1942, she worked out of necessity. We were alone together all those years. She used to pay the next-door neighbor a dollar a day, five days a week for minding me. It was costing her as much to have me minded as it was to pay the rent on the house. You're talking about a take-home [pay] of maybe $30, $35 a week in those days. And ten of it was going for child care and rent. Even though she didn't have a lot of money, I was the best dressed kid in the neighborhood and probably had more toys than any other kid. She was dedicated, and she was doing that on a pretty small pay. If they still had the mills, she'd be working today. Not anyone could do drawing-in. It's more of a skilled job.

She spent a lot of time in the weave room doing drawing-in. The looms are ranked side-by-side. This one weave room that she took me into had banks and rows of them. And it was so noisy, it was unbelievable! My mother had a pretty bad hearing impediment, because of all the years she's spent in the weave room with the looms. Loud, loud, loud, and dozens of them. Row upon row of them. So you had to scream to be heard. I didn't go into the mills all that often with my mother. But the thing that stands out in my mind was that weave room with those noisy machines. I was a small kid, and I was pretty overwhelmed by the whole thing. At a very young age, I had had it.

As it turned out, I wound up working in some factories as a teenager, before I got into sales. [It was] only because I didn't have any training in something else that I worked in the factories, really. I had seen my mother do it. We were living on Lakeview Avenue which is right near Bridge Street heading into downtown Lowell. And there's a bridge right there [over the Merrimack River]. The Central Bridge, it's called, or the Bridge Street Bridge. And right next to it is the Boott mills. And I'd be walking to Lowell High in the morning. It was right across the river from where I lived. And the steam [from the mill] would be floating over the bridge. And [in the winter] it was so cold, that the steam would form tiny little snowflakes that would fall over me. And everytime I'd walk across that bridge and saw those snowflakes falling on me, I'd think of my mother in those wretched mills.

My mother's got the positive attitude, but I've been in those mills, and I've done some jobs other than textile work in the old mills. They became shoe shops and things like that. I've worked in them, and I've seen them. I saw them from a little child, and I had it clear in my mind, when I was young that that wasn't the place for me. I wound up doing some work in them, but no longer than I had to. Once I learned that I could talk people into buying things, that was it for me in the mills.

When she came home from work, how dragged out she was; she was exhausted. I believe as a child she was ingrained with the American work ethic. You know, roll up your sleeves and do it! From the ground level, blood-and-guts type of thing. And she never really thought of herself as having the ability or the talent to do something better. She spent approximately forty-nine years off and on in the mills, when she could have been a federal government secretary. And who knows what else she could have done?

They Were Very, Very Hard on People
in Those Days

Mary Rouses Karafelis

ADMINISTRATIVE SECRETARY

Mary Rouses was the only child in her family to escape mill work. Her mother's skillful negotiations between furious workers and the owners of the Boott mills during a strike in 1941 allowed the mill managers to complete their first War Department contracts. In gratitude, management promised Mary's mother, Soultana Rouses, a personal favor, and she asked that her daughter be given a job in the front office.

Office work elevated Mary Rouses in the eyes of other mill workers. Stylish dress, clean work, and associations with the "higher-ups" made her conscious of the vast social distance between workers in production and those in management. Mary Rouses was grateful that she did not have to face the conditions that her mother confronted every morning at work.

Escape from the mills for Mary Rouses did not free her from the discipline and authority of the ethnic family or its marriage customs. Despite her disappointments, she remembered her parents with deep sympathy and great affection as the adhesive of family life, as neighbors who cooperated with and sometimes protected members of other ethnic families, and as people who fought for justice in the mills.

I GRADUATED FROM Lowell High School in 1941, and there weren't many jobs around for office workers. My mother worked in the mill all her life since she came from Greece. She didn't want me working in the mill. So what happened was she had a chance to get a favor done by John Rogers Flather, the fellow that ran the Boott mill.

In the early part of 1941, these people were going to strike; most of them were foreigners, immigrants who didn't know how to speak English. My mother had gone to night school while she was working in the mill and learned English. The people were going to strike because they were working six days a week and [had] hardly any holidays and the working conditions were terrible and all. So somebody went down and told Mr. Flather, and he came out while they were all walking out, and he wanted to know what the story was. He said to them, Look, look, wait, maybe we can resolve this. They didn't understand, so my mother was translating. She picked this up from working with the French, the Italians, and the Polish. She was a linguist. She learned how to communicate with people.

She told them, Wait; the man wants to talk to us. He said, Pick a committee, have them come and we'll sit around a table, and we'll talk. Don't strike. Maybe we can straighten out the differences. No, they were going to strike. My mother talked them out of it. She said, Look, let's wait and see what he has to offer. You've got children at home; there's no money around. What are you going to do? The children are going to starve. Your family's going to be thrown out of their house. So she talked them into it.

They elected a committee of, I think it was, seven. Every kind of department, like the weaving, the spinning, the machinists. They all sent a representative, and my mother went because she knew how to speak English. They went into his office, and they sat around the table, and he said, What are your demands? My mother presented the demands. They wanted to work five days a week, eight hours a day. If they worked Saturday, they would get overtime. Plus, they wanted certain holidays off, and a raise, okay? The raise plus they would still get the same pay for the less hours—with a little raise on top of it. So he said, Well, let me go to the board [of directors] and see.

So a few days later, he called the committee in, and he presented them with a package. And no, we don't want it! I guess they wanted five cents an hour more, and he was giving them three. It was minimal anyway. The board didn't give as many holidays. So, my mother says, Let me talk to them. Let me find out if we can do something. We had lived in Manchester, and the [Amoskeag] mills closed in Manchester. When we came here [to Lowell] we were starving, depending on relatives to feed us, and my mother didn't want that again. My mother said to them, What if we accept the package as it is; then in six months, he's [going] to give us the other two cents. A few of them held out, but finally they all agreed. They called him in, and he said, All right, in six months. She let them vote so they couldn't turn around and say that she did it. She said, I'm only explaining things to you, but actually she ran the show.

So they told him that they accepted the package, and he said, All right, give me six months. We'll see what we can do for you. When they

Mrs. Soultana Rouses, c. 1955. *Courtesy of Mary Rouses Karafelis.*

were leaving, he shook their hands and thanked them very much. He was a gentleman all the time, my mother said. Everybody walked out, and he called her back and he said, Mrs. Rouses, I would like to tell you something. If ever there is anything I can do for you personally, he said, please feel free to come and see me. No, she said, I'm not that kind. She said, We work together; I'm with them. But remember, he said, the offer stays open.

So they all went back to work. [After six months they got the raise.] I'm graduating high school. I was pretty smart in school. I had taken a business course, and I had almost all A's. My mother says, I don't want to see my daughter in the mill. So she thought about what he said. Well, she thought, I'm not really asking for myself; I'm asking for my child. So she went over. She said to the receptionist, Rita Foye, I'd like to see Mr. Flather. I'm sorry, he's busy. She said, Send my name in; I would like to see Mr. Flather. She said, I can't send your name in; he's in conference. My mother said, Well, I'll sit here until you send my name in; so she sat there. Well, the minute the name was sent in, he came out and he shook her hand. What can I do for you? So they went into his office, and she told him, I'm not asking for myself, but I cannot see my daughter or my children working in the mills. I've had to work in mills all my life, and I don't want that kind of work for them. I'd like it if you would give her a job in the office. He said, I will give her a job in the office, but she has to prove herself. My mother said, She's smart; don't worry about it.

The day after graduation, I went down and asked for him. The girl says, Yeah, go in the conference room. There was this other guy there, Mr. Dombrosk, and Mr. Flather said, I am giving you a job because your mother asked me to, but I want you to know that I am giving you three months to learn it. If you don't learn it in three months, you will be fired; you'll be let go. I said, No problem; I'll learn it. You know how smart kids are, how sure of themselves, right? I had my girlfriend with me, and her mother worked in the mill. I had gall. I said, Do you have a job for my girlfriend? He said, Well, not right now.

So I went to work that Monday. I started at $16 a week for forty hours. First key-punch machines. And I was having a hard time; it was very difficult. Finally after a month, I was there; it was just like using an adding machine. We did the payroll. They would send all these numbers to us. We'd put them in the key-punch, then we'd put them into a big monster machine, and it would print the checks and the information. We figured the percent for Social Security and for whatever taxes and we'd punch the name with all those percents in. Then we'd feed two cards into this machine, and it would figure it out. These were the very first computers. Anyway, by the end of the first year, I was running the whole payroll. Doing the federal forms and mailing the stuff to the IRS. It was over a million and a half dollars then.

With payroll, as always, people have questions. So all these foreign immigrants would come in. They were so honest. If it was over what they thought they should get, they would come in and ask me, Why did they give me more money? If it was less, of course, they would come in. Growing up in a bilingual house, I learned to communicate with people. I became the official interpreter for those people.

I was there almost five years. I had started wiring the computer itself, the circuit board on the big monster Remington-Rand machine. Mr. Dombrosk realized my mechanical ability, and he showed me how to read blueprints to change the inside of the printed circuit board and put it back in the machine to make it work different. Then, unfortunately, my husband came home from the war, and he didn't want me working. In those days, they didn't want their wives working, so he told me he wanted me to quit. So I quit. But if I had stayed there and gone on further, I might have had my own computer company today.

At the beginning, I used to go up into the mills to have lunch with my mother. And I thanked my mother for not having me in there. I never saw anything like it. They had these big boxes, not corrugated boxes, wooden boxes that weighed a ton that they had to fill with bobbins and lift them themselves, women! Lifting them to dump the bobbins into big bins. And not only that, the cotton, the lint in the air. And it was hot, my God! A hundred and forty degrees. And terribly humid! I just thanked my mother every day.

From sixteen years old she worked in the mills when they were twelve and fourteen hours a day. They were getting $12 a week, and they'd work six days a week. My father was seventeen when he came over, but he had come much earlier. He was twenty-nine when he married my mother, and she was sixteen. She eloped with him. It wasn't an arranged marriage. That was a sin. That was a big sin. My father also worked in the mills, but he kept getting fired from one to the other because he would take up a cause. They would pick on some woman or he'd see someone struggling, and he'd go up and help them. They'd say, You're not supposed to be helping her ! If she can't do the job, we'll get somebody who can. They were very, very hard on people in those days. So, my father would tell them to go to blazes, and he'd help the women. So finally after he had opened his mouth enough, they fired him. He went to work for the B and M Railroad after that. He'd had his fill with the mills.

It wasn't so much the mill owners; of course they handed down the orders, but it was the floor superintendents, the floor bosses, that were really hard on the people. None of them dared to talk to my mother like that. She'd handle them good, but they could be very mean. Like I said, if you can't do your job, we'll get someone else that will and blah, blah, blah; there's plenty of people out there. I thank my mother to this day that she didn't let me go and work in the mill.

It was very tough. My middle sister Bessie, she worked there maybe two years, and she told them to shove it. It was very hard work and not much pay. So she went into a dress shop because she could sew. My mother taught us all how to sew, and then she went into a dress shop and got out of the mills. The orders for cloth were dwindling, and they went down South for cheaper labor. The Boott closed down after the war, but the Merrimack was still going. Then they all closed down. My youngest sister Jean had a friend that worked at Raytheon when that was just starting out in South Lowell. As poor as we were, my father made sure we had a typewriter because we were taking business courses in school.

Mary Rouses Karafelis at the Boott mill counting house, 1942. *Courtesy of Mary Rouses Karafelis.*

He paid fifty cents down and fifty cents a week for it. So we all knew how to type. Raytheon hired her, and she worked there for many years.

The girls in the office at the Boott mill would go out to lunch together. Sometimes we had a picnic in the inner courtyard that was all green grass and ivy growing on the walls and at other times, especially when we were paid on Friday, we went out to lunch. We felt like big shots because we didn't work in the mill; we worked in the office. The people, the workers, that I had to deal with that came in the office, they treated me like I was ten levels higher than they were because I was in the office. We dressed much nicer, the heels and the stockings and all that. The best thing of all because I was so good, they brought me up from eighty-three point seven cents an hour or eighty-three cents and seven mils (there's ten mils to a penny) to what the other girls were getting, eighty-four cents an hour. That meant a lot in those days. Oh, I was walking on air! I couldn't wait to get home and tell my mother. I got a three mil raise. That was something in those days when you could buy a pound of butter, a peck of potatoes, bread, and milk for a dollar and still get some change back.

I got married in 1944. In the olden days a girl had to get engaged to get married and have her family involved and all. It was almost a proxy marriage. His mother worked in the mill, and they became friendly, my mother and her. So, my mother was saying something about me, that I worked in the office. Well, right away, his mother said, Oh I want her for a daughter-in-law. So I met him. I didn't want him, but it worked out anyway. I'm married forty years. I didn't want to get married; I wanted to become a career woman. But in those times you were expected to get married and have a family and if you didn't, people thought there was something wrong with you. He was going overseas to fight. He said, I don't want to get a Dear John letter. We have to get married. And I said, I don't want to get married. But you don't argue with your parents. In those days, your parents said, Hey, this is good for you, you're going to do this, you did it. So I got engaged and we got married in 1944.

My mother never spoke ill of anybody that she worked with except their supervisor. They worked for him maybe ten years, and they got to know him so well that they swore at him. He had a hard job because he had the owners behind him telling him, The output's got to be this much, and you work those people until you get it! So he became the bad guy. Even if he wanted to be a good guy, he couldn't; it meant his job. My mother was very friendly with all kinds of nationalities in the mill. I think they banded together, more or less, because they had a common interest, more or less. It was in the mill that they had a common bond, but once they left the mill [at night], they'd say goodbye, and each one went to their own area or their ghetto, and would live within their kind of people. Very rarely did they ever mix socially.

We lived on Dummer Street in the Greek section of the Acre. We moved from Manchester in 1936 to get jobs in the mills. They didn't know any other kinds of jobs. But my mother was far-seeing. She did not want us brought up in just a Greek environment. She said, We've got to break loose and become Americans. So we moved to a neighborhood with two or three Greek families, one Polish and one Irish, but the majority were French people. There were fifteen families in this little complex that we lived in. And every Saturday, one mother of each family would take her turn to go down in the yard, gather all the children together, rake that yard up and clean it, and burn the garbage so that Sunday morning that yard, it was so clean.

There was one young French girl, a very nice woman; she was only in her early twenties. She had had two children, and her husband was a heavy drinker. He didn't drink during the week; he worked. But Saturday and Sunday, he would drink, and he'd come home and beat her up. So one night about two o'clock in the morning, I'll never forget this, bang, bang, bang on the door! My mother got right out of bed and ran to the door and opened it up. She said, What's the matter? The young woman said, He's trying to kill me! So she took her in, locked the door, and put her to bed. She didn't want to sleep. Go in the bed; sleep with my daughter; don't worry about him. She got my father, and she said, If he comes to the door, she says, tell him to go home and take care of the kids and sober up. He's not going to see his wife till tomorrow. By then, he'll be sober, he'll be all right, and it won't be so bad. So the guy came banging at the door, and my father opens the door. My father was a big, tall man. What do you want? He says, I want my wife! What for? You hit her; you beat her; no good. So he says, I want my wife. You're not going to get your wife.

The next day, the young woman got up in the morning, and my mother wouldn't let her go alone. My mother went with her. When my mother came back, she said, Everything is fine now. He was sobered up and holding his head when we walked in. He was practically crying. So, my mother said, I gave him a talking to. I told him you better not touch her again, because I'll have the police up here. In those days, the policeman was your friend; we were brought up that way.

When I went to school, I didn't have any problems, but my second sister, she was a terror. She came home one day and said to my mother, The teacher told me to do something; I told her I wouldn't. What? I told her I wouldn't. She says, Come here. Wham! She gave her one. She said, I want you to understand. Your teacher is your second mother. Your teacher has you longer than I do. She is trying to teach you what's right and wrong, and you're going to listen. And even if you're right, you bite your tongue, and you do what she tells you. I don't care whose fault it was, your teacher is always right. And she drilled that into us, and I brought up my own kids that way.

This is the upbringing that we had in an ethnic home. The parents were always right. You never could tell your parents, No, you're wrong. You'd like to. You wanted to many times, but you don't dare. Not because they'd hit you, because my parents were very good. My mother wouldn't hit too much. She was the one that would hit, but she didn't hit a lot. When she was making pastry, she might take the long dowel that

we made the pita with and crack you on the legs or on the behind where
it doesn't show if you got black and blue. You knew, the minute she
looked at you. If she said, Sit; you sat.

My father, he just said something once. Strong. And you didn't cross
him. I couldn't wear lipstick or shorts till I was eighteen. I'd see him
coming; I was on the porch, and I had shorts on; I'd see him coming. I
had to run in and put a skirt on. Each one had their chore. We were
three girls, so we'd do the dishes one night, every third night, and my
father was the cook. He used to be a cook before he went to work in the
mills, and he would love to teach us. And because of that, I can cook
anything. They were exhausted when they got home from work at night,
but they still knew they had a responsibility to their children, and they
did the best they could.

And clean! You had to keep your house clean. We didn't have the best
of everything. We had linoleum on the floors that was worn almost
through to holes, almost no patterns left, just the backing. But that had
to be scrubbed every other day. We lived on the third floor, and every
Saturday, one of the children would scrub the hall stairs with lye so that
the wood looked like new. We kept those hallways swept and clean. My
mother came from the Greek villages where they kept things clean. She
carried it over to America, and she passed it on to me.

Once [in 1936] I needed a pair of shoes so bad because there were no
soles on my shoes. We didn't have the money to buy them. So my
mother says to my father, Someone at work told me if you go back of the
city hall, they have a place there, an office, and you tell them that she
needs shoes and you can't afford them, they'll give you a paper, and you
go down and buy a pair for her. My father says, I'm not going. She said,
You've got to go, George. What are we going to do? The girl hasn't got
any shoes. She's got to have shoes.

So he took me down. I remember this; I must have been twelve. We
sat down and waited. A stern woman called us over, and she asked him a
lot of questions. How much do you make? How much does your wife
make? How much are your bills? Finally my father got very disgusted,
and he said to her, Look, if I had enough money to buy her a pair of
shoes, I wouldn't be here. She said, Well, I'm sorry, but we got to make
sure that you don't have enough money to buy her a pair of shoes. My
father took me and left. We went home and told my mother, and they
decided to borrow money from relatives to buy me a pair of shoes. The
immigrants had pride, that's what they had. Pride, and they wanted to

do better for their kids. If you're going to get married and have children, your first duty is to your children.

One day when my sister Bessie was sixteen, she came home with a piece of paper, and she says to my mother, Sign this paper. I'm not going to school any more; I'm going to work. My mother says, You want to go to work? And you don't want to finish high school? Lady, she says, you're going to finish high school. She says, No I'm not! She says, Yes, you are; and she gave her a good one. My father comes in. What are you hitting the girl for? Here, you deal with it. He said, Bessie, wait a minute; sit down. There's one thing you've got to understand; without education today, you will go nowhere. You may not get more than high school, but high school is good. You will finish high school whether you like it or not, and you will get good marks. And if you don't, he said, *I* will hit you, not your mother. And he never hit us, so coming from him. . . . He was very stern. We were afraid he'd kill us, and he never hit us, never laid a hand on us. She went to school. She finished. My mother made sure.

In those days, a family was a family. What one had, the other one shared. We didn't resent that we'd give in our paycheck. My paycheck went right in on Friday. No cashing. I had a five-dollar allowance. And you had to do with that. Everybody pooled everything they had. I started walking because that way I saved money. It's only a mile and a quarter, why give them the ten cents on the bus? That's ten cents each way, that's twenty cents a day, that's a dollar a week. Why should I give them that? A girl couldn't leave her father's house, no matter, unless she was married. It was up to your parents to find you someone, and that's what they usually did. If they didn't, it was terrible. Although a lot of families prospered considerably because the daughter's paycheck was still coming in, and there was no husband to give it to.

College was for the boys. The girls will work to put the boys like my brother Chris through college, poor as we are. We don't have enough, but we will all work hard to put the boy through college because the boy is going to be the mainstay of the family. But my brother never wanted to go to college. He worked the second shift in the mill; he wanted to be a policeman. I put my son through Boston University. My whole paycheck went there, my whole paycheck. Later he said to me, Ma, I want to go to the University of Connecticut for graduate school. And I said, Okay, I'll work. You go. He finished in June 1984 and got a very good job.

My mother was very proud of him. She had ten grandchildren. Not one of them smoked pot; not one of them a drunk; not one of them in trouble with the police. Every one of them is a very good kid and respects their elders. Grandchildren, I'm talking about. She kept this family together. Anything these kids wanted, they'd go up to see "Babou." She worked very hard when she was young. Her body kind of broke down because of it, but anything the kids wanted, she never said no. Babou, my pants are too long. I just bought a new pair of slacks, and I want to wear them tonight. Bring them up, honey; don't worry about it. Grandchildren.

Glossary

Battery A device attached to an automatic loom that feeds full bobbins as they are needed into the shuttle during the weaving process. *Battery hands* fill the device with full bobbins.

Beam A large wooden cylinder several feet long on which lengths of warp threads are wound in parallel rows before the process of slashing, after which the beam is fitted into the back of the loom.

Bobbin A hard wood core of various kinds with a hole drilled up the center on which yarns are wound. Bobbins are put on spindles in spinning machines of all types.

Bobbin-boy Someone who delivers full bobbins and collects and cleans the empty bobbins from the spinning and weaving machines.

Carding A process that cleans the cotton or wool lap, separates the fiber, and produces a soft, tubular roll or sliver, which is coiled into a can. A *card tender* or *carder* feeds laps into the machine, keeps it clean, and removes full cans of sliver. (See fig. B)

Change-over man A cotton mill worker who removes an empty warp beam from the loom and inserts a full beam. For similar work in a silk mill, see *warp rigging*.

Cleaning Removing the fly lint and loose bunches of cotton from a spinning frame to avoid breakage or defects called slubs in the yarn.

Cloth boy A person who removes the roll of cloth from the loom after the weaving process.

Combing A straightening process that removes short fibers and dirt or specks in a cotton or wool sliver by recombining several slivers through a mechanism with fine teeth (combs or pins). The result is a combed sliver with long parallel fibers. The machines are operated by *comber tenders* or *combers*.

Count The numerical designation of the weight of yarn or sliver that changes according to product specifications.

Creeler or filling hand Helper to a carpet or silk weaver who sets up the various colors of wool or silk yarn so that they are ready to be placed by hand into the shuttles of the looms.

Creels Frameworks that hold spools wound with warp yarn. They are used in the warping process to assemble the yarn on the warp beam. (See fig. E)

Crompton and Knowles loom A heavily constructed woolen or silk loom, more sturdy than a cotton loom. It has a dobby head, which gives it the capacity to operate many harnesses and produce fancy weaves.

Dobby head A mechanism attached to a loom to operate multiple harnesses for complicated weaving patterns such as letters on towels.

Doffing Removing bobbins spun full of yarn from a machine and replacing them with empty ones. The job is done by a *doffer*.

Draper looms Looms whose key feature is a filling bobbin changer or battery, which discharges an empty bobbin and replaces it automatically with a full one without stopping the loom. It may operate the harnesses through the action of cams or with a dobby head.

Drawing frame   A machine with four or five pairs of rollers operating at progressively faster speeds. It is used to draw or recombine several slivers, thus producing more uniform and straighter fibers.

Drawing-in   Threading the warp yarn from the warp beam through the eyes of the heddles and the openings or dents in the reed. This was skilled work that required excellent eyesight and was done by *drawing-in girls*. These workers were replaced by drawing-in and knot-tying machine operators. (See p. 108)

Drop wires   Drop wires are sensors through which the warp yarn passes that stop the loom immediately if there is breakage.

Duck   Medium- or heavy-weight cotton canvas often used for military purposes.

Filling hand   See *Creeler.*

Fixer   General term for a skilled mechanic in the mills who repairs and overhauls textile machinery.

Give-backs   Concessions made by unions on wages or benefits during contract negotiations with management.

Greige or grey cloth   Fabric as it emerges from the loom. It is sold before it undergoes any bleaching, dyeing, printing, or finishing process.

Hander-in   Someone, usually a learner, who helps a drawing-in girl by sitting on the opposite side of the harnesses and handing each end of the yarn to be pulled through the heddles.

Harness   A metal frame on a loom that contains the heddles carrying the warp yarns during weaving. By lifting or lowering the harnesses in the loom, the shed is formed. (See fig. F)

Jacquard loom   A weaving machine that uses programmed instructions from punch cards to manipulate the warp yarns, one by one, to produce intricate and highly stylized patterns in cloth.

Jig   A cauldron used to dye or bleach cloth in steam-heated water.

Jiggsie   The operator of a jig; a jig tender.

Knot-tying machine   A mechanism that ties knots to connect the warp yarn ends in a full beam to those in a nearly empty warp beam. Once tied, the knots are pulled through the harnesses and reed in preparation for weaving. This eliminates drawing-in work.

Lap   A continuous, loosely compressed sheet of cotton fiber, about an inch thick and either twenty or forty inches wide, wound into a cylindrical roll, ready to be fed into the carding machines.

Loom fixer   A skilled mechanic assigned responsibility for preparing the looms for operation and keeping them functioning properly in one section of the mill.

Mending   Skilled women's work that reconstructs the pattern in defective or damaged woolen or worsted cloth. (See p. 129)

Mule spinning   A process of producing fine filling yarn from a large complicated spinning machine that moves back and forth along tracks in the mill floor. The *mule spinner* manipulates the machine to meet specifications for the yarn. He draws out and twists a length of yarn and then winds it up, repeating the cycle several times each minute. The operator must piece-up broken ends, piece-in new roving, and doff the full bobbins. Mule spinning requires more skill than ring spinning. (See p. 169)

Pick A single sideways movement of a shuttle across the shed formed in the loom by movements in the harnesses. A pick is also one thread of the filling in weaving.

Pick-counter or pick clock A device mounted on looms that records the amount of production by registering each movement of the shuttle during one shift.

Picker-stick A wooden arm in a loom that propels the shuttle from one shuttle box into the opposite shuttle box across the shed made in the warp yarn.

Picking A general process of cleaning and opening matted raw cotton that produces a continuous lap ready for use on a card.

Piece-rate system A managerial policy that offers money incentives to stimulate more production.

Piecework The calculation of wages by measured amounts of production.

Piecing-up Joining two ends of sliver, roving, or yarn with a twist or roll of the fingers. For many operations, piecing-up can be done while the machine is running.

Quilling Rewinding yarn onto filling bobbins suitable for the shuttles of silk looms. The work is done by a *quiller.*

Reed A comblike device on a loom that battens or bangs the filling yarn hard against the woven cloth after each movement of the shuttle to tighten the weave.

Roving A process that reduces sliver produced by carding and drawing to a suitable size for spinning.

Scouring Degreasing raw wool with solvents in preparation for carding.

Second hand Foreman or second person in charge of a room in a mill.

Seconds Defective yarn or cloth that fails to meet management standards and is sold at cut-rate prices.

Shed An opening made by movement in the harnesses of the loom for the shuttle to pass through carrying the filling yarn. (See fig. F)

Short hours In the 1920s and 1930s, young mill workers between the ages of fourteen and sixteen were limited by state law to working forty hours per week with one afternoon of school. At sixteen they could work "long hours" or the full forty-eight-hour week.

Shuttle The boat-shaped device in the loom that carries the filling bobbin through the shed opening made in the warp. It is made of hard wood and has pointed metal ends.

Side-cam A simple loom with two to seven harnesses for basic or simple weaving. The harnesses are controlled by cams located at one end of the loom.

Slashing The application by a *slasher* of starch or size to a sheet of warp yarn produced in the warping process to protect the warp yarn during the weaving process. (See p. 270)

Sliver A ropelike strand of soft cotton about the diameter of a broom stick. In cotton production, "sliver" is pronounced with a long "i"; in worsted production, with a short "i."

Smash-piecing The intricate, painstaking work, done by a *smash-piecer*, of repairing damaged warp yarns and piecing them up while they are still in the loom.

Sparehand A learner or temporary worker. Sometimes called a tender or, in Lancashire, a tenter.

Speed-up To increase the speed of machinery or the pace of work.

Spooling A winding process that transfers long lengths of warp yarn from spinning bobbins to a spool that is used in the warping process. The person who does this job is a *spooler*.

Stretch-out To assign additional work or more machines without increasing the work force.

Sweeper An unskilled worker who collects and cleans up the excess lint and dirt under machines and throughout the mill buildings.

Time-study men People who study the efficiency of each operation in the textile process and measure both the time and the motions expended, with the purpose of redesigning work so that mill workers can do it faster. Their calculations are used to establish piece rates.

Top mill A mill that specializes in cleaning and carding wool and selling it off as slivers or "top" to yarn mills that specialize in spinning.

Traveler A small piece of hardened steel or bronze wire designed to travel on the flanged track of the spinning ring to impart twist to the yarn.

Twill A diagonal weave that produces a strong, durable fabric.

Twisting A process of combining two or more parallel yarns into a ply yarn or cord for greater strength and smoothness, carried out by a *twister*.

Unifill machine A mechanism that replaced the automatic bobbin changer or battery and the battery hand. It winds its own bobbins while the loom runs and replaces the empty ones without stopping.

Velvet cutting The cutting with special knives of a piece of cotton cloth woven double or face-to-face connected by the pile. The result is two pieces of cloth, each with one side of pile.

Warping The assembly of hundreds of parallel warp yarns on to the warp beam in preparation for slashing. The process is done by a *warper*. (See fig. E)

Warp rigging The insertion by a *warp rigger* of the heavy full warp beam into the back of the looms in preparation for weaving.

Warp yarn Yarn spun on ring spinning machines (see fig. D). It has enough twist to give it strength and elasticity and is coated with starch and wound on a loom beam. Warp yarn also comprises the lengthwise system of yarns in woven fabric.

Weaver's knot A small, quickly tied knot that becomes tighter the more it is pulled and slips easily through the heddles and reed in a loom.

Weft yarn Filling yarn that runs across the width of the warp yarns and comprises the crosswise system of yarns in woven fabric.

Worsted Yarn made of combed wool and spun by the worsted process that gives a harder twist than "woolen," producing worsted fabric with more resiliency, a smoother finish, and a clearer surface than woolen fabric.

Winding　The mechanical transfer of yarn from one size or form of package to another, such as from bobbins to cones or tubes. The process is done by a *winder.*

Index